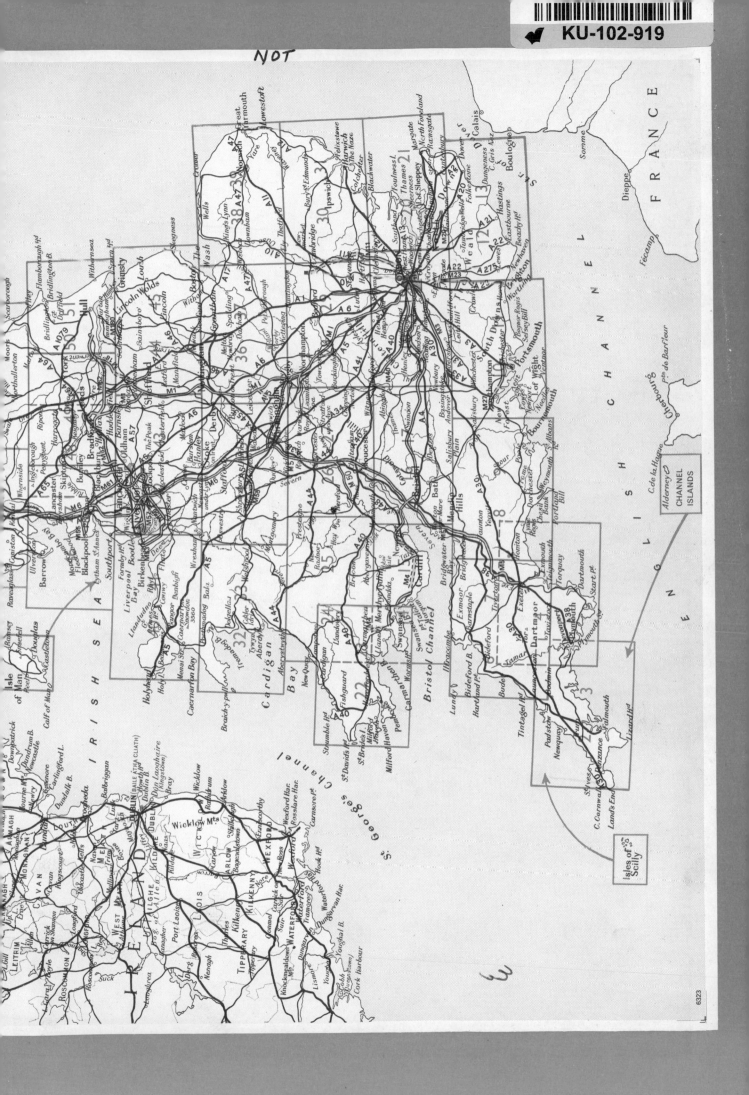

Bartholomew

Road Atlas Britain

Contents
1:300 000 maps
Route planning maps
Town Plans
Index

Sommaire
Cartes au 1:300 000
Cartes de préparation d'itinéraires
Plan de villes
Index

Inhalt
Karten 1:300 000
Streckenplanungskarten
Stadtpläne
Index

Indices
Carte con scala 1:300 000
Carte programmazione tragitto
Piante delle città
Indice

Printed and Published in Scotland
Copyright © John Bartholomew & Son Ltd 1976
ISBN 0 85152 727 2
6323

1:300 000

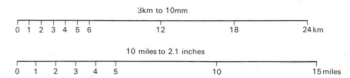

3km to 10mm

0 1 2 3 4 5 6   12   18   24 km

10 miles to 2.1 inches

0 1 2 3 4 5   10   15 miles

Motorway Autoroute Autobahn Autostrada	**'B' Road** Route secondaire 'B' Straße Klasse 'B' Strada secondaria	**Principal Civil Airport** Aérodrome civil principal Verkehrsflughafen Aeroporto civile principale
Interchange Echangeur Anschlußstelle Intercambio	**Single track road** Route à voie unique Straße, einbahnig Strada ad una carreggiata	**Railway (passenger)** Chemin de fer (passagers) Eisenbahn (Personenverkehr) Ferrovie (Passeggeri)
Limited Interchange Echangeur limité beschränkte Anschlußstelle Intercambio limitato	**Other Serviceable roads** Autres routes practicables Nebenstraße Altre strada utilizzabili	**Canal** Canal Kanal Canale
Service Area Zone de service Tankstelle und Raststatte Area di servizio	**Mileage (between circles)** Distance (entre cercles) Entfernung in Meilen (zwischen den Kreisen) Distanza in miglia (tra i cerchi)	**Church** Eglise Kirche Chiesa
Under Construction En construction im Bau In costruzione	**Track** Piste Fahrweg Strada non pavimentata	**County boundary** Limite de comté Grafschaftsgrenze Confine di contea
Projected Prévu geplant Progettato	**Path** Chemin Pfad Sentiero	**Height (in feet)** Hauteur (en pieds) Hohe Altitudine (piedi)
Dual Carriageway Route principale à voies séparées Autostraße, zweibahnig Doppia carreggiata	**Car ferry** Bac pour autos Autofähre Nave traghetto per automobili	**Page Continuation** Continuation à la page Anschlußseite Pagina di continuazione
'A' Road Route principale 'A' Straße Klasse 'A' Strada principale	**Other ferries and sea routes** Autres bateaux de passage et voies maritimes andere Fähren und Seeverbindungen Altri punti di traghetto e rotte	**Certain built-up areas** Terrain bâti bebaute Fläche Agglomerati urbani

Feet
3000
2000
1000
500
100
Sea level
Below sea level
Feet

A　　　　B　　　　C　　　　D

ISLES OF SCILLY
25 Miles South-West
of Land's End

St Martins
Bryher　Tresco　Eastern Is
Samson　St Marys
Hugh Town
Annet　Gugh　To Penzance
St Agnes
Western
Rocks

0　4　8　12 Miles

1

2

3

4

5

6

Trevose Head
Crugmee
Harlyn
Trevose
Trevone
Pad
Treyarnon
St
Shop
Trego
Park Hd
Pentire
Penrose
Bedruthan Steps
St Ervan
St Evil
Mawgan Porth
15
Watergate
Bay
Tregurrian
Vale
Mawgan
Maw
NEWQUAY
St Columb
7
A 3059
Towan Hd
Newquay Bay
Newquay Porth
St Columb Minor
Colan
White
Newquay
The Gannel
L.C. Sta.
A 392
A 392
Kelsey Hd
W Pentire
Crantock
A 3075
Penhale Pt.
Ligger Pt.
Cubert
St Enoder
Newlyn East
Cha
Perran
Penhale
Bay
Sands
A 3016
A 30
A 30
12
Mitchell
Perranporth
Rose
Newlyn
Carland
B 3285
Goonhaven
Downs
A 3059
B 3284
St Agnes Hd
Perranzabuloe
Zelah
Truthan
Tregear
A 3075
Penhallow
St Allen
St Erme
Trispen
St Agnes
Mithian
Callestick
A 30
8
11
B 3277
Trelas
Porthtowan
Mount
Tregavethan
Shortlanesend
Hawke
End
Kenwyn
Blackwater
B 3284
Kenwyn
Portreath
B 3300
B 3277
Truro
A 39
A 30
Scorrier
Chacewater
9
A 390
St Clement
Illogan
St Day
A 390
Kea
Malpas
St Michael
B 3301
4
A 39
Penkevil
Godrevy Is
Redruth
B 3298
A 3047
Godrevy Pt.
Gwithian
Pennance
Gwennap
Perranwell
Sta.
King
Harry Ferry
Red R.
Carn Naun Pt.
Roseworthy
Camborne
Lanner
A 393
Devoran
Keock
10
The Island
St Ives
Connor Downs
7
A 39
Perranarworthal
Zennor
St Ives
Gurnards Hd
Bay
Carbis Bay
Barrack
Troon
Four Lanes
Ponsanooth
A 393
Mylor Br
St Just
Treen
Halse
Carbis Bay Sta.
Phillack
Carnhell
Lane
town
Uny Lelant
Green
Stithians
Penryn
Flushing
St Mawes
B 3306
Sta.
Hayle
Gwinear
Res.
Long
Burnhouse
Towednack
Trencrom Hill
St Erth Sta.
Rosewarne
Downs
Mabe
13
A 30
Praze-an-Beeble
Edgcumbe
Falmouth
Amalebra
Canon's
St Erth
Crowan Beacon
B 3290
Newmill
Town
B 3302
Porkellis
B 3291
B 3306
Lanyon
Townshend
Crowan
Castle
Morvah
Madron
Crowlas
B 3280
10
Wendron
A 39
Falmouth
Boscaswell
PENZANCE
Ludgvan
B 3302
Crown Town
Bay
Trewellard
Heamoor
A 30
Longrock
Relubbus
Pendennis Pt.
St Anthony
St Just
Gulval
Marazion
Godolphin
A 394
in-Roseland
Cross
Zone Pt.
A 3071
A 3071
Tremethick Cross
St Michaels Mt
Goldsithney
Trescowe
Sithney
Constantine
Mawnan
Cape
Res.
Perranuthnoe
13
Smith
Rosemullion Hd
Cornwall
Sancreed
Drift
Germoe
Breage
Port
St Just
10
Catchall
Ashton
A 394
Navas
Helford River
Mawnan
Whitesand
Crows-an-wra
Helston
Gweek
Helford
Nare Pt.
Bay
Paul
B 3304
B 3291
St Anthony
The Brisons
A 30
Mousehole
B 3293
Sennen Cove
Porthleven
Manaccan
Lands
Sen'en
B 3288
Trewavas Hd
Looe
St Martin's
Porthallow
End
Trevescan
Boleigh
Pool
Green
Newtown
Mounts Bay
St Buryan
Zennor Cove
Berepper
10
Porthoustock
B 3315
Treen
Mawgan
Manacle Pt.
Porthcurno
St Levan
B 3293
St Keverne
Gwennap Head
Logan Rock
Cury
Lowland Pt.
11
Gunwalloe
B 3294
To Isles of Scilly
Poldhu Cove
Radio Sta
B 3083
Post Off.
Goonhilly Downs
Coverack
Mullion Cove
Porth Mellin
Ruan Major
Predannack
Wollas
Ruan Minor
Grade
Cadgwith
Kynance Cove
Black Hd
Lizard
Lizard Point

The Edinburgh Geographical Institute

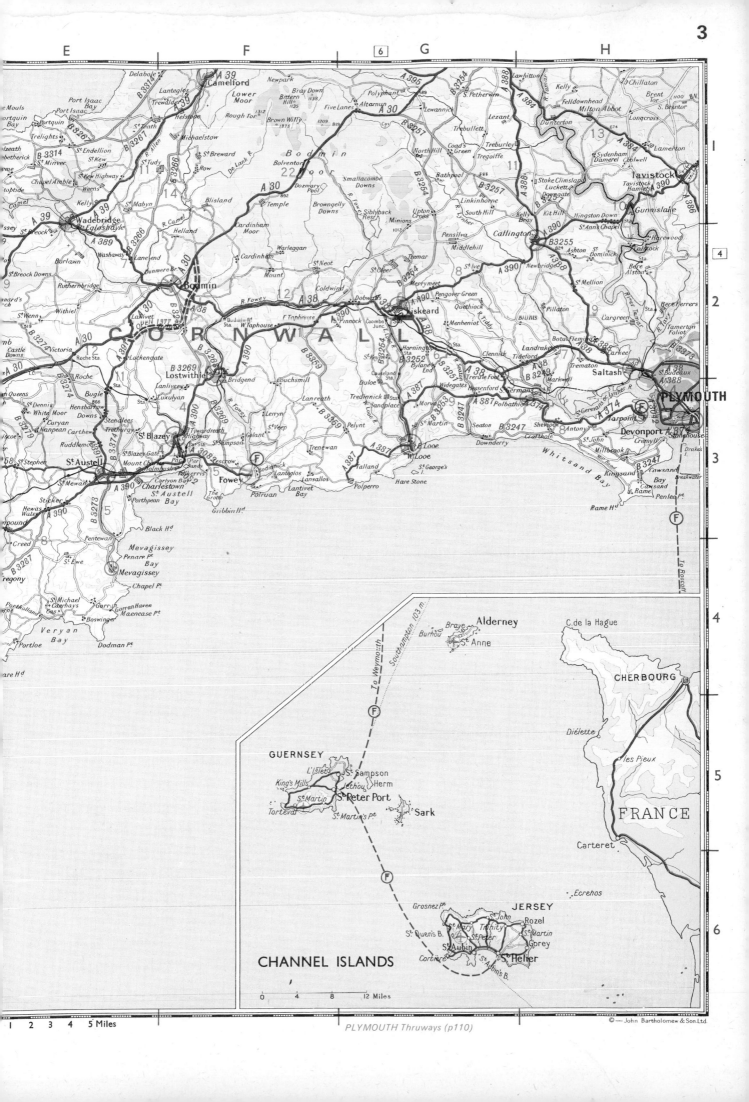

CORNWALL

CHANNEL ISLANDS

0   4   8   12 Miles

1 2 3 4 5 Miles

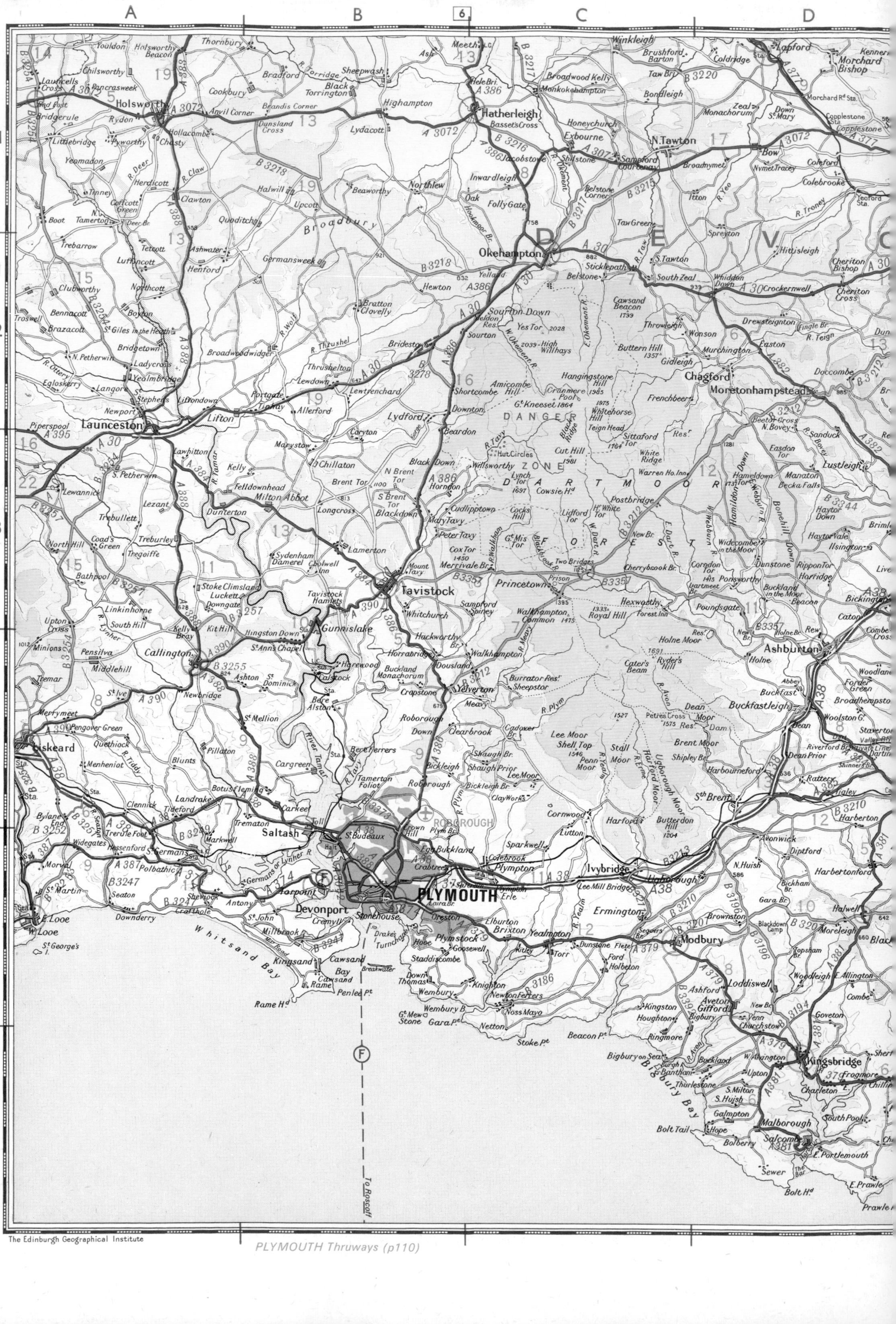

The Edinburgh Geographical Institute

PLYMOUTH Thruways (p110)

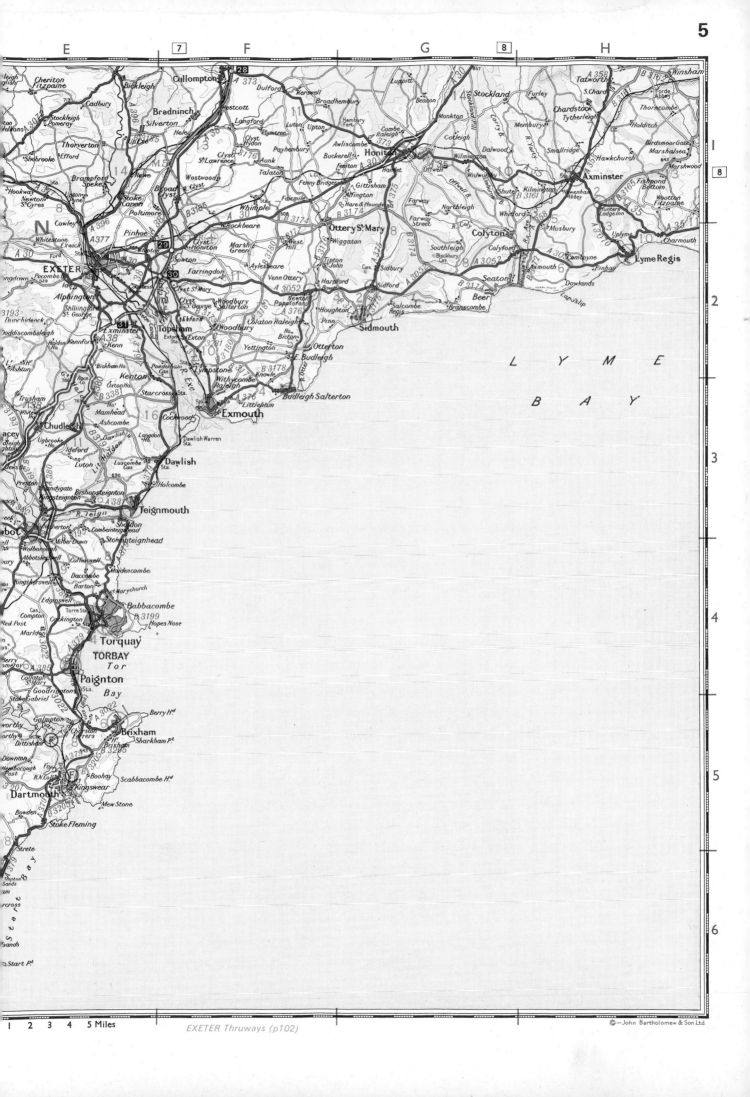

6

1

North West Pt
Lundy
Shutter Pt. Rat Island

Ilfracombe
Combe Martin Bay
Widmouth Hd
Bull Pt. Lee B. Lee Hele
Morte Pt. Mortehoe Berrynarbor Sterridge
B 3343
Woolacombe B 3231
Morte Bay
W. Down Bittadon
Baggy Pt.
857
Croyde Georgeham Milltown Muddiford
Saunton Knowle Marwood Youlston Kingsheanton
B 3231
Braunton Prixford
Saunton Sands Braunton Burrows
Wrafton
Ashford A 39
Pilton

2

BARNSTAPLE
OR
BIDEFORD BAY
Barnstaple Bar
River Taw
Bickington Barn
A 39 A 3
Fremington
The Neck
Appledore Instow St John's Chapel Tawstock Landke
Westward Ho! B 3236 Westleigh Eastleigh Bishop
Northam Loveacott Newton Tracey
Bideford East-the-Water Alverdiscott Fishley Barton

Hartland Pt.
Damehole Pt.
Gallantry Bower
Hartland Quay
B 3231
Clovelly Clovelly Bay
Stoke Hartland Clovelly Cross Buck's Mills
Ford Fairy Cross Yarnscombe Langridge
Horns Cross Littleham Landcross
Goldworthy A 39 Weare Giffard High Bullen Sherwood Green
Milford Eddistone Buck's Cross Parkham Monkleigh B 3227
Elmscott Tosberry Cranford Priory
Woolfardisworthy (Woolsery) Almiston Cross Buckland Brewer Frithelstock Gt Torrington St Giles in the Wood
Melbury Frithelstock Stone Stevenstone Ho. Kingscott
Taddiport Roboro

3

Welcombe Meddon Ashmansworthy R. Torridge E. Putford Torrington B 3220 Beaford
14 Langtree 592
Morwenstow Shop E. Youlstone W. Putford Stibb Cross B 3227
Higher Sharpnose Pt. Woodford Bradworthy Bulkworthy Peters Marland Merton
Lower Sharpnose Pt. Coombe Sutcombe Brendon 17 Newton St Petrock Woollaton Heanton Satchville
Kilkhampton Tamar Lake Youldonmoor Cross Milton Damerel Huish North Town
Stibb 14 Youldon R. Waldon Shebbear Buckland Filleigh Meeth
Poughill Chilsworthy Holsworthy Beacon Thornbury Bradford R. Torridge Sheepwash Ash Hele Bri.
Grimscott Launcells Cross Pancrasweek Cookbury Brandis Corner Black Torrington Highampton
Bude Stratton 307 5 Holsworthy A 3072 Anvil Corner Dunsland Cross Lydacott 13 Hatherleigh
Launcells Red Post Rydon Hollacombe Brandis Corner A 3072 Basset's Cross
Bude Bay A 3073 Bude Aqueduct Bridgerule Pyworthy Chasty B 3218 A 386 Okehampt
Helebridge Marhamchurch Littlebridge R. Deer R. Claw Halwill Upcott Beaworthy
Budds Titson Yeomadon Herdicott Broadbury Oak Folly Gate

4

5

Poundstock Week Orchard R. Bude Tinney Clawton Quoditch Northlew Inwardleigh
Whitstone Boot Tamerton Deer Br. 13 Ashwater Germansweek Hewton
Cambeak Crackington Haven Wainhouse Corner Jacobstow 15 Trebarrow Tettott Henford Bratton Clovelly A 30
Crackington Maxworthy Caudworthy Clubworthy Luffincott Northcott Boyton R. Wolf Lewdown A 30
Tresparrett Posts 18 Higher Langdon Troswell Bennacott St Giles in the Heath Bridgetown Broadwoodwidger Thrushelton 19 B 3278 16
Boscastle B 3263 Tresparrett Canworthy Water Brazacott Yeolmbridge Bridestowe Amicombe Hill
Trevalga Lesnewth Otterham Warbstow Trossell N. Petherwin Ladycross Portgate Lewtrenchard Shortcombe
Tintagel Hd B 3262 Penwenham Tremaine R. Ottery B 3254 Langore Stephen's Lifton Downton Lydford
Tintagel B 3266 Hallworthy Egloskerry Newport Liftondown Galt Beardon
Trewarmett Davidstow A 395 Downhead Piperspool Launceston Lifton Allerford Dow Yes P
Rockhead B 3263 Tremail R. Inny St Clether Laneast A 395 A 30 Lawhitton Marystow Black Down Willsworthy
Delabole 16 Newpark Bray Down Polyphant S. Petherwin Kelly Chillaton Horndon Lynch
Camelford Lower Moor Bittern Hills Altarnun Felldownhead Brent Tor DAN
Lanteglos Trewalder Five Lanes A 30 Lewannick 11 13 Milton Abbot S. Brenton
Helsto Rough Tor

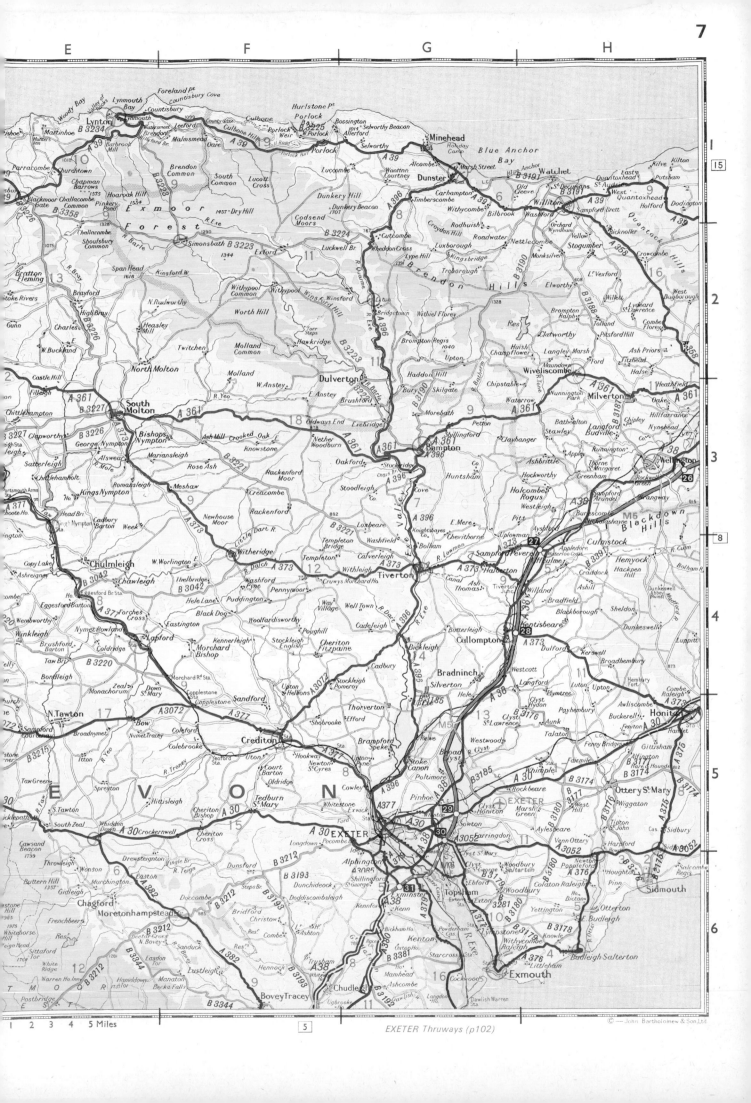

A 15 B 16 C D

SOMERSET

Vale of Taunton Deane

Blackdown Hills

Quantock Hills

Easty Quantoxhead · St Audries · West Quantoxhead · Holford · Kilve · Kilton · Burton · Putsham · Fairfield Ho. · Shurton · Stringston · Stogursey · Stockland Bristol · Otterhampton · Huntspill Level · Pawlett · Catcott Burtle · R. Brue · Westhay Moor · Westhay · Up. Godney · Polsham · Coxley · Bowlish · **Shepton Mallet** · Doulti

Bicknoller · Dodington · Nether Stowey · Fiddington · Combwich · Coultings · Rodway · Brymore Ho. · Down End · Dunball · Knowle Hall · Woolavington · Cossington · Edington · Chilton · Catcott · Shapwick · Meare · Queens Sedge Moor · **Glastonbury** · Isle of Avalon · N. Wootton · Pilton · Cannards Grave · Prestleig

Crowcombe · Over Stowey · Spaxton · Enmore · Goathurst · Halswell Ho. · Woolmersdon · **Bridgwater** · Battle of Sedgemoor 1685 · Sutton Mallet · Moorlinch · Greinton · Ashcott · Street · Walton · Overleigh · Baltonsborough · Parbrook · Ditcheat · Lamy

Willett · West Bagborough · Merridge · Aisholt · Durleigh · N. Petherton · Huntworth · Parrett · Westonzoyland · Drain · King's Sedge Moor · Henley Corner · Dundon · Compton · Butleigh · Barton · St David · Alhampton · Castle Cary Sta. · Ansford · Cast

Lydeard St Lawrence · Combe Florey · Cothelstone · Toulton · Thurloxton · North Newton · Northmoor Green or Moorland · Othery · Middlezoy · Greylake · High Ham · Low Ham · Littleton · Kingweston · Copley Wood · Ifford · R. Cary · B 3152 · Lovington · B 3153 · Galham

Ash Priors · Fitzhead · Halse · Heathfield · Staplegrove · Bathpool · Creech St Michael · North Curry · West Monkton · Lyng · Isle of Athelney · Stathe · Aller · Pitney · Somerton · Kingsdon · **Long Sutton** · King's Moor · Long Load · B 3151 · Barrow · N. Barrow · Popple Br. · Cadbury · S. Cadbury

Milverton · Norton Fitzwarren · Oake · Rushton · Durston · Stoke St Gregory · Oath · Curry Rivel · Langport · Huish Episcopi · Pibsbury · Pitney · Northover · Yeovilton · Bridgehampton · Podimore · N. Camel · Queen Camel

Chipley Pk. · Nynehead · Bradford · **Taunton** · Wilton · Trull · Henlade · Stoke St Mary · Thornfalcon · Ham · Fivehead · Swell · Drayton · Muchelney · Thorney · Witcombe · Limington · Ashington · Mudford · Yeovil Marsh · Trent · Marston Magna · Corton Denham · Sandford Orcas · Poyn

Wellington · W. Buckland · Angersleigh · Blackmoor · Corfe · Pitminster · Bagdon · Staple Fitzpaine · Bickenhall · Curland · Windmill Hill · Isle Abbots · Kingsbury Episcopi · Hambridge · Westport · **Martock** · Stapleton · Coat · Ash · Tintinhull · Chilthorne Domer · Stoke sub Hamdon · Montacute · Thorne · **Yeovil** · Nether Compton · **Sherborne** · Ohorne

Rockwell · Wrangway · Clayhidon · Rosemary Lane · Stapley · Churchstanton · Otterford · Buckland · Bishops Wood · Broadway · Ilton · Isle Brewers · Barrington · Lambrook · Shepton Beauchamp · Bower Hinton · Norton sub Hamdon · Odcombe · Preston Plucknett · Barwick · Bradford Abbas · Thornford · Lillington

Hemyock · Hackpen Hill · Sheldon · Dunkeswell · Smeathorpe · Churchingford · Northay · Howley · Whitestaunton · Ilminster · Donyatt · Dowlish Wake · Cricket Malherbie · Chillington · Hinton St George · Merriott · Haselbury Plucknett · Hardington Mandeville · Pendomer · Sutton Bingham · Closworth · Ryme Intrinseca · Yetminster · Beer Hackett

Dunkeswell · Luppitt · Upottery · Yarcombe · Marsh · Ford · Combe St Nicholas · Wadeford · Cudworth · Chaffcombe · Chard · Cricket St Thomas · Clapton · Seaborough · Mosterton · Cheddington · W. Chelborough · Eversfield · Holwell · Melbury Osmond · Chetnole · Leigh · Holnest

Awliscombe · Buckerell · Fenton · Combe Raleigh · Stockland · Monkton · Cotleigh · Wambrook · Tatworth · S. Chard · Thorncombe · Blackdown · Burstock · Broadwindsor · **Beaminster** · Tollerdown Gate · Uphall · Rampisham · Up. Cern · Cerne Abbas · Sydling St Nicholas

Honiton · Gittisham · Alfington · Hamlet · Offwell · Widworthy · Wilmington · Dalwood · Smallridge · Chardstock · Tytherleigh · Membury · Hawkchurch · Holditch · Birdsmoor Gate · Marshalsea · Pilsdon · Stoke Abbott · Mapperton · Toller Whelme · Hooke · Wraxall · Chalmington · Cattistock

Ottery St Mary · Wiggaton · Farway · Northleigh · Farway Street · Shute · Kilmington · Newenham Abbey · **Axminster** · Musbury · Wootton Fitzpaine · Marshwood · Pilsdon · Netherby · Bettiscombe · Bowood · Waytown · N. Poorton · Melplash · Powerstock · Toller Porcorum · Toller Fratrum · Wynford Eagle · Maiden Newton

Colyton · Southleigh · Blackbury Cas. · Colyford · Combpyne · Uplyme · Whitchurch Canonicorum · Marshwood · Salway Ash · N. Milton · Nettlecombe · Eggardon Hill · Compton Abbas · Frampton · Grimston

Sidbury · Sidford · Branscombe · Seaton · **Beer** · Rousdon · Dowlands · Landslip · Pinhay · Charmouth · **Lyme Regis** · Golden Cap · Chideock · Seatown · **Bridport** · Eype · West Bay · Bothenhampton · Waditch · North Hill · R. Bride · Shipton Gorge · Litton Cheney · Long Bredy · Winterbourne Abbas · **Dorc**

Sidmouth · Salcombe Regis · Branscombe · Burton Bradstock · Burton Mere · Swyre · Punknowle · Lit. Bredy · Black Down · Abbotsbury Cas. · Abbotsbury · Abbey · Portisham · Bronkham Hill · Rodden · **Martinstown** · Win

L Y M E   B A Y

West Fleet · Chesil Bank · Fast Fleet · Langton Herring · Chickerell · Radi · Broadw · Upwe · We · B · For

Wyke Regis · Portland · Fort

0 1 2 3 4 5 M

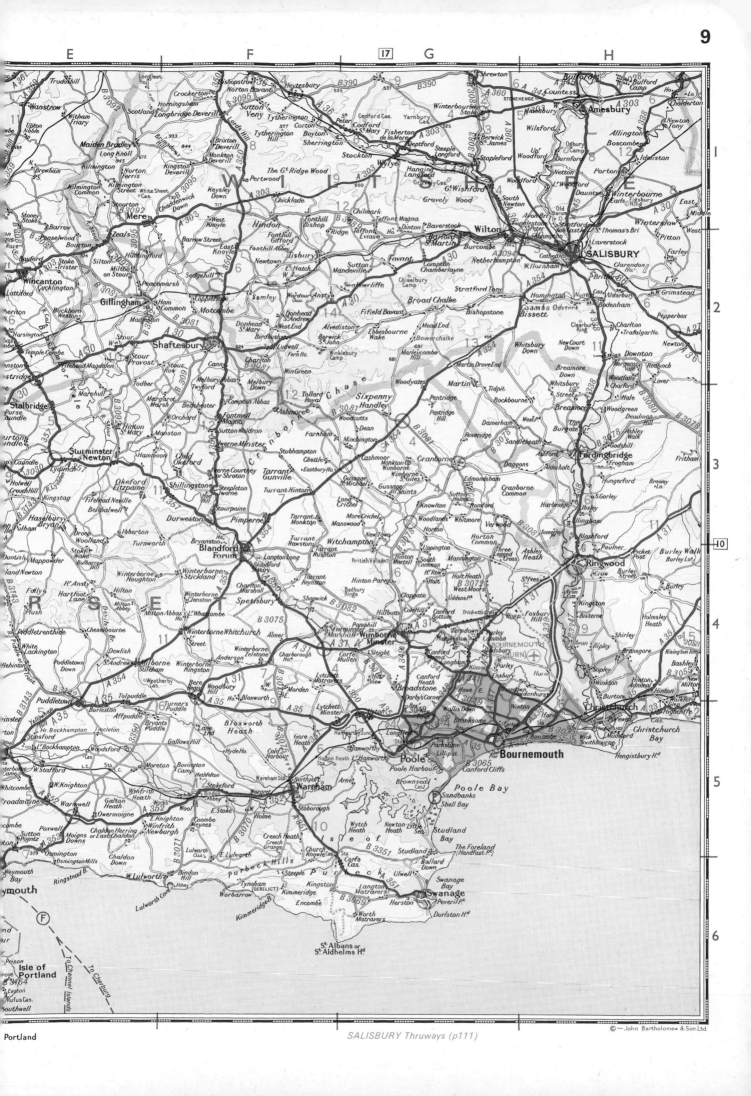

© — John Bartholomew & Son Ltd.

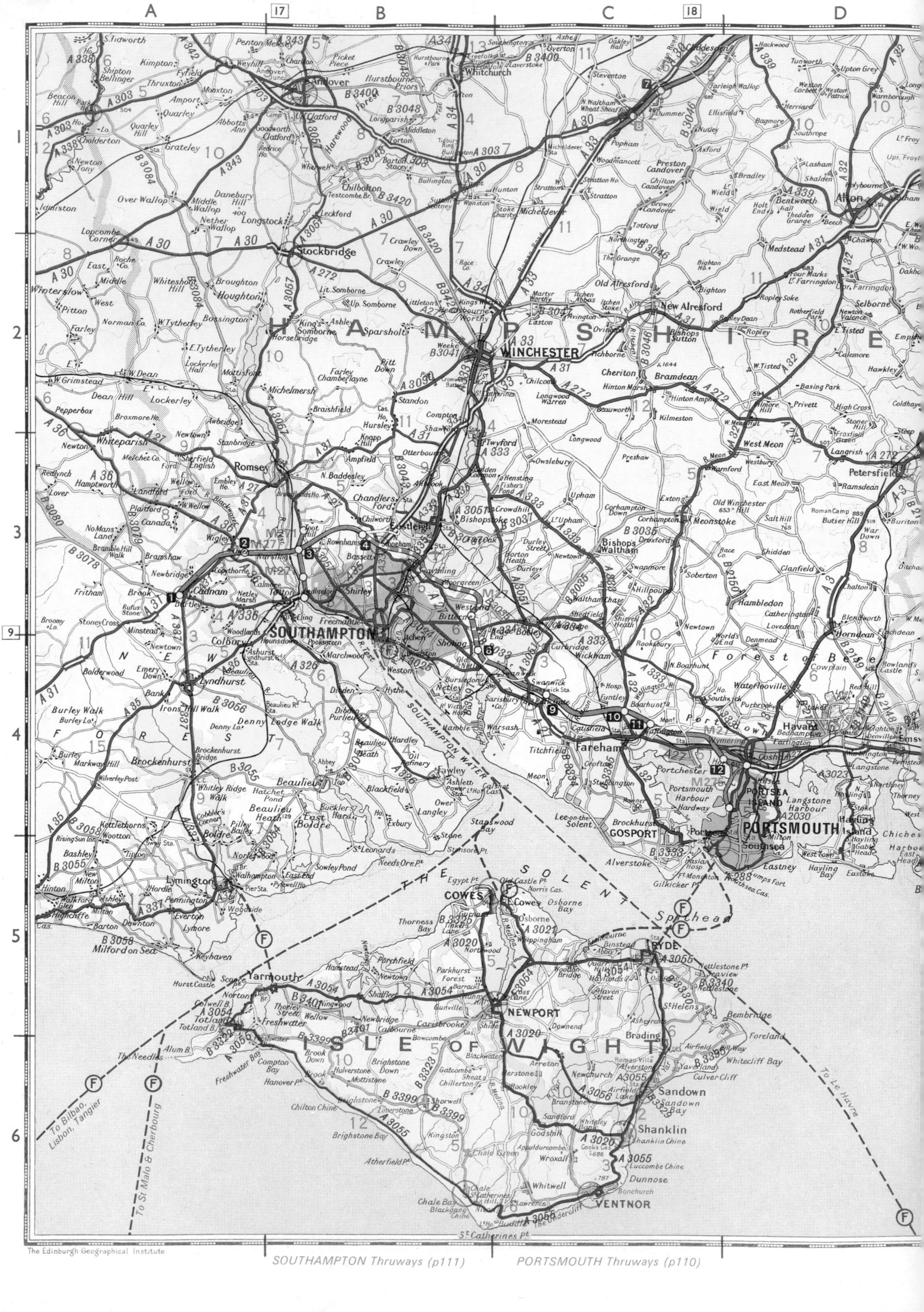

A B C D

HAMPSHIRE

WINCHESTER

New Alresford

Andover

Whitchurch

Stockbridge

Romsey

Eastleigh

SOUTHAMPTON

Lyndhurst

Brockenhurst

Lymington

Petersfield

Havant

PORTSMOUTH
Southsea

GOSPORT

Fareham

Portchester

N E W   F O R E S T

Milford on Sea

Yarmouth

Freshwater

The Needles

I S L E   O F   W I G H T

Cowes

Newport

RYDE

Sandown

Shanklin

VENTNOR

Brading

Bembridge

THE   SOLENT

Spithead

SOUTHAMPTON   WATER

To Bilbao,
Lisbon, Tangier

To St Malo & Cherbourg

To Le Havre

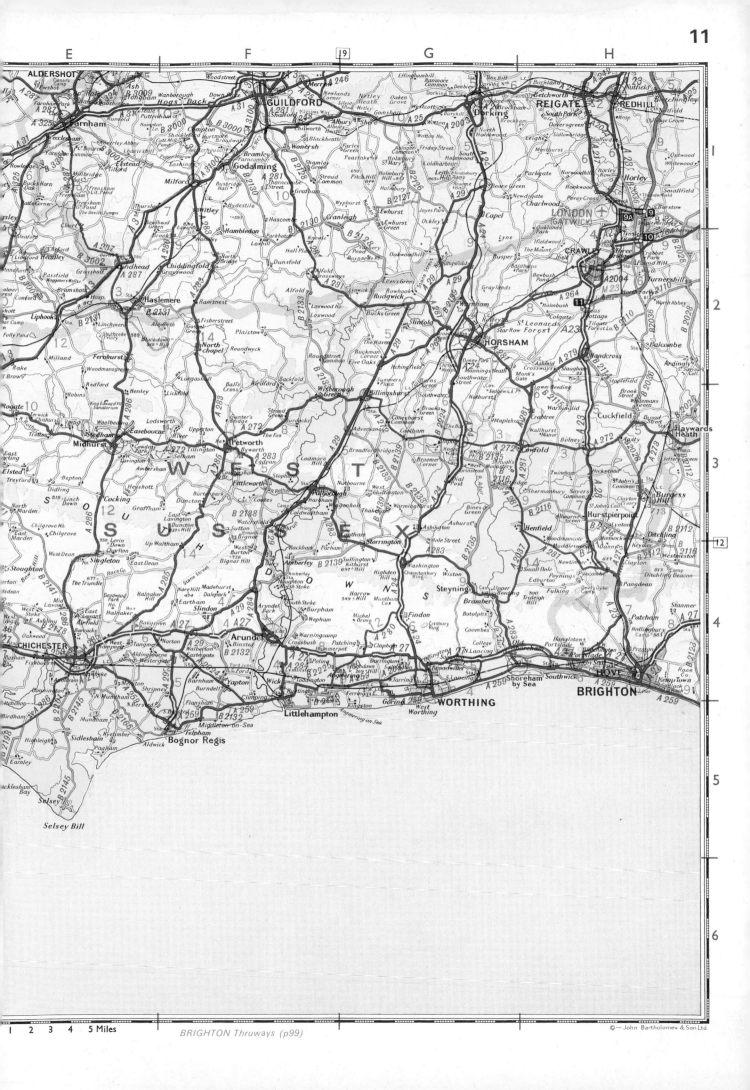

©—John Bartholomew & Son.Ltd.

I 2 3 4 5 Miles

A   B   20   C   D

SUTTON CROYDON Orpington SEVENOAKS Wrotham ROCHESTER CHATHAM GILLINGHAM

REDHILL Westerham Sundridge TONBRIDGE MAIDSTONE

Edenbridge Lingfield Southborough Hadlow Yalding

EAST GRINSTEAD ROYAL TUNBRIDGE WELLS Marden Cranbrook Goudhurst

Forest Row Hartfield Frant Lamberhurst Wadhurst Hawkhurst

Ashdown Forest Crowborough Mayfield Burwash Etchingham Battle

Cuckfield Haywards Heath Nutley Rotherfield Heathfield Robertsbridge

Burgess Hill Uckfield Cross in Hand Herstmonceux BEXHILL

Hurstpierpoint Ditchling Ringmer East Hoathly Hailsham ST LEONARDS HASTINGS

LEWES Glynde Polegate Pevensey Westham

BRIGHTON HOVE Newhaven Seaford Alfriston EASTBOURNE

Peacehaven Cuckmere Haven Beachy Head

The Edinburgh Geographical Institute

BRIGHTON Thruways (p99)

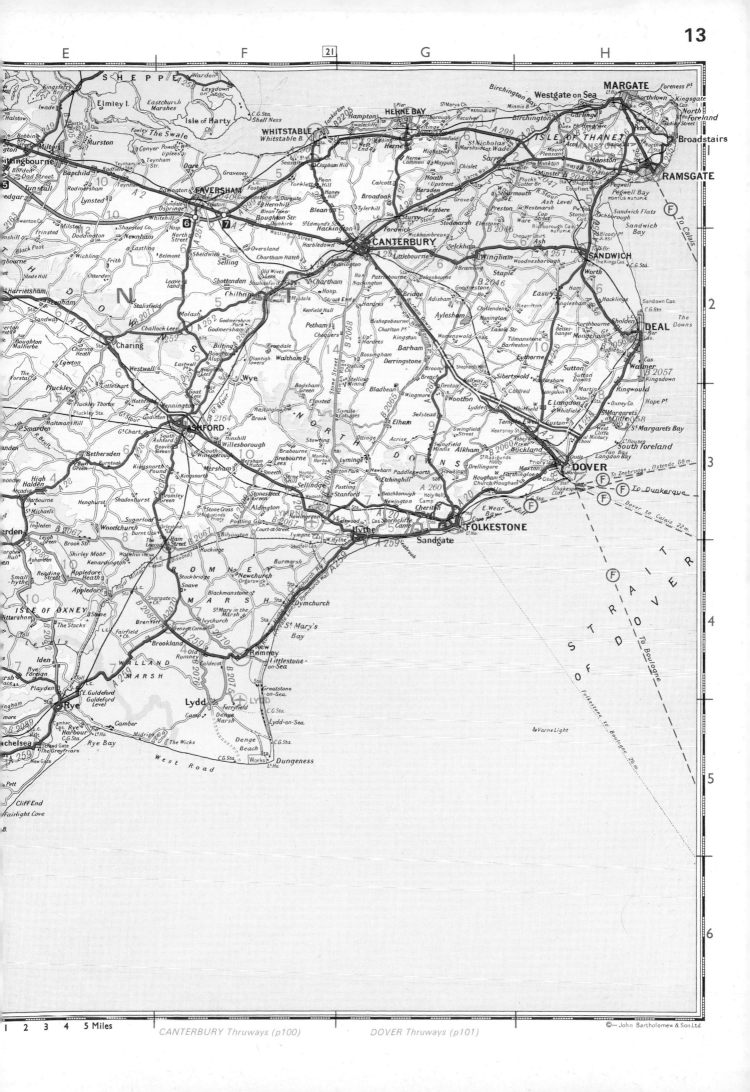

E F 21 G H

SHEPPEY

Warden
Kingsferry Br.
Leysdown on Sea
Elmley I.
Eastchurch Marshes
Isle of Harty
The Swale
Conyer
Uplees
Oare
Graveney

WHITSTABLE
Whitstable B.
Seasalter
Swalecliffe
Tankerton

HERNE BAY
Hampton
Herne
Studd Hill
Reculver
Beltinge

Birchington Bay
Westgate on Sea
Birchington
Minnis B.

MARGATE
Foreness Pt.
Northdown
Kingsgate
North Foreland

Broadstairs

RAMSGATE

ISLE OF THANET

Milton
Murston
Conyer
Teynham
Powder Wks.

FAVERSHAM
Ospringe
Preston
Boughton Str.
Dunkirk

Blean
Tylerhill
Broadoak
Hoath
Westbere
Sturry

CANTERBURY

Monkton
Minster
Manston
Acol

St Nicholas at Wade
Sarre
Chislet

Sandwich Flats
Richborough
Sandwich Bay

SANDWICH
Worth

DEAL
The Downs
Walmer
Kingsdown
Ringwould
Hope Pt.

Sittingbourne
Bapchild
Tunstall
Lynsted
Rodmersham
Teynham

Doddington
Newnham
Eastling
Selling

Chilham
Chartham
Shottenden

Bridge
Bekesbourne
Patrixbourne
Bishopsbourne
Kingston
Barham
Derringstone

Wingham
Staple
Woodnesborough
Goodnestone

Eastry
Northbourne
Mongeham
Sholden

Harrietsham
Lenham
Charing
Westwell
Wye

Waltham
Petham
Elham
Lyminge
Stelling Minnis

Womenswold
Nonington
Aylesham
Wootton
Alkham

Sibertswold
Coldred
Eythorne
Sutton

St Margaret's at Cliffe
St Margaret's Bay
South Foreland
Langdon Bay

Pluckley
Smarden
High Halden
Biddenden

ASHFORD
Willesborough
Mersham
Sellindge
Stanford

Brabourne
Smeeth
Hastingleigh

Swingfield
Buckland

DOVER
To Zeebrugge Ostende 68 m.
Shakespeare Cliff
Dover to Calais 22 m.
To Dunkerque

Bethersden
Woodchurch
Appledore
Brookland

ROMNEY MARSH
Newchurch
Dymchurch
St Mary in the Marsh
St Mary's Bay

HYTHE
Sandgate
FOLKESTONE
Cheriton

ISLE OF OXNEY
WALLAND MARSH

RYE
Rye Harbour
Camber
Winchelsea

New Romney
Littlestone on Sea
Greatstone on Sea
Lydd
Lydd-on-Sea
Dungeness
Denge Beach

STRAIT OF DOVER

Varne Light

To Boulogne

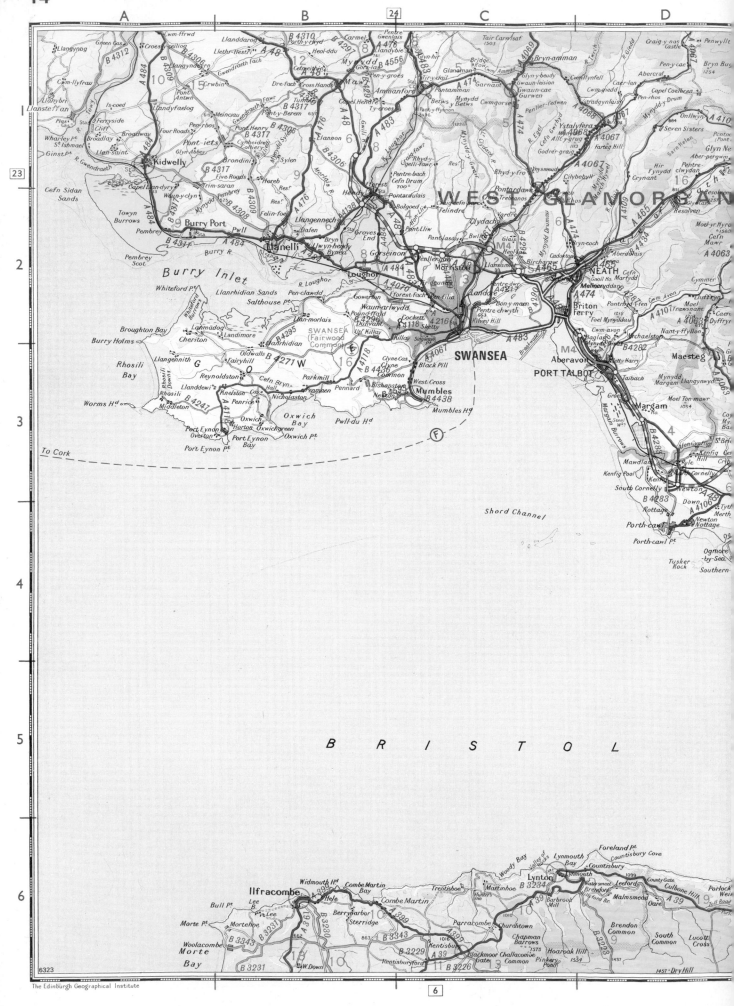

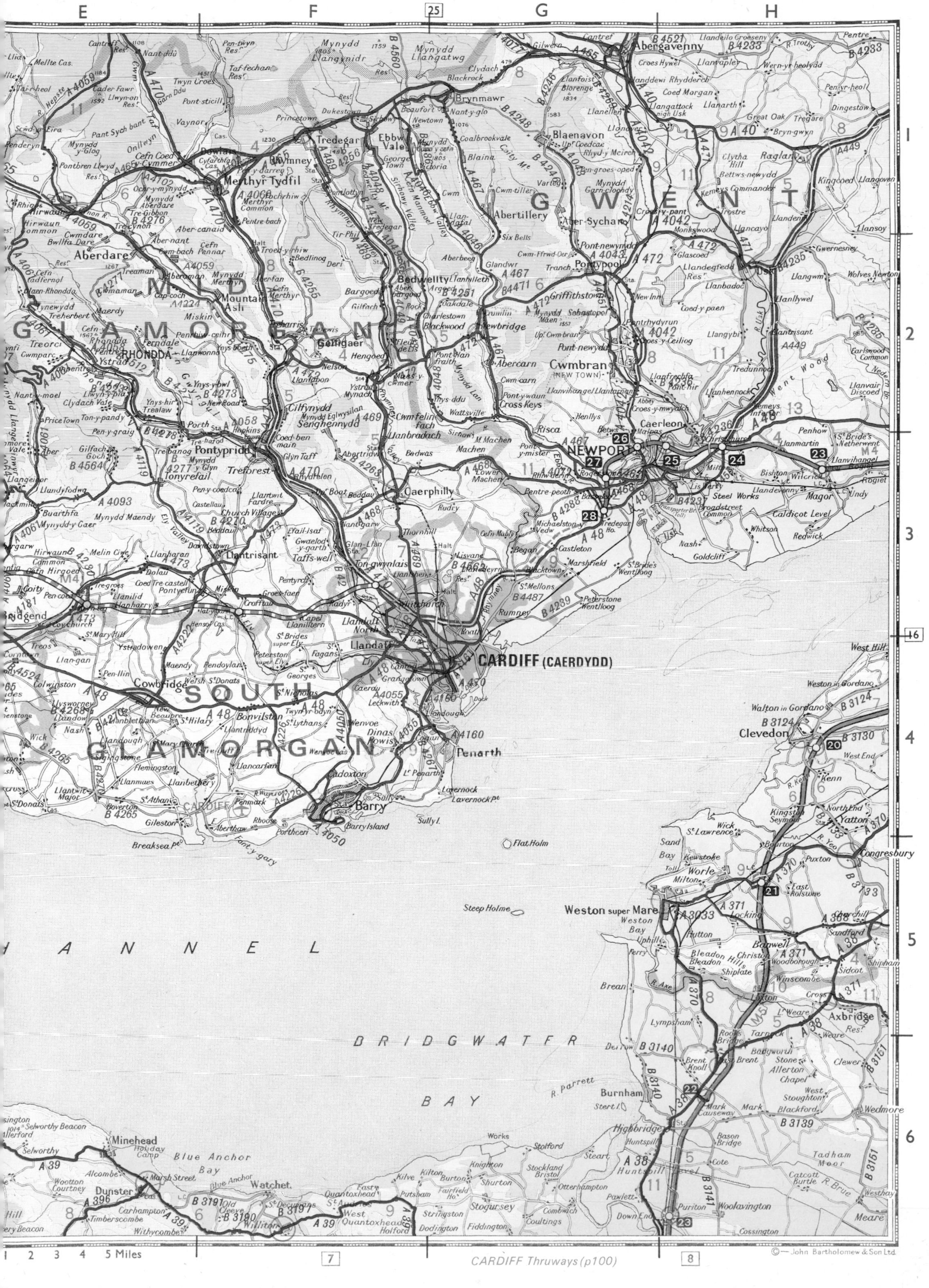

E   F   G   H

I

GWENT

Abergavenny

Brynmawr   Blaenavon

Tredegar   Ebbw Vale

Merthyr Tydfil   Abertillery   Aber-Sychan

Aberdare   Pontypool

MID

GLAMORGAN

Bedwellty   Griffithstown

Gelligaer   Newbridge

RHONDDA   Blackwood

Cilfynydd   Abercarn   Cwmbran (NEW TOWN)

Senghenydd   Cross Keys

Porth   Llanbradach   Caerleon

Pontypridd   Machen   Risca

Treforest   Caerphilly   **NEWPORT**

Church Village   Rogerston

Llantrisant   Rumney   Marshfield

M4   St Mellons   Castleton

Llandaff   **CARDIFF (CAERDYDD)**

Cowbridge   Llandaff North

SOUTH

GLAMORGAN

Bonvilston   Clevedon

Dinas Powis   Penarth   Walton in Gordano

Wenvoe   Yatton

Cadoxton   Congresbury

Barry   Lavernock

Barry Island   Worle

Flat Holm   Weston super Mare

Steep Holme   Locking   Axbridge

C H A N N E L

Bleadon   Winscombe

B R I D G W A T E R

B A Y

Burnham   Highbridge

Minehead

Blue Anchor Bay   Watchet   Mark

Dunster   Williton   Puriton

1 2 3 4 5 Miles

7   *CARDIFF Thruways (p100)*   8   ©— John Bartholomew & Son Ltd.

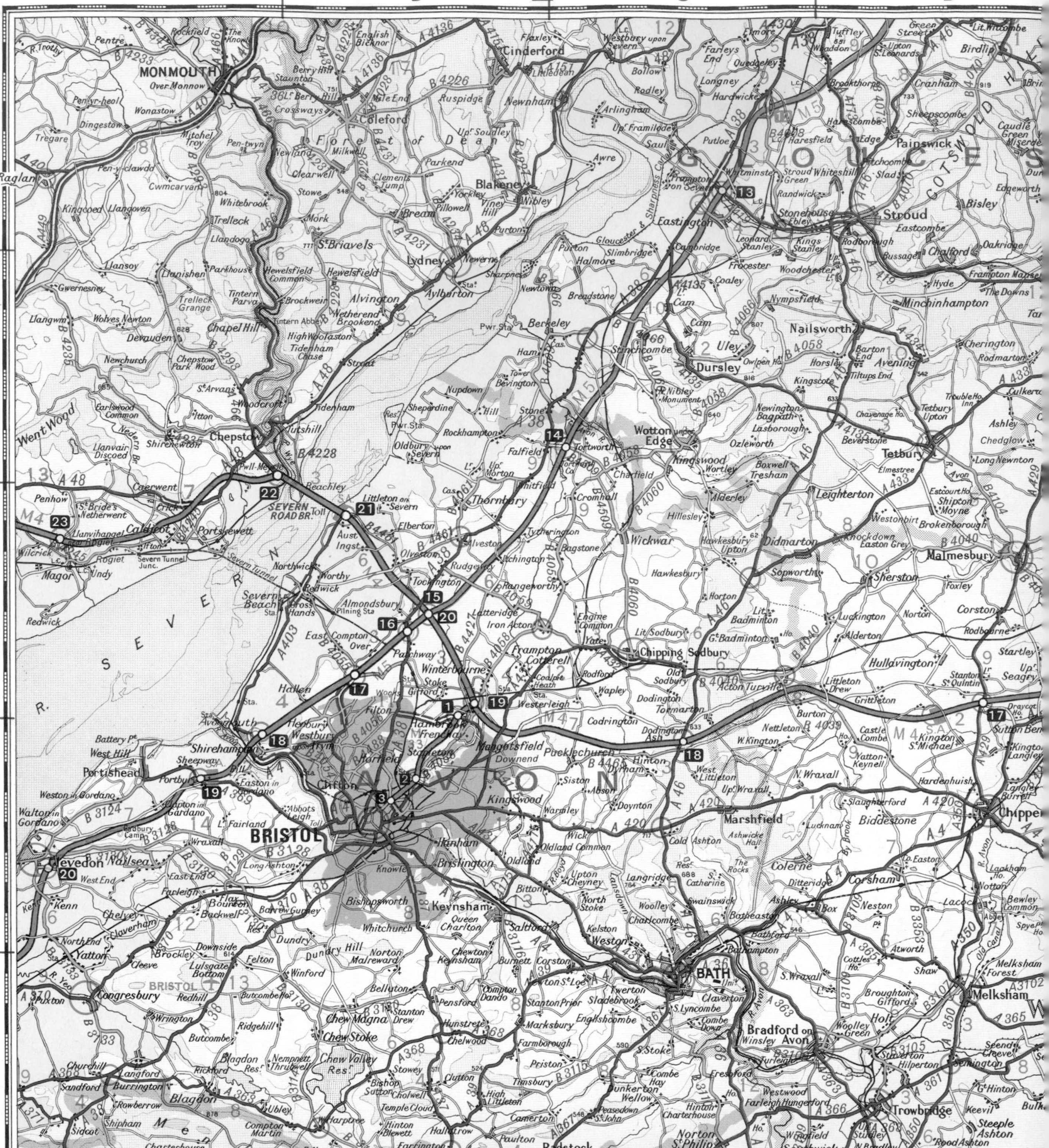

A   B   26   C   D

1

2

3

13

15

4

5

6

MONMOUTH

Cinderford

Coleford

Lydney

Blakeney

Newnham

Chepstow

Berkeley

Dursley

Nailsworth

Stroud

Painswick

Tetbury

Malmesbury

Sherston

Wotton under Edge

Thornbury

Chipping Sodbury

Clevedon

Nailsea

BRISTOL

Keynsham

Bath

Corsham

Melksham

Marshfield

Colerne

Chipping

Congresbury

Chew Magna

Chew Stoke

Chew Valley Res.

Radstock

Trowbridge

Westbury

Warminster

Axbridge

Cheddar

Wells

Shepton Mallet

Midsomer Norton

Frome

Bradford on Avon

Winsley

SEVERN R.

AVON

FOREST OF DEAN

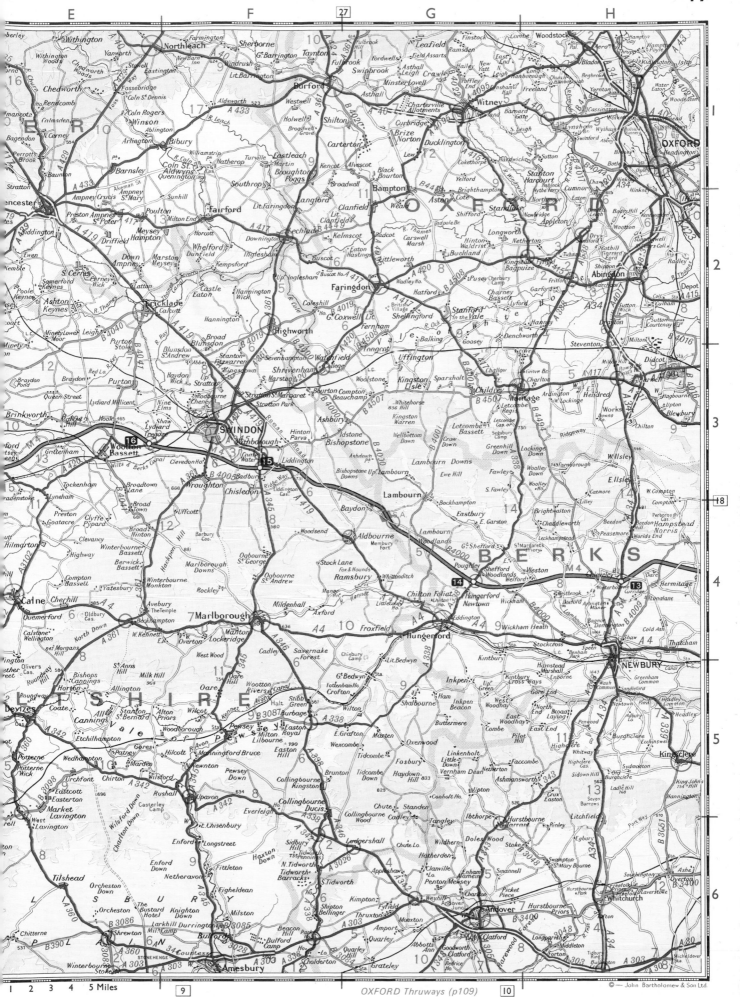

St Johns Rd

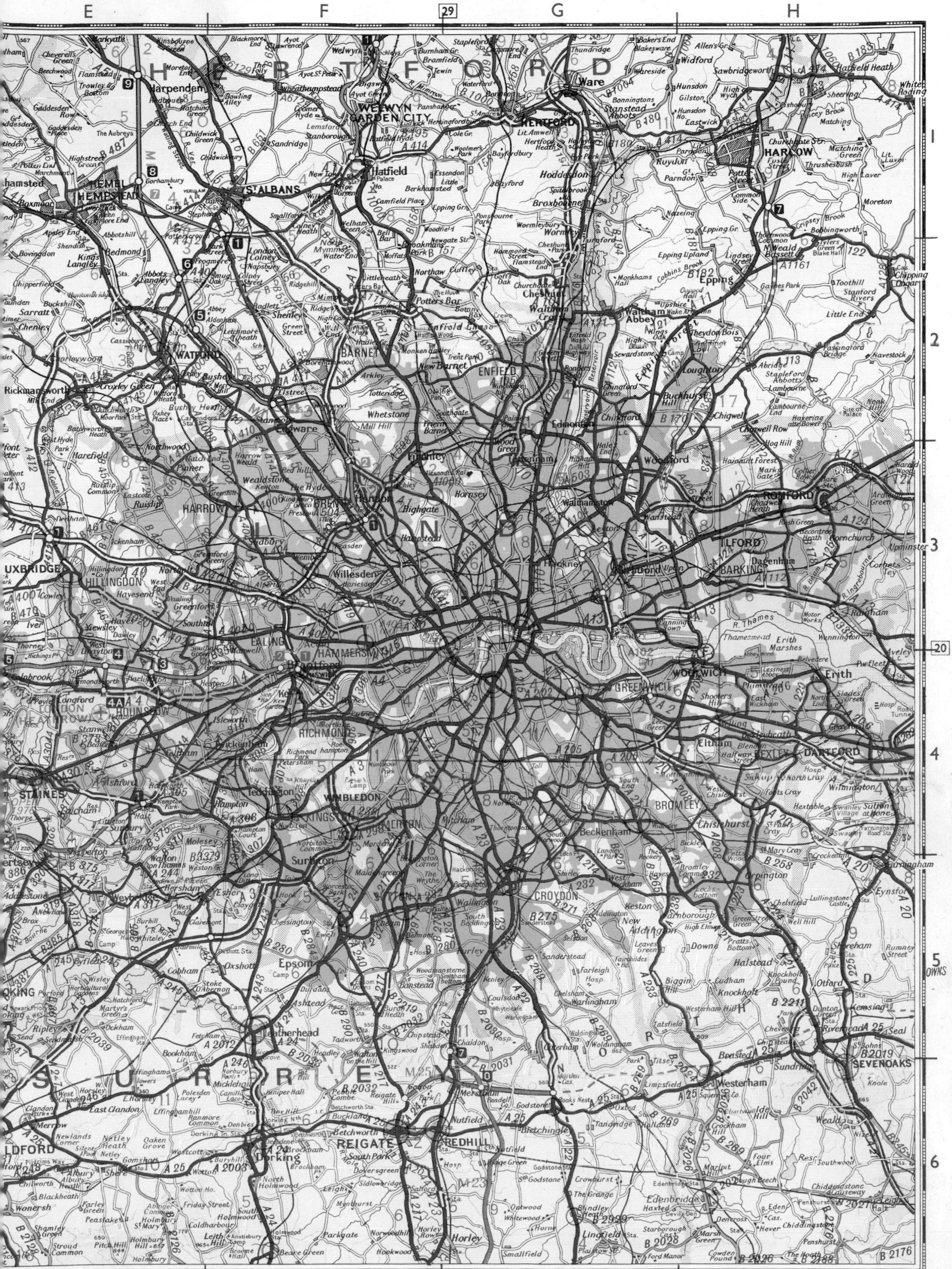

E   F   29   G   H

HERTFORD

Harpenden
WELWYN GARDEN CITY
Ware
Hertford
HEMEL HEMPSTEAD
St. ALBANS
Hatfield
Hoddesdon
Broxbourne
HARLOW
Chipping Ongar
WATFORD
BARNET
ENFIELD
Epping
Waltham Abbey
Loughton
Buckhurst Hill
Chigwell
Edmonton
Chingford
Woodford
ROMFORD
Upminster
HARROW
Highgate
Walthamstow
ILFORD
Dagenham
BARKING
UXBRIDGE
HILLINGDON
EALING
HAMMERSMITH
Hackney
R. Thames
Erith
HEATHROW
HOUNSLOW
RICHMOND
WOOLWICH
GREENWICH
Eltham
BEXLEY
DARTFORD
STAINES
WIMBLEDON
KINGSTON
MITCHAM
BROMLEY
Chislehurst
Orpington
Weybridge
SUTTON
CROYDON
Beckenham
Esher
Epsom
Leatherhead
SURREY
Westerham
SEVENOAKS
GUILDFORD
Dorking
REIGATE
REDHILL
Oxted
Horley
Lingfield

1 2 3 4 5 Miles   11   See Pages 106-107   Signposted N. & S. Circular Roads & Ring Road ——   12   © — John Bartholomew & Son, Ltd.

A 29   B   30   C   D

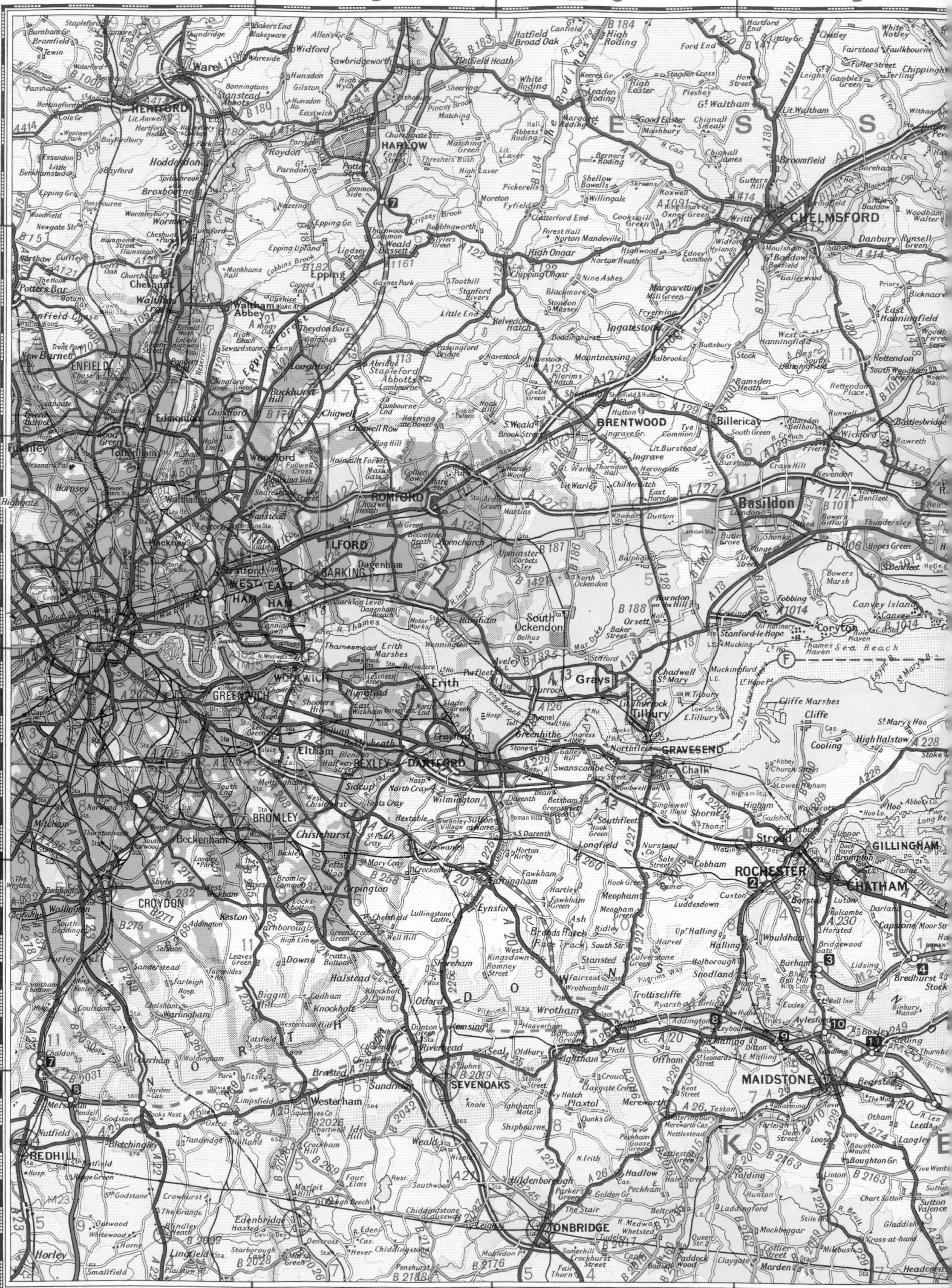

E S S E X

Signposted N. & S. Circular Roads & Ring Road ————   12   *See pages 106-107*

The Edinburgh Geographical Institute

E F 31 G H

Inworth Layer Marney Abberton Langenhoe Langenhoe Hall Roughe Heath Gt Holland Little Clacton Frinton-on-Sea
B 1022 Layer Breton Peldon B 1027 Holland on Sea Sandy Pt.
Tiptree Gt Wigborough Brightlingsea St Osyth Clacton Holland Cliff
Tiptree Heath Lit. Wigborough B 1029 Priory Coppens Gr. CLACTON-ON-SEA
Tolleshunt Knights Virley Salcott Chan. Ivy Ho. B 1032
B 1023 Tolleshunt D'Arcy MERSEA I. St Cleres Hall St Osyth Marsh Sands Pier
Gt Totham Salcott Sunken West Mersea E. Mersea Jaywick Martello Tower
Tolleshunt Major Tollesbury Quarters Spit Mersea Flats Colne Pt.
Goldhanger Shinglehead Pt Wallet Gunfleet Gt Gunfleet Lt.
Broad Street Green Heybridge The Stumble RIVER BLACKWATER Sales Pt. St Peter's Flat Knoll Kings Channel or East Swin Little Sunk
Heybridge Basin Osea Northey Bradwell Waterside St Peter's Chap. Bachelor Spit
Stansgate Abbey Bradwell-on-Sea East Swin Middle Sunk
Steeple Dengie Flats Buxey Sunk Sand
St Lawrence Tillingham Middle Deep Black Deep
Mundon Tillingham Marshes Dengie Hall Middle Light East Barrow
Mundon Hill Dengie Asheldham Foulness Sands
B 1012 Latchingdon Southminster Dengie Marshes Ray Sands Barrow 2
Althorne Ostend Sta. Whitaker Chan.
Bridgemarsh East Wick Holliwell Pt.
Burnham on Crouch Foulness Pt. South West Reach Barrow Deep To Gothenburg
Canewdon River Crouch Courtsend N. Newlands West Barrow Black Deep Lt.
Ashingdon Paglesham Churchend Maplin Light Duke of Edinburgh Chan. Lt. Duke of Edinburgh Chan.
Rochford Wallasea I. River Roach North Shingles
Gt Stambridge Potton Island Rugwood Hd. Maplin Notice Buoy West Shingles
SOUTHEND Barling Rushley E. Wick Sands Notice Buoy West Barrow 3
Sutton Little Wakering Shelford Creek New England Cr. Black Deep Lt.
Southchurch Gt Wakering Havengore South Shingles Princes Chan. Lt.
Southend North Shoebury Havengore Cr. West Swin Mouse Knob Chan. Alexandra Chan. Princes Channel
Thorpe Bay Shoeburyness Artillery Range Buoys Oaze Girdler Light To Flushing
Shoebury Ness Oaze Deep Red Sand Gilman Princes Channel

THAMES Nore Sand The Flats The Cant E. Spaniard Margate Sand 4
London Stone Nore Light Spaniard
Isle of Grain Sheerness Margate Hook
Port Victoria Dock Yard Minster Warden Pt. Margate Hook MARGATE Foreness Pt.
Queenborough Halfway Houses Warden Birchington Bay Westgate on Sea Northdown North Foreland Kingsgate Cas.
SHEPPEY Eastchurch Leysdown on Sea St Marys Ch. Minnis B. Birchington ISLE OF THANET Cantium Prom.
Elmley I. Eastchurch Marshes C.G. Sta. Shell Ness Hampton Herne Bay Reculver Manston Broadstairs
Milton Isle of Harty The Swale Swalecliffe A 299 St Nicholas Acol Manston RAMSGATE 5
Sittingbourne Conyer WHITSTABLE Whitstable B. Herne Monkton Pegwell Bay To Calais
Bapchild Teynham Seasalter Clapham Hill Hoath Chislet Minster Sandwich Flats
Lynsted Ore Graveney Yorkletts Broadoak Upstreet Stourmouth SANDWICH Sandwich Bay
FAVERSHAM Preston Honey Hill Tylerhill Westbere Ware Worth
M 2 Davington A 2 Boughton Str. Blean Fordwich Stodmarsh Ash
Ospringe Hernhill Dunkirk Hackington Wickhambreaux Woodnesborough Deal
Sheldwich Selling CANTERBURY Littlebourne Wingham Staple 6
Newnham Eastling Chartham Hatch Harbledown Ickham B 2046 Eastry
Doddington Belmont Overland Ibanington Bekesbourne Goodnestone Worth
Stalisfield Shalmsford Chartham Patrixbourne Adisham Knowlton Ham DEAL
Molash Chilham Nackington Bishopsbourne Aylesham Nonington Northbourne The Downs
Charing Godmersham Park Kenfield Hall Charlton Kingston Wingmore Sutton
Westwell Boughton Petham Barham Eastling Ringwould
Wye Bilting Chequers Derringstone Broome Sibertswold Kingsdown
Pluckley Crundale Bossingham Stelling Minnis Denton Walmer
Littlehart Goat Lees Bladbean Wootton E. Langdon Hope Pt. A 258

1 2 3 4 5 Miles CANTERBURY Thruways (p100) 13 © — John Bartholomew & Son, Ltd.

A B C D

1

To Rosslare

F

Strumble Head *Carreg Wastad (French landed A.D.1797)* *Porth Sychan*

2

Pen Brush *Pen Cleddau* Crincoed Pt *Fishguard Bay* Dinas Hd Dinas Island *Newport Bay* Berry Hill Cardigan Island Mount Ch.

Cemaes Hd Port Cardigan Gwbert-on-Sea Verwick Trema

Pen-yr-Afr Pwll Granant Tre-Rhys St Dogmaels CARDIGAN

B 4546 B 4582 A 487

Goodwick Sta. Lower Town Dyffryn FISHGUARD

Llanwnda Trefasser Pen Bwch-du Manorowen St Nicholas

Dinas Bwlch Mawr Newport Carn-ingle Common Nevern

Moylgrove Tredrissi Glan-rhyd Monington Cilgerran

Velindre farchog Tre-Wilym Eglwyswrw Bridell Llantood Rhos-hill

Newchurch Bridell Blaenffos Boncath

3

Pen Morfa Ynys Deullyn Aber-castle Granston St Nicholas

Pen Clegyr Porth-gain Trevine Mathry Jordanston Castle Morris Newbridge

Aber Eiddy Llanrhian Croes-goch Llanreithan Welsh Hook St Lawrence

St David's Head Treleddyd-fawr Tretio A 487 Triglemais Llanhowel Solva Llandeloy

Pen Llechwen Rhodiad Caer farchell Middle Mill Hayscastle

Whitesand Bay Whitchurch Pen-y-cwm Brawdy Hayscastle Cross

Carreg Rhoson St John Rhosson ST DAVIDS Solva A 487

Ramsey Island Dinas fawr Green Scar Newgale

Ynys Bery Llethr Roch Br. Roch Camrose

Scleddau Tre-cwn Letterston Wolf's Castle Little Newcastle Castlebythe

Llanychaer Br. Pontfaen Cilrhedyn Br. Morvil Woodstock Slop Ambleston

Mynydd Melyn Mynydd Caregog Foel Eryr Mynydd Castlebythe Tufton

Bryn-berian Tafarn-y-bwlch Maenclochog New Moat

Mynydd Presely Prescelly Top or Foel Cwm cerwyn 1760 Clyn ford Foel Drych Pentre-galar

Hermon Glandwr Llanglydwen Derwyn Eglwys

Henry's Moat Rosebush Mynachlog ddu Hebron

Maenclochog Llandissilio Llangolman Llanfallteg

Llys-y-fran Res. Llys-y-fran Llanycefn Cilymaenllwyd Login Llanboidy

D Y F E D

Pen-ffordd Clarbeston Bletherston Rhyd-y-Wrach

Woodstock Walton East Clarbeston Road Gelly Clynderwen Castelldwyran

15

4

St Brides Rickets Head Nolton Haven Nolton Keeston Br. Keeston

ST BRIDES BAY

Haroldston West Portfield Gate Greenhill Merlins Br. Prendergast HAVERFORDWEST

The Nab Head Broad Haven Little Haven Talbenny Walton West Rosepool Tiers Cross Broadway

Tangiers Pelcomb Pelcomb Cross Lambston Crundale Fenton Br.

Wiston Llawhaden Canaston Br. Robeston Wathen Narberth Whitland

Uzmaston The Rhos Slebech Hall Picton Pk. Minwear Landshipping

Woodbine Lower Freystrop Freystrop Cross Llangwm Martletwy Yerbeston Reynalton

Pope Hill Johnston Sardis Hill Mountain Houghton Benton Bishops Templeton

A 40 A 478 Velfrey Princes Gate Tavernspite Crunwear

Cold Blow Ludchurch Lampeter Velfrey Crinow Llanteague Marros

Garland Stone Wooltack Pt Skomer Midland Marloes Sandy Haven Herbrandston

5

Mew Stone Gateholm Hooper's Pt The Stack Skokholm Dale Dale Pt

Broad Sound The Head St Ishmael's Hubberston Refinery MILFORD HAVEN Waterston

St Ann's Head Thorn I. Angle Angle B. Pwllcrochan Rhoscrowther Hundleton

Sheep I. B 4320 Newton Castlemartin Maiden Wells Kingsfold Hoggeston

Neyland Llanstadwell PEMBROKE DOCK Pembroke Ferry PEMBROKE Lamphey

MILFORD HAVEN Rosemarket Steynton Burton Cosheston Carew Milton

Honeyborough Lawrenny Cresswell Redberth Jeffreston Begelly Kilgetty

W. Williamston Cresselly Redberth Hill Williamston Stepaside

A 4075 A 477 A 478 B 4318 Saundersfoot Saundersfoot Bay

Carew Cheriton St Florence Gumfreston Woodside Monkstone Pt

Manorbier Sta. Jameston New Hedges TENBY Tenby Roads

Freshwater West Castlemartin Warren Merrion Orielton Cheriton Trewent Pt

Blucks Pool St Petrox Court Stackpole Manorbier Penally Giltar Pt

Linney Hd Bosherston Buckspool Stackpole Hd Broad Haven Lydstep Caldy Sd

The Wash Saddle Hd St Govan's Hd Old Castle Hd St Margaret's I. Caldy I.

St Catherine's I. The Ridgeway A 4139

C A

6

To Cork

F

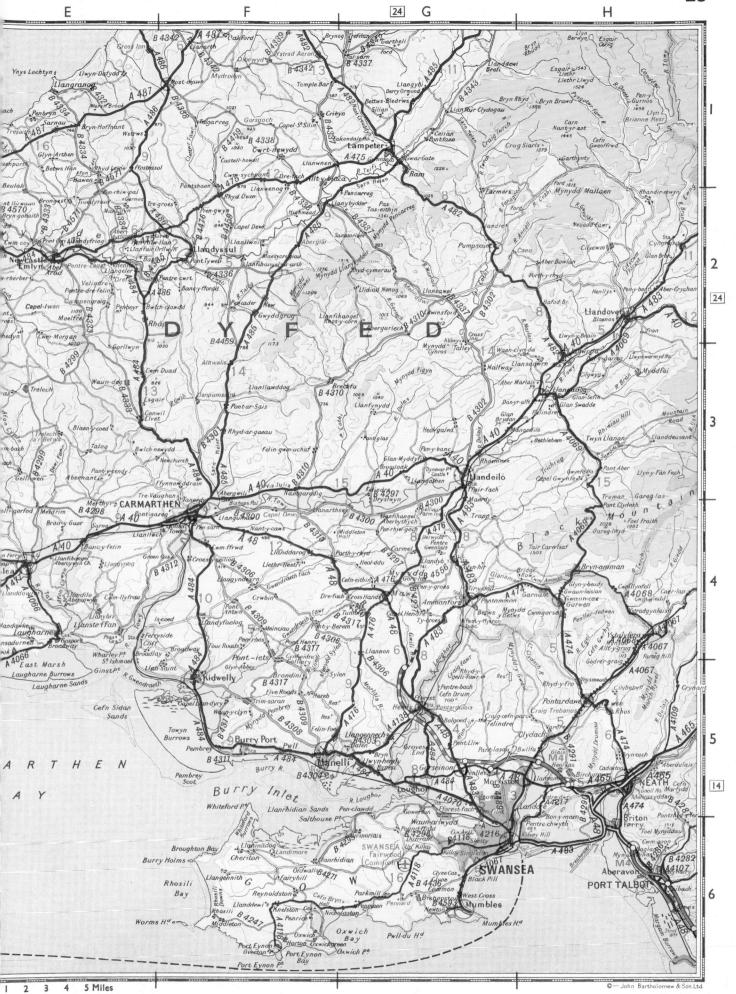

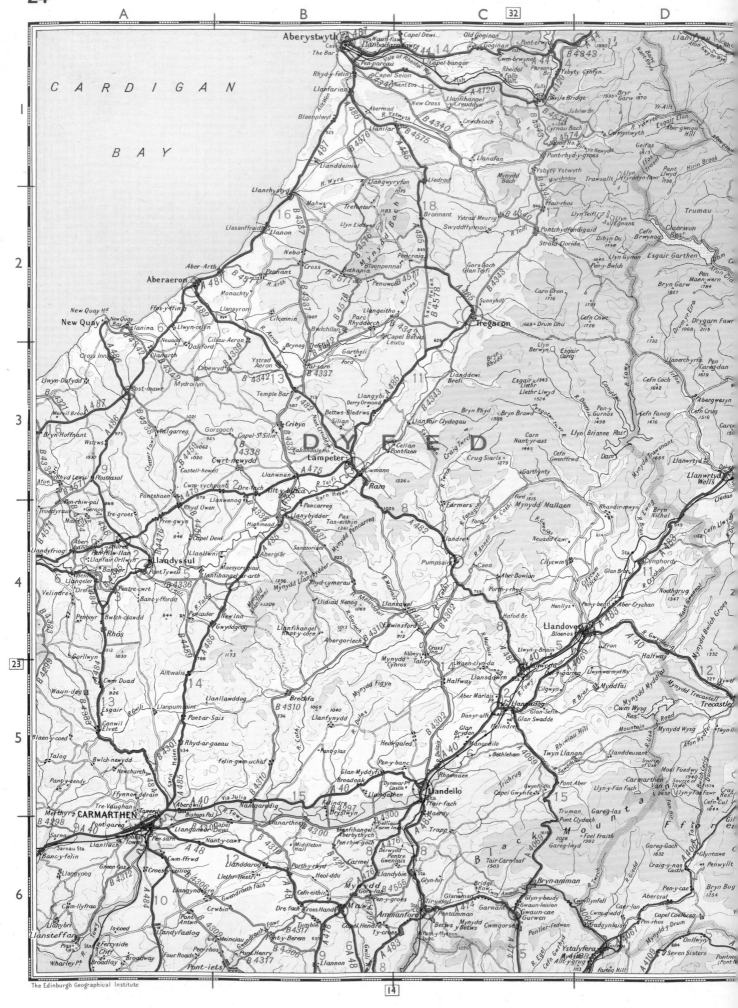

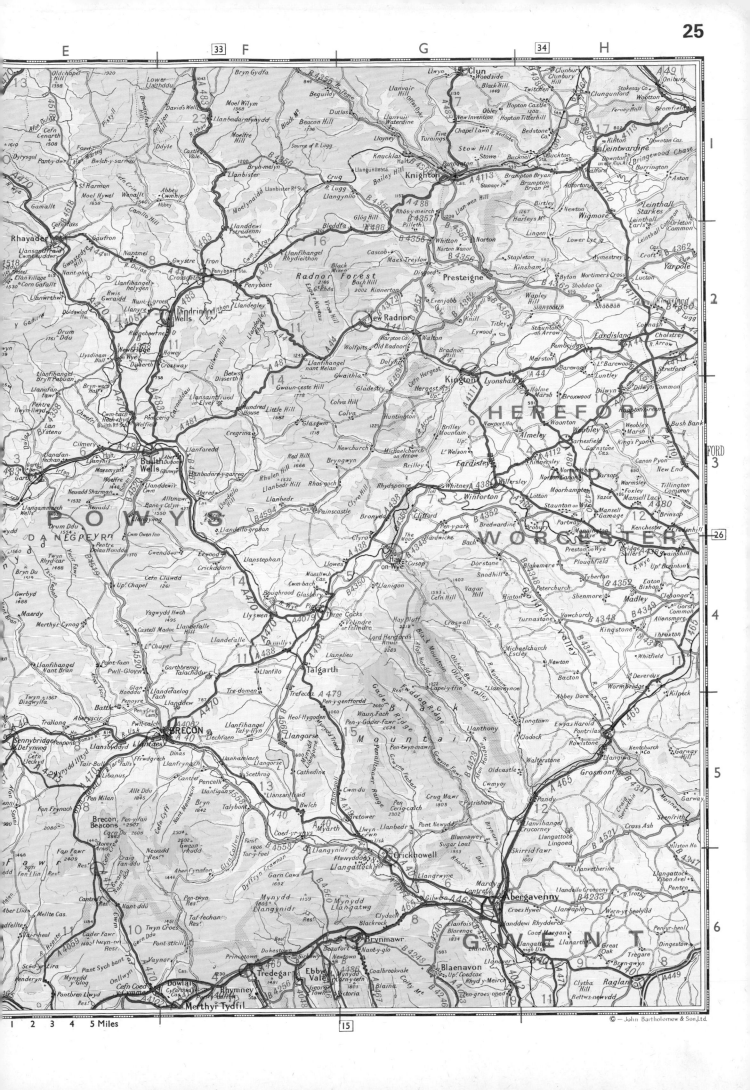

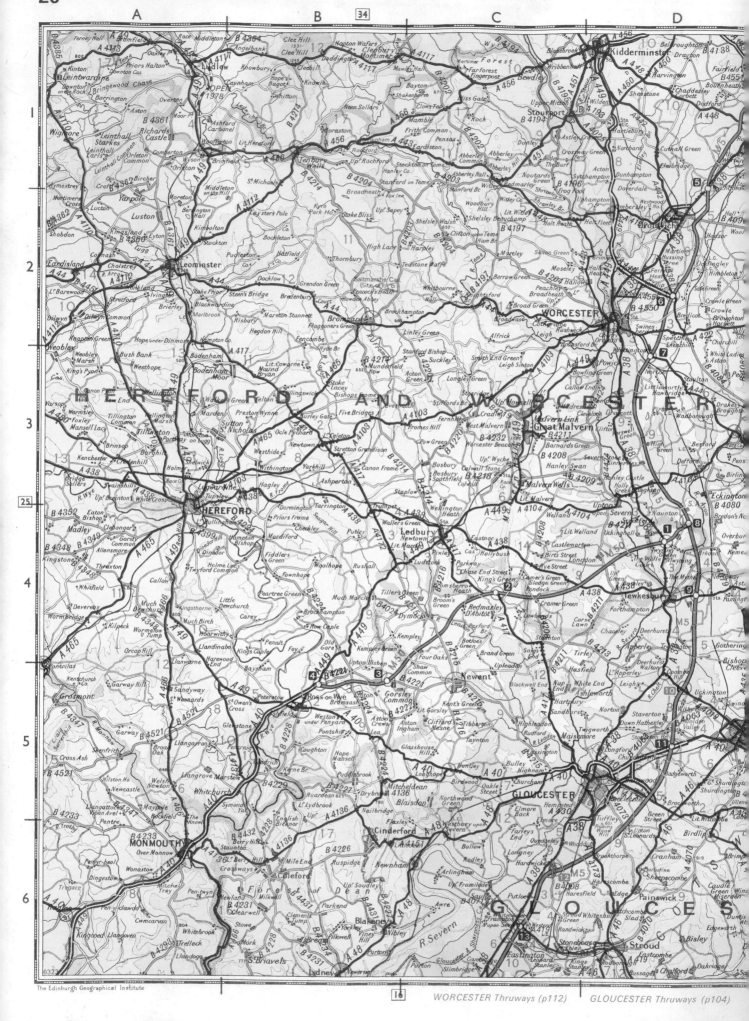

WORCESTER Thruways (p112)   GLOUCESTER Thruways (p104)

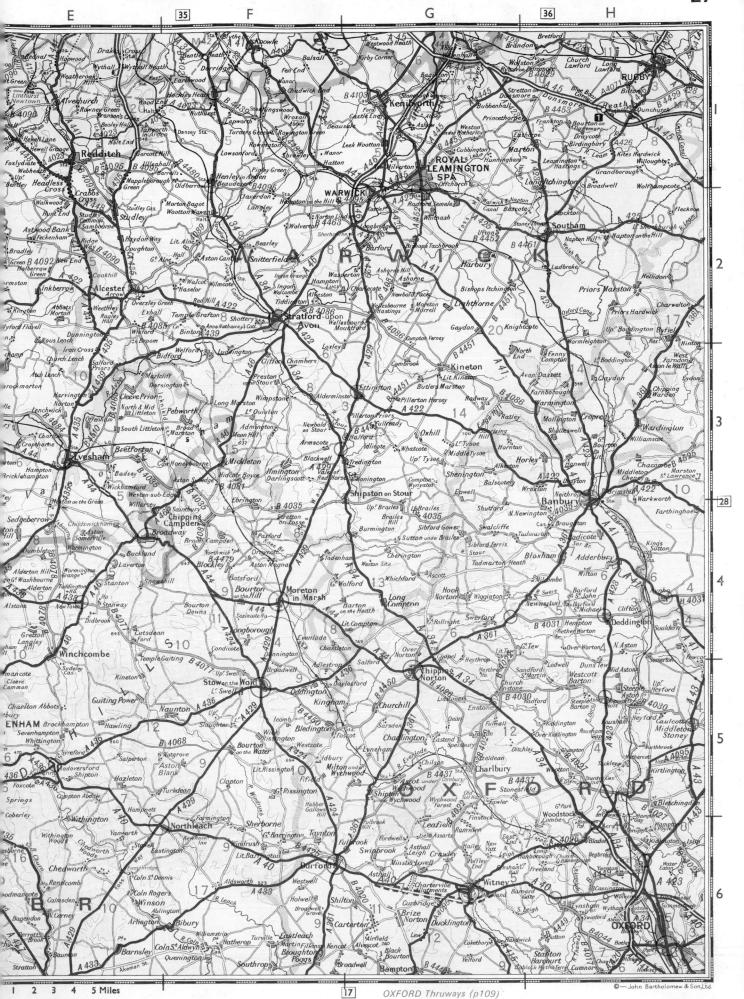

OXFORD Thruways (p109) © — John Bartholomew & Son, Ltd.

NO RIGHT TURN FROM
M1 TO M45 (WEST)

NO LEFT TURN FROM
M45 TO M1 (NORTH)
AT JUNCTION 17   36

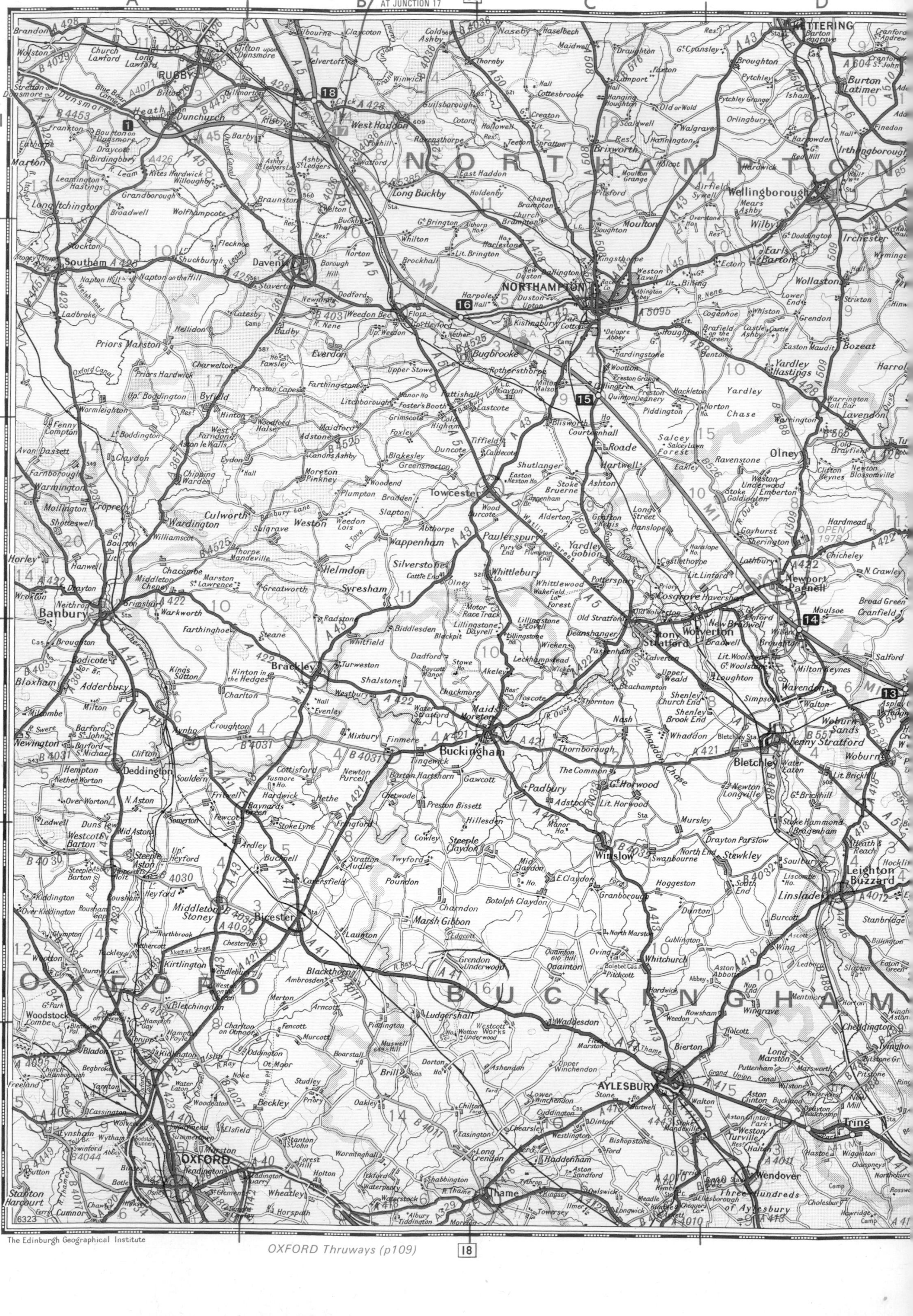

A   B   C   D

1

2

3

4

5

6

NORTHAMPTON

OXFORD   BUCKINGHAM

Rugby
Banbury
Northampton
Wellingborough
Kettering
Burton Latimer
Irchester
Wollaston
Olney
Newport Pagnell
Milton Keynes
Stony Stratford
Wolverton
Bletchley
Fenny Stratford
Woburn
Leighton Buzzard
Linslade
Towcester
Brackley
Buckingham
Bicester
Winslow
Aylesbury
Thame
Wendover
Tring
Oxford
Deddington
Southam
Daventry
Woodstock

27

Oxford

The Edinburgh Geographical Institute

OXFORD Thruways (p109)

18

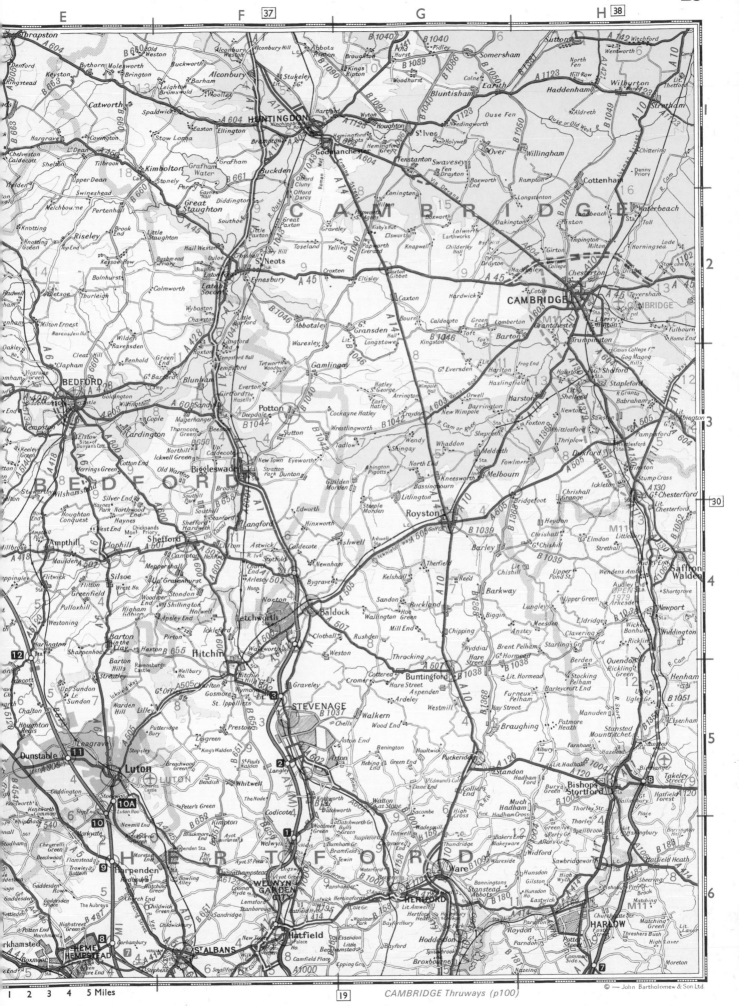

CAMBRIDGE Thruways (p100)

© — John Bartholomew & Son Ltd.

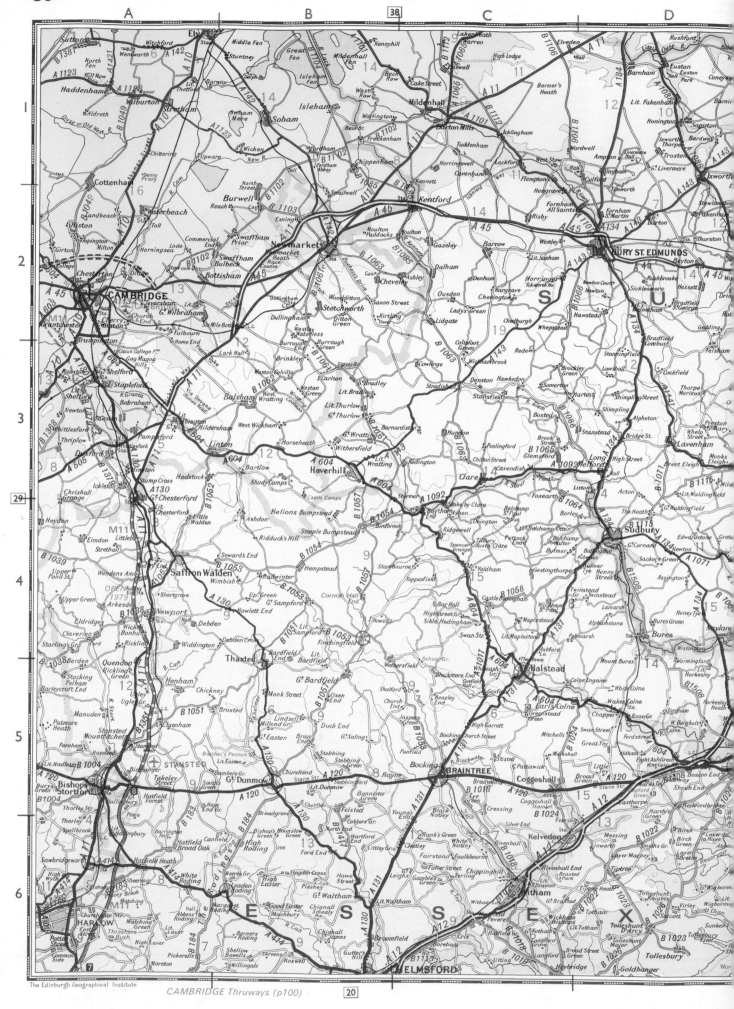

CAMBRIDGE Thruways (p100)

20

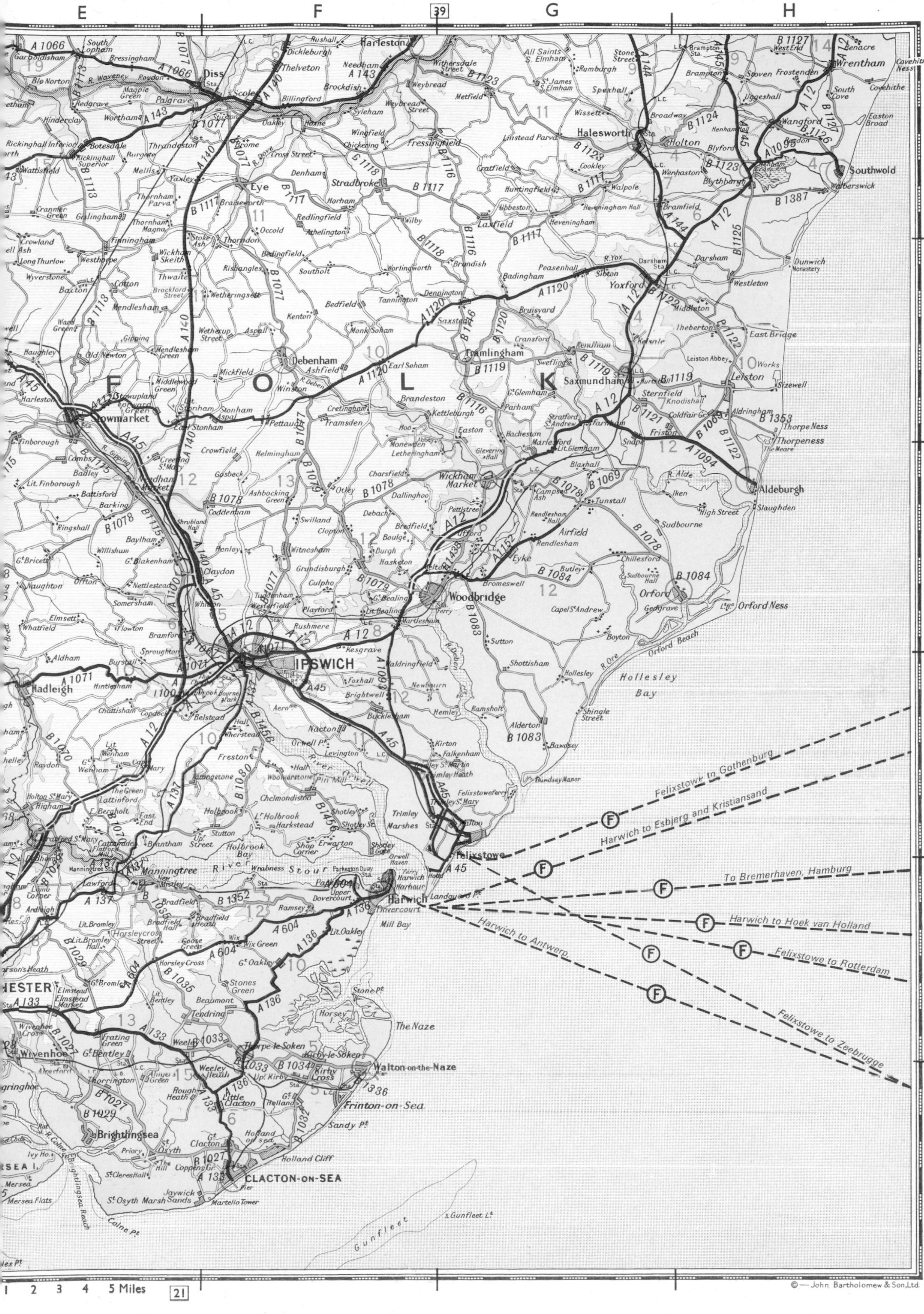

E F 39 G H

FOLK

IPSWICH

Diss
Harleston
Halesworth
Southwold
Walberswick
Wrentham
Eye
Debenham
Framlingham
Saxmundham
Leiston
Aldeburgh
Stowmarket
Needham Market
Woodbridge
Orford
Orford Ness
Hadleigh
Felixstowe
Harwich
Dovercourt
Manningtree
Brightlingsea
Wivenhoe
CHESTER
Walton-on-the-Naze
Frinton-on-Sea
CLACTON-ON-SEA
Hollesley Bay
The Naze

Felixstowe to Gothenburg
Harwich to Esbjerg and Kristiansand
To Bremerhaven, Hamburg
Harwich to Hoek van Holland
Harwich to Antwerp
Felixstowe to Rotterdam
Felixstowe to Zeebrugge

River Stour
River Orwell

Gunfleet

1
2
3
4
5
6

1 2 3 4 5 Miles   21

© — John Bartholomew & Son, Ltd.

A   B   C   40   D

1

Trevor
Y Gyrn-ddu
1712
Yr Eifl
1849 The Rivals
Mynydd Cennin
859
Bryncir
Garn Dolbenmaen
A 4085
Pass of Aber-Glaslyn
Pont Aber-Glaslyn
Nantmor
Moel Ddu
1811
Moelwyn
2327
Moelwyn Bach
2334
Tan-lan
Gris Powe
Sta.
Llithfaen
Llanaelhaearn
Llyn Glasfryn
Cefn-caer-ferch
Dolbenmaen
Penmorfa
A 498
Afon Glaslyn
Tan-lan Rhyd
Garreg
A 410
B 4411
Morfa Nefyn
Edern
Greestfordd
Nefyn
Garn Bodfean
B 4354
Botfuan
Y Ffôr
Llanarmon
Llangybi
Llanystumdwy
Pentre-felin
Tremadog
Porthmadog
Penrhyndeudraeth
Festiniog Rly
B 4417
Rhos-y-llan
Tudweiliog
Dinas
Madryn Cas.
1217
Carn Fadryn
Rhyd-y-clafdy
Efail-newydd
Abererch
Holiday Camp
Cricieth
Moel-y-Gest
Borth-y-gest
Portmeirion
A 496
Traeth Bach
Tal-sarnau
Eisingrug
2046
Penllech
Porth Colmon
Llangwnnadl
Aber
Llaniestyn
Sarn Mellteyrn
Bryncroes
Pig Street
Pwllheli
Penrhos
South Beach
Llanbedrog
Llanbedrog Pt.
TREMADOG BAY
Harlech Pt.
Llanfihangel-y-traethau
Harlech
B 4573
Llanfair
556
Y Graig ddfwg
Afon
2

Methlem
Rhos-hirwaun
406
Llandegwning
965
Mynydd Rhiw
Llangian
A 4499
St Tudwal's
Abersoch Bay
Llanbedr & Pensarn Sta.
Gwynfryn
Nant-Col
2475
Y Llet
2333
Rhinog Fawr
2362
Llidiardour
B 4413
Bwlch-y-Rhiw
Rhydolion
Llanengan
Sarn bach
East St Tudwal's I.
West St Tudwal's I.
Llandanwg
Llanbedr
Morfa Dyffryn
Moelfre
1932
Moelfre
Llyn Bodlyn
Diphwys
2462
Mynydd Anelog
628
Llanfaelrhys
Porth Neigwl or Hell's Mouth
333
Porth Ceiriad
Pencilan Hd.
Llanenddwyn
Dyffryn
Sta.
Afon Ysgethin
Tal-y-bont
A 496
Llawr Llech

St Mary's Ch.
Aberdaron
Aberdaron B.
Pen-y-cil
Bardsey Sd.
Llanddwywe
Llanaber Halt
1459
Caer Deon
3

St Mary's Abbey
Bardsey
Barmouth
BARMOUTH BAY
Afon Mawddach
Morfa Mawddach
Fairbourne
Fairbourne Sta.
13
Arthog
Bry
Bro

Friog
Pen-y-Garn
1504
Craig-y-Llyn

Sta.
Llwyngwril
Afon
1280
4

Llangelynin
B 4493
Rhos-Irfaine
Llanegryn
Afon Dysynni
B 4405
Dol go
Foel Cocyn
1013
Tenfanau Sta.
6
Aber Dysynni
Brynocrug
Pandy
Broad Water
Tywyn
Trum Gelli
1743
Happy Valley
Corlan Fraith
A

C A R D I G A N
837
914
Gogan
Aberdyfi
A 493
R. Dyfi
Aberdyfi Halt

Twyni Bach
Traeth Maelgwyn
Ynys-las Sta.
Fochn
5

B A Y
Borth Sands
Llancynfelyn
Tre
Borth
Talybont
Upr Borth
Dol-y-bont
Llanfihangel Genau-r-glyn
297
Sarn Cynfelyn
Llangorwen
Cwm Cynfelyn
B 4572
Bow Street
Penrhyn-coch
Rhy
A 4159
6

Aberystwyth
Waun-fawr
Capel Dewi
Llanbadarn-fawr
Castell
The Bar
A 487
Pen-parcau
A 44
Capel
Rhyd-y-felin
Capel Seion
Nant Eos
Llanfarian
12
Llanilar
B 4575
Blaenplwyf
Abermad
R. Ystwyth
A 485
A 487
116
B 4340
B 4576
18
A 485

B A Y

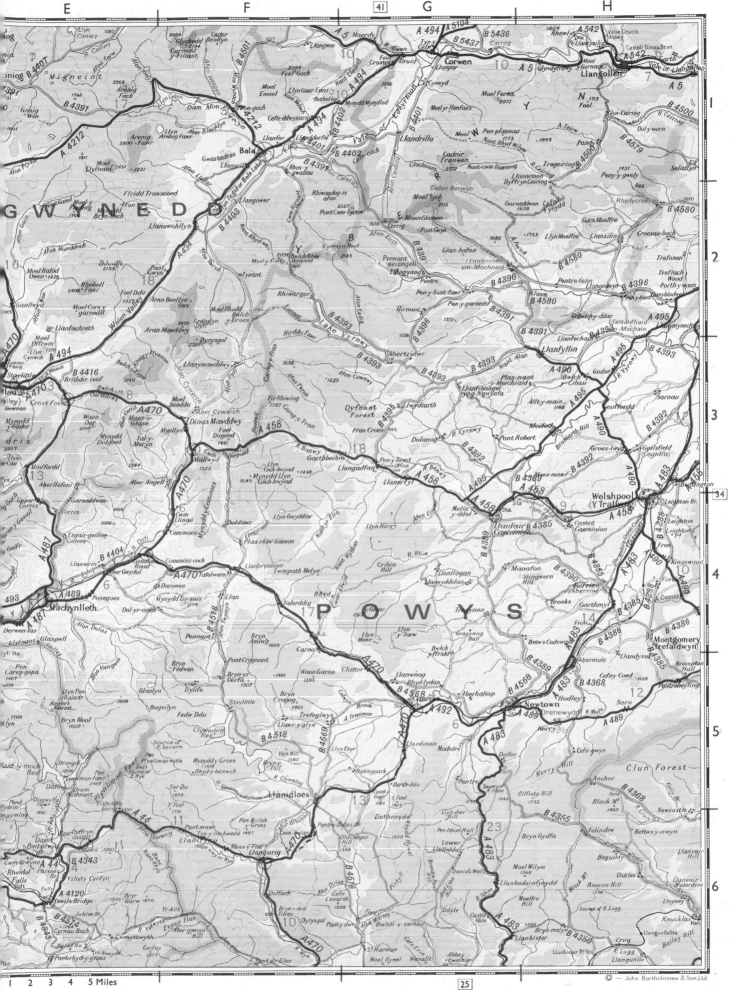

© — John Bartholomew & Son Ltd.

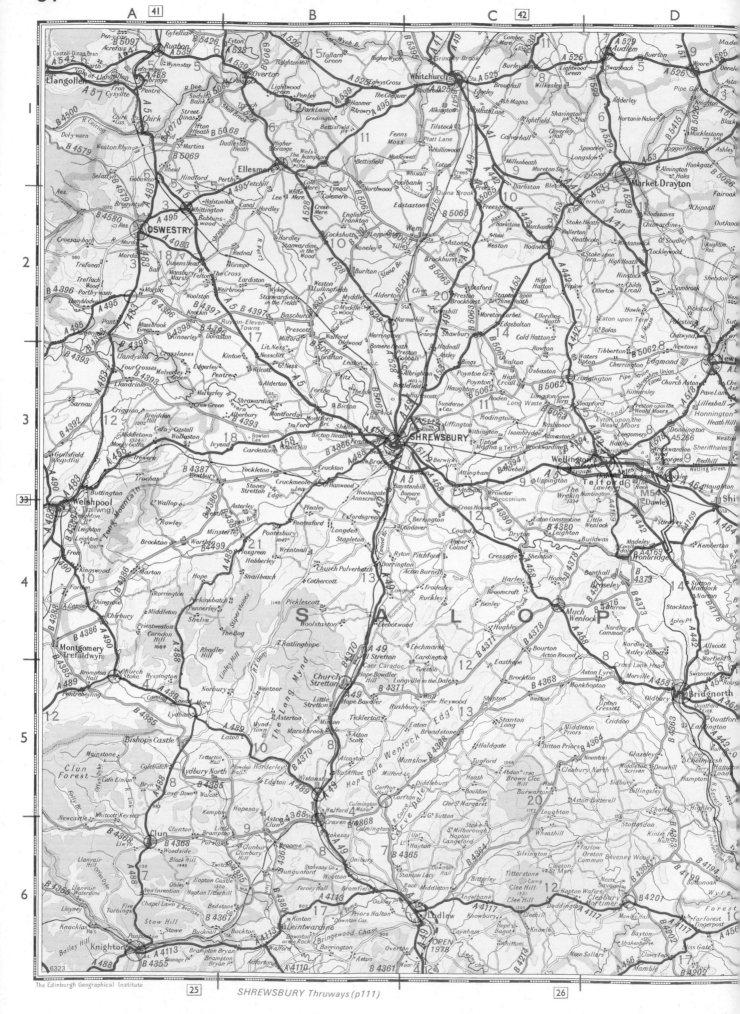

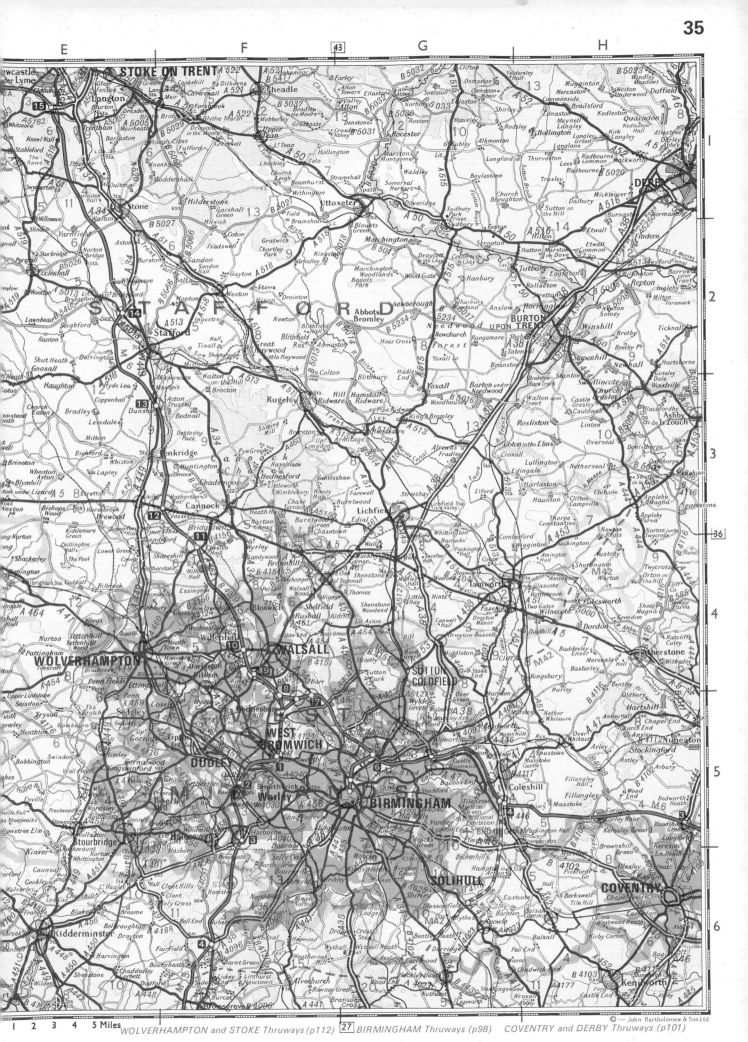

© — John Bartholomew & Son Ltd.

A   B   C   D

NOTTINGHAM

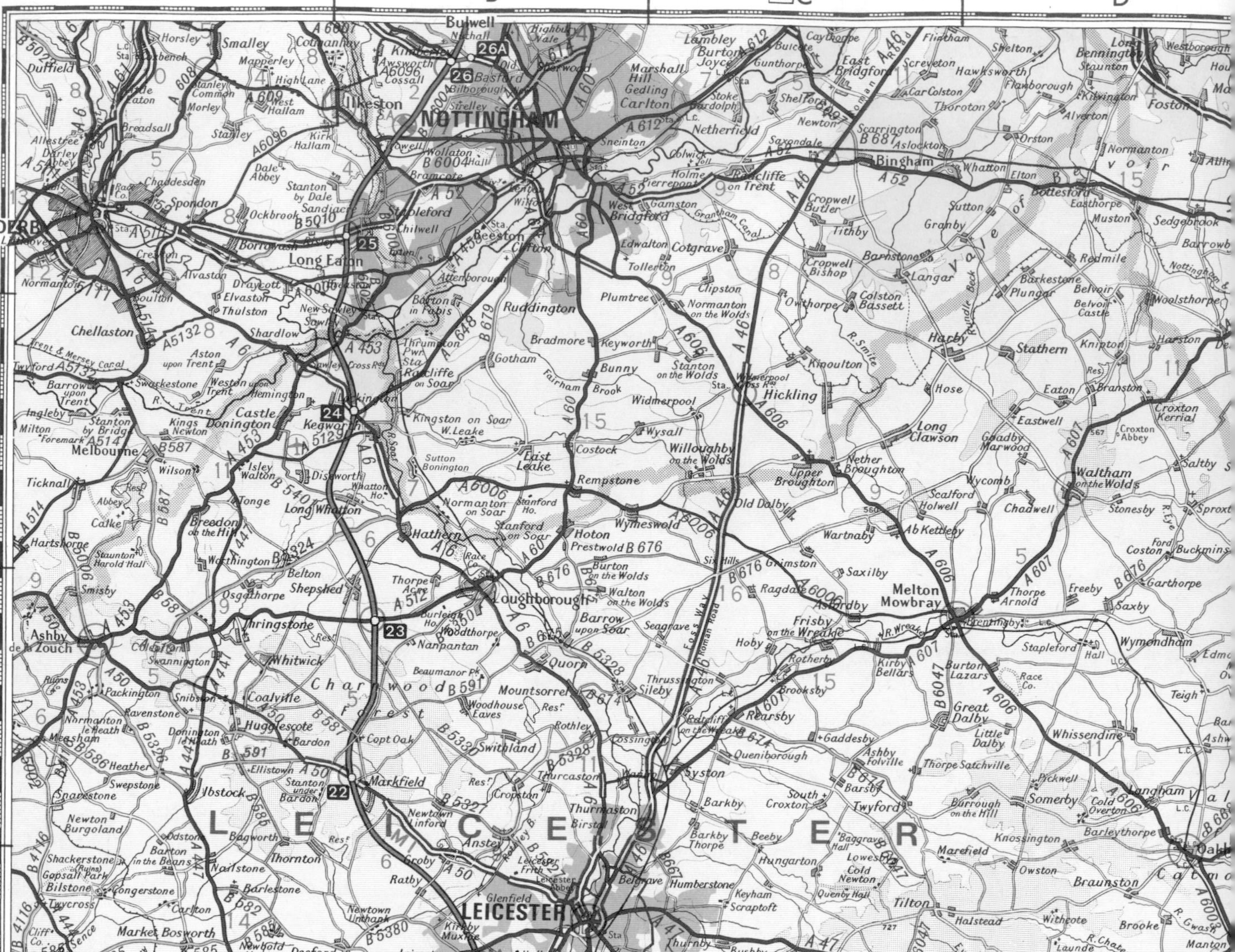

DERBY

LEICESTER

LEICESTERSHIRE

Loughborough

Melton Mowbray

COVENTRY

Nuneaton

Hinckley

Rugby

Market Harborough

Uppingham

COVENTRY and DERBY Thruways (p101)   *LEICESTER Thruways (p105)*   **28** *NOTTINGHAM Thruways (p109)*

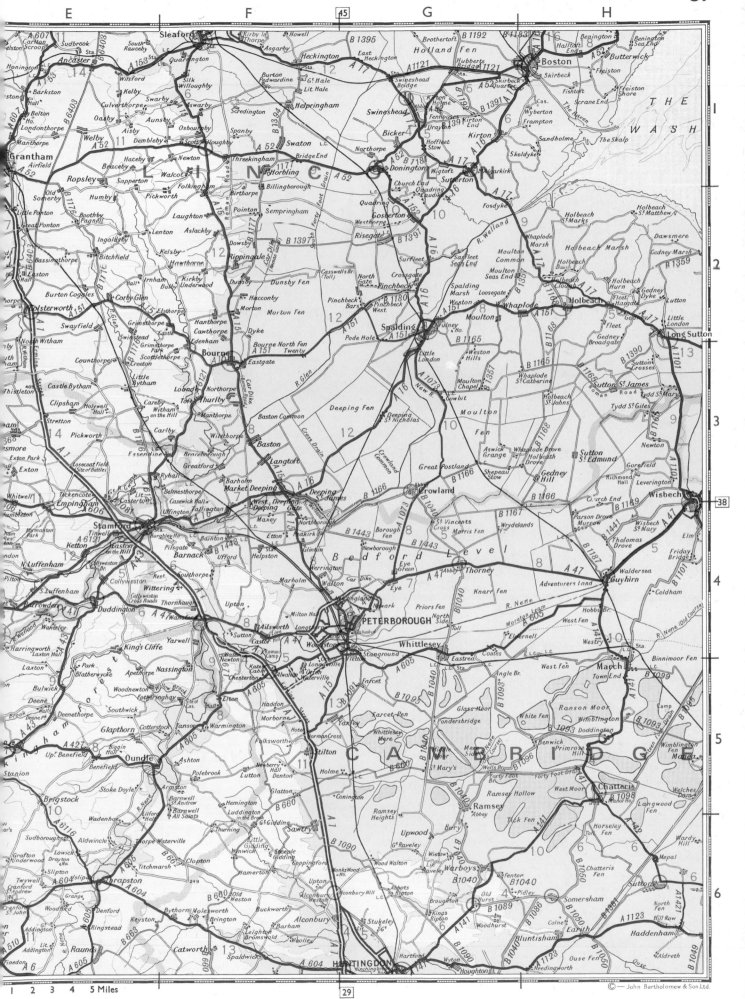

1 2 3 4 5 Miles

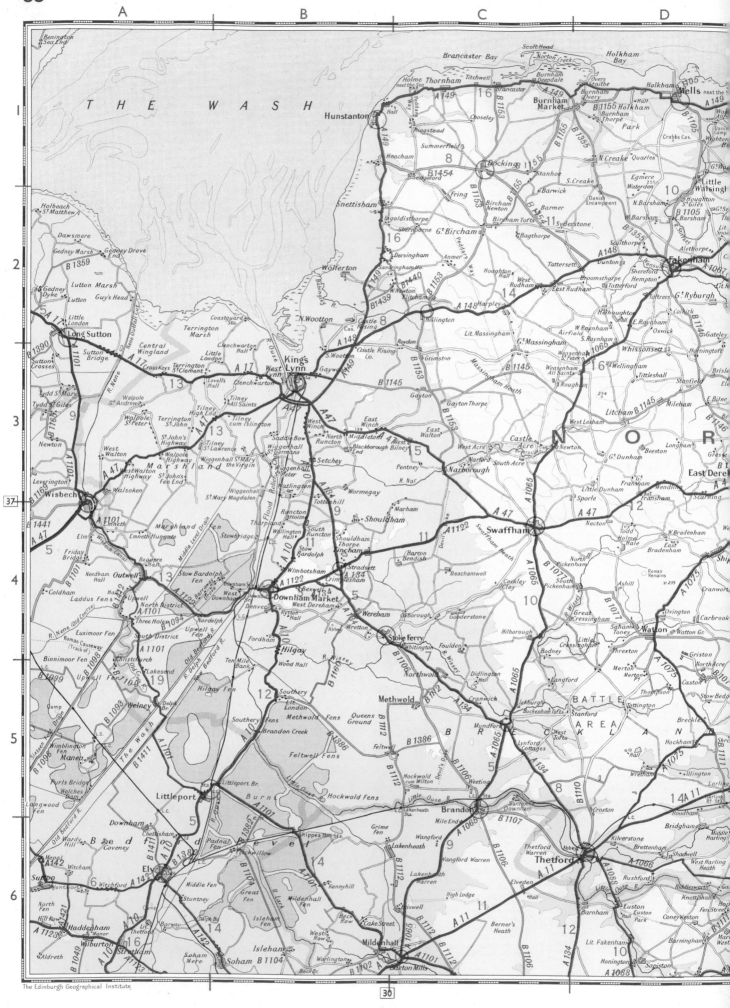

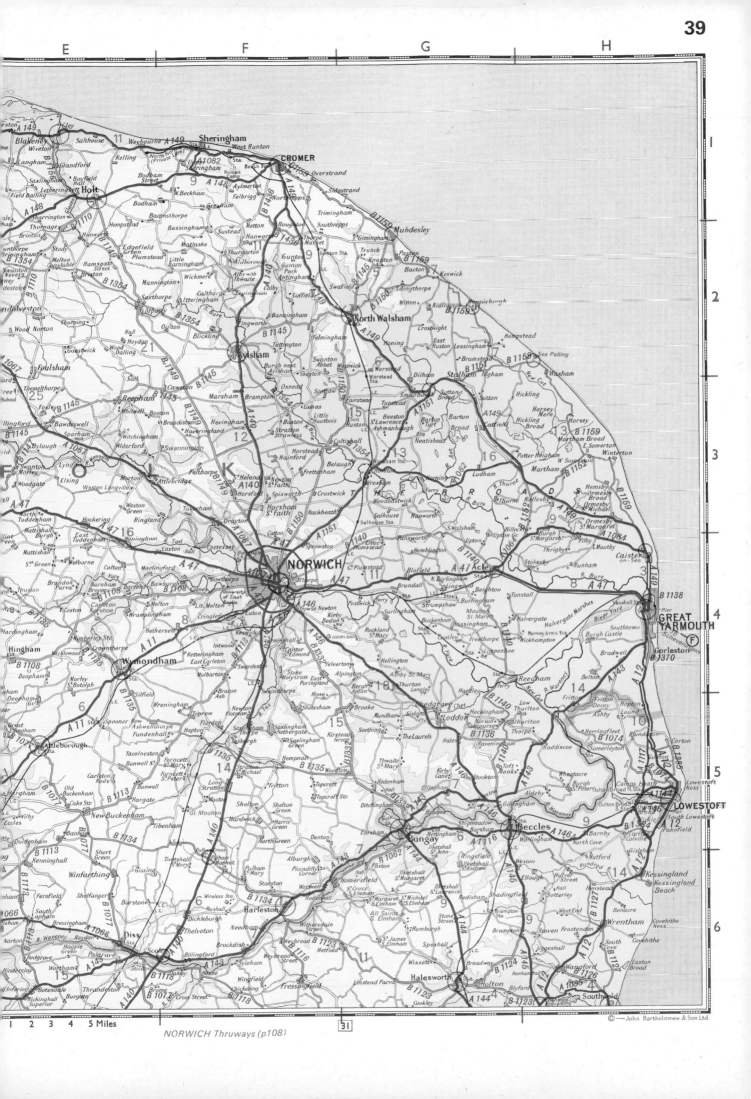

© —John Bartholomew & Son Ltd.

1 2 3 4 5 Miles

A   B   C   D

1

To Dublin

2

The Skerries
O L¹ Ho.
Carmel Hd
Cemaes B.
Llanlleiana (Site of)
Porth Wen B.
Works
Nèuadd
Bull B.
Bull Bay
Amlwch
Point Lynas
L¹ Ho.
Cemaes Bay
A 5025
Borwen
B 5111
Llaneilian
Tre'gele
Llanfair
ynghornwy
Bodewryd
Penysarn
Church B.
Llanfechell
Parys
Mount
Nebo
Ynys Dulas
Rhyd-wen
Llanrhyddlad
Rhos-y-bol
Llanwenllwyfo
Dulas B.
B 5111
A 5025
Lligwy Bay

3
To Dun Laoghaire
F
Llanfaethlu
Llanbabo
Cors-y-Bol
Alaw Res.
Penrhos
Lligwy
Moelfre
A 5025
Llanfwrog
Llanddeusant
Llanerchymedd
Llanallgo
A 5108
N. Stack
Holyhead
Mount
720
HOLYHEAD
Sadl.
Llantrisant
Llyn Llywenan
Coedana
Llanfihangel
Tre'r-Beirdd
B 5110
Llanddona
L⁵ Ho.
S.
Stack
Llaingoch
B 5112
ANGLESEY
Capel Coch
Brynteg
17
Benllech
Red Wharf
Bay

Kingsland
Penrhos
Llanfachraeth
Trefor
Llangwyllog
B 5110
Llanbedr
goch
Red Wharf
Bwrdd
Arthur
Penmon Priory
Puffin I.
or Priestholm
B 5109
Valley
5025
B 5109
Llangwyllog
B 5111
Rhos-meirch
B 5109
Mynydd
Llwydiarth
Llanddona
Llangoed
CONWY BAY
Caer-geiliog
Llynfaes
Tyn-Ion
Talwrn
Llanfaes
Baron
Hill
Tre-Arddur Bay
A 5
Bryngwran
Bod-ffordd
Cefni
Res.
B 5109
Llansadwrn
Bryn-
minceg
Beaumaris
HOLY
ISLAND
Four Mile Br.
Airfield
Llangefni
Penmynydd
R. Braint
Llandegfan
Pier
Lavan Sands
Rhoscolyn
Gwalchmai
A 5
Heneglwys
A 5114
Port Penrhyn
Llanfaelog

SOUTHPORT

Ainsdale
Woodvale

Barton

Formby Point
Freshfield
Gt. Altcar
Formby

Ince Blundell

Hightown

Little Crosby
Thornton

Blundellsands

Crosby
Waterloo
Seaforth

LIVERPOOL

To Belfast
To Douglas

BAY

MERSEYSIDE BOOTLE

New Brighton
WALLASEY

Rock Channel
Mockbeggar Wharf

LIVERPOOL

East Hoyle Bank

Hoylake
Saughall Massie
Upton
Greasby
Frankby

Birkenhead

Prenton
Oxton
Port Sunlight

Hilbre Pt.
Hilbre I.

West Kirby

Caldy
Irby

New Ferry

Bebington

Point of Air

Thurstaston

Gayton
Barnston
Brimstage
Thornton Hough

Heswall

Raby
Willaston

Pier
Gwespyr
A 547
Prestatyn
Llanasa

Flynnon groes
Mostyn Quay

Rhyl
B 5119
Meliden
Morfa-bach

Kinmel Bay
Morfa Rhuddlan

Llannerch-y-mor

Whitford
Mertyn
A 548

Greenfield
Walwen

Neston

Gayton Sands

Lit. Neston
Ness

Burton

Rhuddlan
Marian
Lloc
Carmel

Bagillt

Pentre-chwiad
White Sands

Puddington
Shotwick

Rhyd-y-foel
Abergele
A 55
Bodelwyddan
Rhualit

Pantasaph

Holywell

Flint

Steel Works

St. Asaph
St. George Kinmel

Babell
Pentre Halkyn
Pistyll

Halkyn Mountain
Halkyn

Flint Mountain

Connah's Quay

Moelfre isaf
Marli
Cefn Meiriadog

Tremeirchion
Licswm
Walwen

Northop

Shotton
Queen

Sandycroft

Moelfre-uchaf
Llannefydd
Trefnant
Moel-y-Parc
Nannerch

Rhosesmor

Northop Hall

Henllan
Waen

Cilcain
Gwernaffield

Buckley
Drury

Broughton

Denbigh
Kilford
Llandyrnog

Moel Llys-y-coed

Mold

Pant-y-fawnog
A 5118
Buckley Sta.

Llanynys
Tafarn-y-gelyn

Nercwys
Pont-blyddyn

Nantglyn
Rhewl
Llanbedr Dyffryn Clwyd

Llanferres
Treuddyn
Rhos-y-brwyner
Caergwrle

Bylchau
Llanrhaeadr
Pentre

Hirwaen

Moel Findeg

Frith

Ruthin

Llanfwrog

Eryrys
Pant-y-ffordd

Llanfynydd
Cefn-y-bedd

Sportsmen's Arms Inn
Llyn Bran

Bontuchel

Clocaenog

Efenechdyd

Llanfair Dyfryn Clwyd

Cyffylliog

Hope
Stryt's Br.

CLWYD

Pentre-celyn

Bwlch-gwyn

Southsea

Rhydtalog

New Broughton

Alwen Reservoir

Craig bron-banog

Derwen

Llanelidan

Mynydd Cricor

Pentrebwlch

Esclusham Mountain

WREXHAM

Cerrigydrudion

Betws Gwerful Goch

Gwyddelwern

Peny-Stryt

Rhostyllen

Rhoslannerchrugog

Johnstown

Maerdy

Ty-mawr

Vernant

Ruabon Mountain

Gyfelia

Ruabon

Corwen
Llangar
Druid
Bonwm

Llantysilio Mountain

Valle Crucis Abbey
Castell Dinas Bran

Llangollen
Vale of Llangollen

Glyndyfrdwy

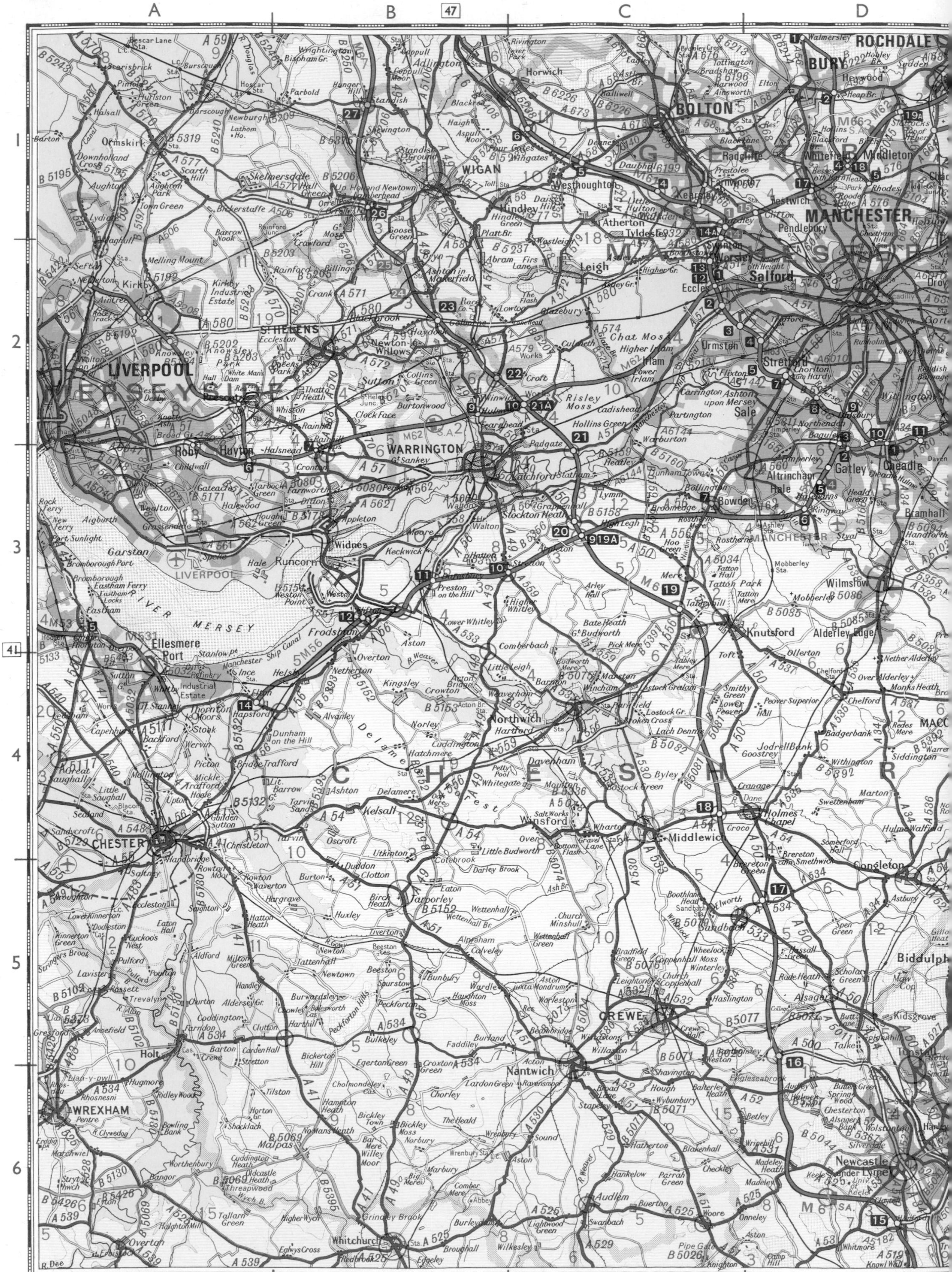

A
B
C
D
47
41
34
1
2
3
4
5
6
ROCHDALE
BURY
BOLTON
Horwich
WIGAN
Ormskirk
Skelmersdale
MANCHESTER
Salford
Eccles
Leigh
ST HELENS
LIVERPOOL
MERSEYSIDE
Prescot
Huyton
WARRINGTON
Widnes
Runcorn
RIVER MERSEY
Ellesmere Port
Frodsham
Altrincham
Sale
Stretford
Cheadle
Knutsford
Wilmslow
Alderley Edge
Northwich
Winsford
Middlewich
Holmes Chapel
Congleton
Sandbach
CHESTER
CREWE
Nantwich
Tarporley
Malpas
Whitchurch
WREXHAM
Holt
Audlem
Alsager
Kidsgrove
Newcastle under Lyme
Biddulph
CHESHIRE
GREATER MANCHESTER
Delamere Forest
Macclesfield

The Edinburgh Geographical Institute

CHESTER Thruways(p101) STOKE Thruways(p112)
LIVERPOOL Thruways(p105)
MANCHESTER Thruways(p108)

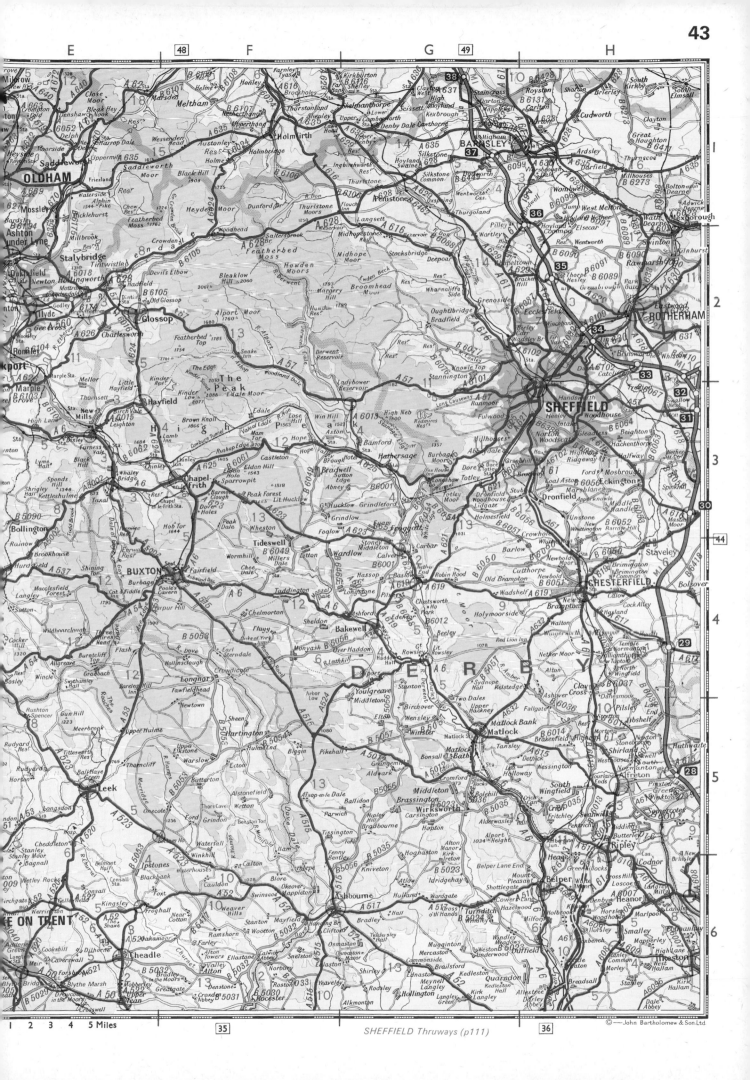

© — John Bartholomew & Son Ltd.

1 2 3 4 5 Miles

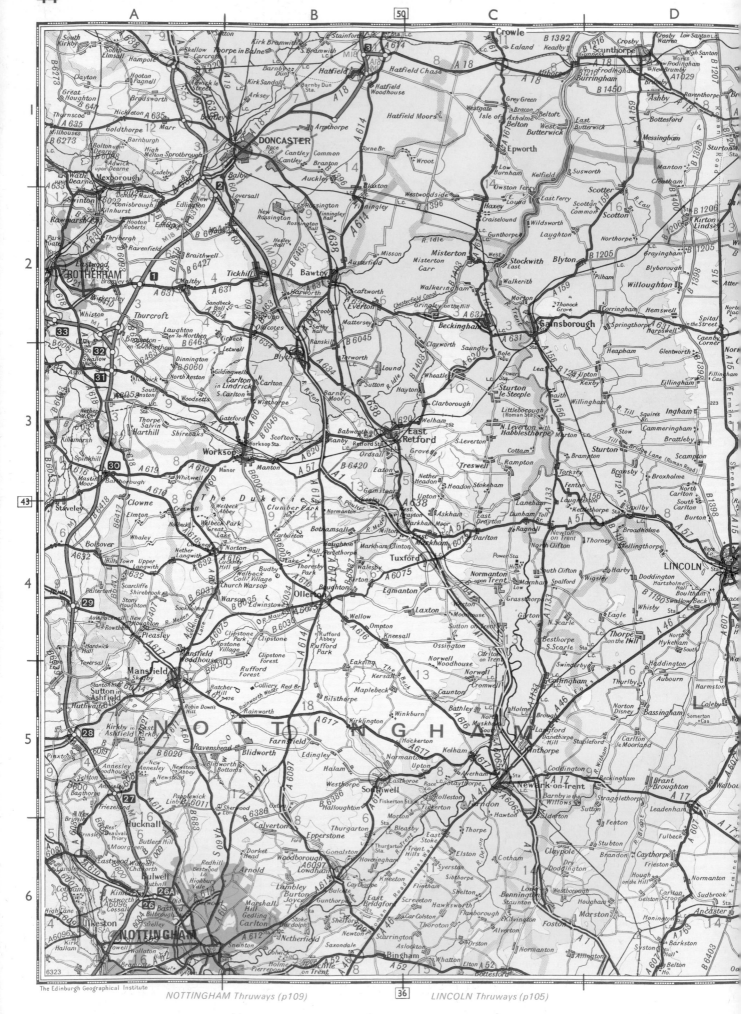

E · F · 51 · G · H

GRIMSBY · Cleethorpes · Scartho · Humberston · Spurn Head

Immingham to Gothenburg · Hull to Rotterdam & Zeebrugge · Immingham to Amsterdam

Elsham · A160 · Croxton · Ulceby Chase · Kirmington · Brocklesby · Brocklesby Park · Keelby · Stallingborough · Healing Sta. · West Marsh · Old Clee · Beaconthorpe Pier · Low Water Mark · Sandhaile Flats

Wrawby · Barnetby le Wold · Bigby · Searby · Great Limber · Riby · Riby Grove · Aylesby · Laceby · Bradley · A1098 · B1219 · New Waltham

Howsham · Cadney · North Kelsey · Grasby · Clixby · Swallow · Cabourne · Irby upon Humber · Beelsby · Barnoldby le Beck · Waltham · Holton le Clay · Brigsley · Ashby cum Fenby · Tetney · North End · South End · North Coates · Grainthorpe Haven · Somercotes Haven · Lifeboat Sta. · Donna Nook

South Kelsey · Moortown · Nettleton · Caistor (Roman Sta.) · Rothwell · Cuxwold · Hatcliffe · East Ravendale · Grainsby · Waithe · Marsh Chapel · Eskham · Wragholme · Meals · North Somercotes

Holton le Moor · Thornton le Moor · North Owersby · Normanby le Wold · Claxby · Thoresway · Croxby · Swinhope · Wold Newton · Cabeby Hall · Ludborough · North Thoresby · Fulstow · Grainthorpe · Covenham St. Bartholomew · Conisholme · Church End · Saltfleet

Kingerby · Usselby · Osgodby · Walesby · Kirmond le Mire · Binbrook · Binbrook Hall · North Ormsby · Utterby · Fotherby · Covenham St. Mary · Yarburgh · South Somercotes · Saltfleetby St. Clement · Saltfleetby All Saints

Dale Br. · West Rasen · Middle Rasen · Market Rasen · North Willingham · Ludford Parva · Ludford Magna · Kelstern · A631 · North Elkington · South Elkington · Lit. Grimsby · Alvingham · North Cockerington · South Cockerington · Grimoldby · Saltfleetby St. Peter · Theddlethorpe All Saints · Theddlethorpe St. Helen

Toft next Newton · Newton by Toft · Faldingworth · Friesthorpe · Lissington · Sixhills · Girsby Manor · Burgh on Bain · Gayton le Wold · Welton le Wold · Hallington · Louth · A157 · Manby · Little Carlton · Legbourne · Castle Carlton · Great Carlton · Gayton-le-Marsh · Mablethorpe · Gibraltar

Snarford · Wickenby · Holton cum Beckering · East Torrington · West Torrington · South Willingham · Benniworth · Donington on Bain · Withcall · Raithby · Haugham · Muckton · Burwell · South Reston · Tothill · Authorpe · Strubby · Maltby le Marsh · Thorpe · Withern · Sutton on Sea · Trusthorpe

Snelland · Wragby · Holton · East Barkwith · Panton · Market Stainton · Asterby · Cawkwell · Maidenwell · Burwell · Claythorpe · Aby · Beesby · Hannah · Saleby · Markby

Sudbrooke Holme · Newball · Apley · Langton by Wragby · Hatton · Great Sturton · Sturton Hall · Baumber · Hemingby · R. Bain · Ranby · Belchford · Farforth · Oxcombe · Ruckland · White Pit · Ketsby · Swaby · S. Thoresby · Belleau · Rigsby · Alford · Bilsby · Huttoft · Anderby Creek

Barlings · Kingthorpe · Stainfield · Minting · Gautby · Waddingworth · Wispington · Edlington · W. Ashby · Fulletby · Tetford Hill · Tetford · Somersby · Brinkhill · Driby · Farlesthorpe · Ulceby Cross · Mumby · Cumberworth · Willoughby · Hogsthorpe · Sloothby · Anderby · Chapel St. Leonard

Cherry Willingham · Fiskerton · Toll Bri. · Thimbleby · Horsington · Langton · Thornton · Horncastle · Low Toynton · High Toynton · Greetham · Hagworthingham · Aswardby · Harrington · Langton · Skendleby · Claxby · Welton le Marsh · Audlethorpe · Ingoldmells

Heighington · Branston · Branston Booths · Bardney · Bucknall · Martin · Daldeby · Mareham on the Hill · Hameringham · Asgarby · Mavis Enderby · Hundleby · Old Bolingbroke · Spilsby · Halton Holgate · Partney · Scremby · Ashby by Partney · Gunby · Orby · Burgh le Marsh · Bratoft · Irby in the Marsh · Addlethorpe

Nocton · Potterhanworth · Potterhanworth Booths · Nocton Fen · Southrey · Stixwould · Reeds Beck · Roughton · Wood Enderby · Claxby Pluckacre · Mimingsby · Moorby · Hareby · Revesby Abbey · Hagnaby · Keal Cotes · E. Kirkby · Toynton All Saints · Toynton St. Peter · Lit. Steeping · Gt. Steeping · Thorpe Culvert · Firsby · Croft · Skegness

Dunston · Nocton Delph · Kirkstead · Woodhall Spa · Kirkby on Bain · Haltham · Wilksby · Mareham le Fen · Revesby · E. Keal · W. Keal · Stickford · Midville · Eastville · Fendike Corner · Wainfleet Bank · Wainfleet · Keys Toft · Croft Marsh · Havenhouse Sta. · Steeping R. · Thorpe St. Peter

Martin · Timberland Dales · Thorpe Tilney Dales · Tattershall Thorpe · Tumby · New Bolingbroke · Stickney · Hobhole Drain · East Fen · Lade Bank · Wrangle Bank · Friskney · Friskney Eaudike · Gibraltar · Gibraltar Pt.

Scopwick · Kirkby Green · Timberland · Walcot · Tattershall · Coningsby · Moor Side · Tumby Woodside · Carrington · Northlands · Wrangle Lowgate · Wrangle · Leake · Leuke Fold Hill · Old Leake · Leake Hurns End

Rowston · Digby · Billinghay · Walcot · Tattershall Br. · Dogdyke · Hawthorn Hill · Scrub Hill · New York · West Fen · Sibsey · Leverton · Leverton Outgate

Ashby de la Launde · Bloxholm · Dorrington · Ruskington · North Kyme · South Kyme · Wildmore Fen · West Fen Drain · Thornton le Fen · Frithville · Fishtoft Drove · Langriville · Boston Long Hedges · Leake Common Side · Benington · Benington Sea End · Renington

Braucewell · Roxholm · Anwick · R. Slea · Car Dike (Roman Canal) · Amber Hill · Brothertoft · Langrick · Holland Fen · Halltoft End · Butterwick · Boston Deeps

Sleaford · Haverholme Priory · Ewerby Thorpe · Ewerby · Howell · Asgarby · Heckington · East Heckington · Hubberts Bridge · A1121 · Boston · Skirbeck · Skirbeck Quarter · Fishtoft · Freiston · Freiston Shore · Scrane End

Quarrington · Silk Willoughby · Swarby · Scredington · Helpringham · Gt. Hale · Lit. Hale · Swineshead Bridge · Swineshead · Fenhouses · Kirton · Kirton Holme · Wyberton · Frampton · Cas.

1 2 3 4 5 Miles

© — John Bartholomew & Son Ltd.

37

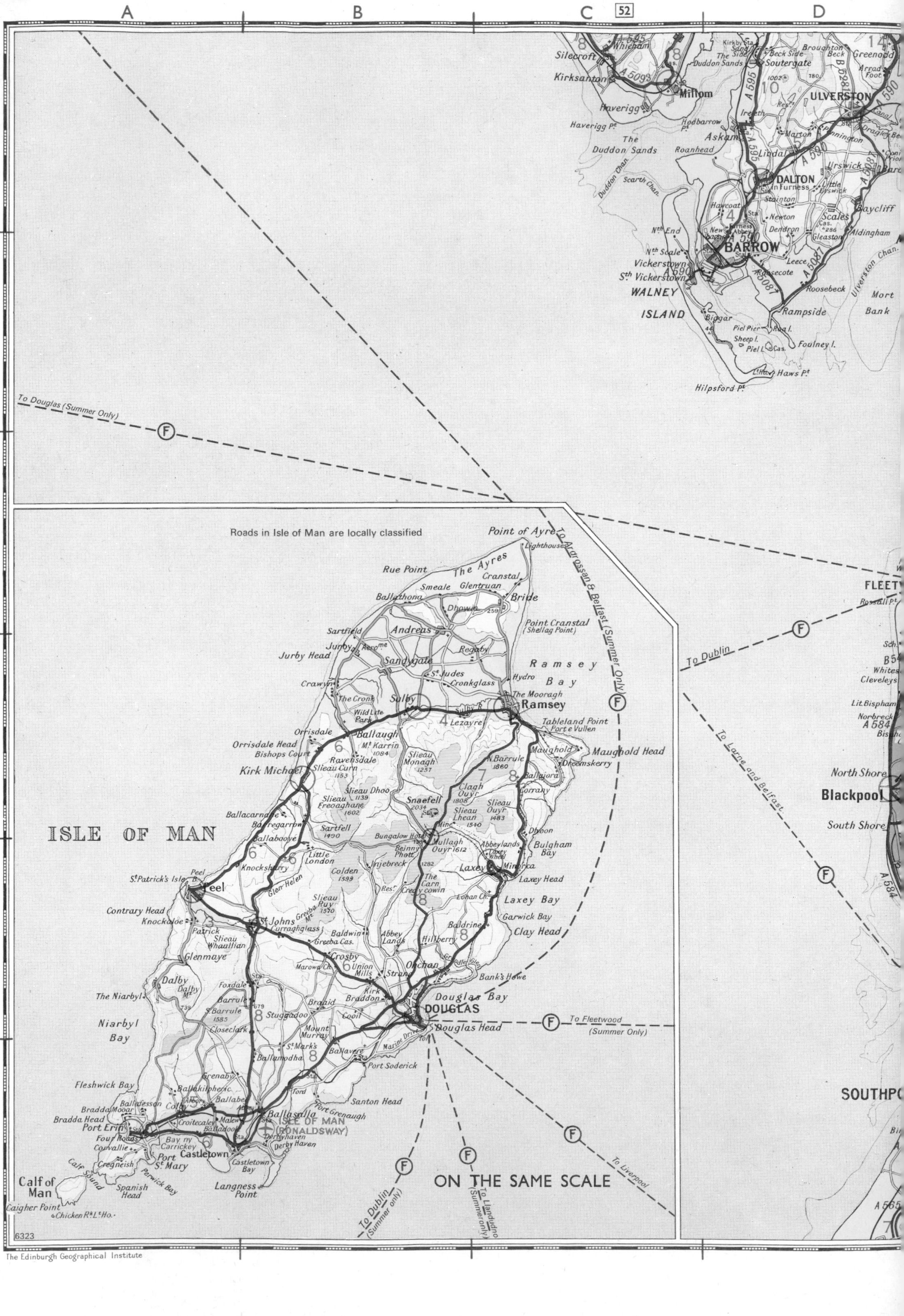

A   B   C   52   D

1

2

3

4

5

6

Isle of Man map:

Roads in Isle of Man are locally classified

ISLE OF MAN

Point of Ayre
Lighthouse
The Ayres
Rue Point
Cranstal
Smeale Glentruan
Ballaghona
Dhowin
Bride
Point Cranstal
(Shellag Point)
Sartfield
Andreas
Aesome
Regaby
Jurby
Jurby Head
Sandygate
St. Judes
Cronkglass
Ramsey Bay
Crawyn
The Cronk
Sulby
Ramsey
The Mooragh
Hydro Ho.
Wild Life Park
Lezayre
Tableland Point
Port e Vullen
Orrisdale
Ballaugh
Mt. Karrin 1084
Slieau Monagh 1257
Maughold
Dreemskerry
Maughold Head
Orrisdale Head
Bishops Court
Ravensdale
Slieau Curn 1153
N. Barrule 1860
Ballajora
Kirk Michael
Slieau Dhoo 1139
Cronany
Slieau Freoaghane 1602
Snaefell 2034
Clagh Ouyr 1808
Slieau Ouyr 1483
Ballacarnane
Bregarrow
Sartfell 1490
Slieau Lhean 1540
Dhoon
Ballabooye
Little London
Beinny Phott
Bungalow Hotel
Mullagh Ouyr 1612
Abbeylands
Bulgham Bay
Knocksharry
Colden 1599
Injebreck
The Carn
Creg ny cowin
Laxey
Minorca
St. Patrick's Isle
Peel
Glen Helen
Slieau Ruy 1570
Greeba Mt.
Laxey Head
Contrary Head
St. Johns
Curraghglass
Baldwin
Garwick Bay
Knockaloe
Greeba Cas.
Laxey Bay
Patrick
Slieau Whaallian
Crosby
Abbey Lands
Baldrine
Clay Head
Glenmaye
Marown Ch.
Union Mills
Onchan
Dalby
Foxdale
Strang
Dalby Mt.
Kirk Braddon
Folieu Glen
Bank's Howe
The Niarbyl
Barrule
Braaid
Cooil
Douglas Bay
Barrule 1585
Stuggadoo
Mount Murray
Douglas
Niarbyl Bay
Closeclark
St. Mark's
Ballahavare
Douglas Head
Greenaby
Ballamodha
Port Soderick
Fleshwick Bay
Ballakilpheric
Ballabeg
Santon Head
Bradda Mooar
Colby
Croitcaley
Malew
Ballasalla (ISLE OF MAN) (RONALDSWAY)
Port Grenaugh
Bradda Head
Ballafesson
Ballabooie
Derbyhaven
Port Erin
Four Roads
Bay ny Carrickey
Derby Haven
Cooivallie
Port St. Mary
Castletown
Castletown Bay
Cregneish
Spanish Head
Langness Point
Calf of Man
Caigher Point
Chicken R. L. Ho.

To Douglas (Summer Only)
To Ardrossan & Belfast (Summer Only)
To Larne and Belfast
To Dublin
To Fleetwood (Summer Only)
To Liverpool
To Dublin (Summer only)
To Llandudno (Summer only)

ON THE SAME SCALE

6323

Cumbria/Lancashire inset map:

Silecroft
Whicham
Kirksanton
Millom
Haverigg
Haverigg Pt.
Hodbarrow Pt.
The Duddon Sands
Scarth Chan.
Duddon Chan.
Kirkby
Beck Side
Broughton
Greenodd
Soutergate
ULVERSTON
Askam
Dalton in Furnure
Lindal
Urswick
Little Urswick
Haycoat
Newton
Dendron
Scales
Gleaston
Bardsea
Baycliff
Aldingham
Nth. End
Nth. Scale
BARROW
Newbiggin
Leece
Vickerstown
Sth. Vickerstown
Roose
Roosebeck
WALNEY ISLAND
Biggar
Rampside
Mort Bank
Piel Pier
Roa I.
Sheep I.
Piel I. Cas.
Foulney I.
Lifling Haws Pt.
Hilpsford Pt.
FLEETWOOD
Rossall Pt.
Cleveleys
Lit. Bispham
Norbreck
North Shore
Blackpool
South Shore
SOUTHPORT

The Edinburgh Geographical Institute

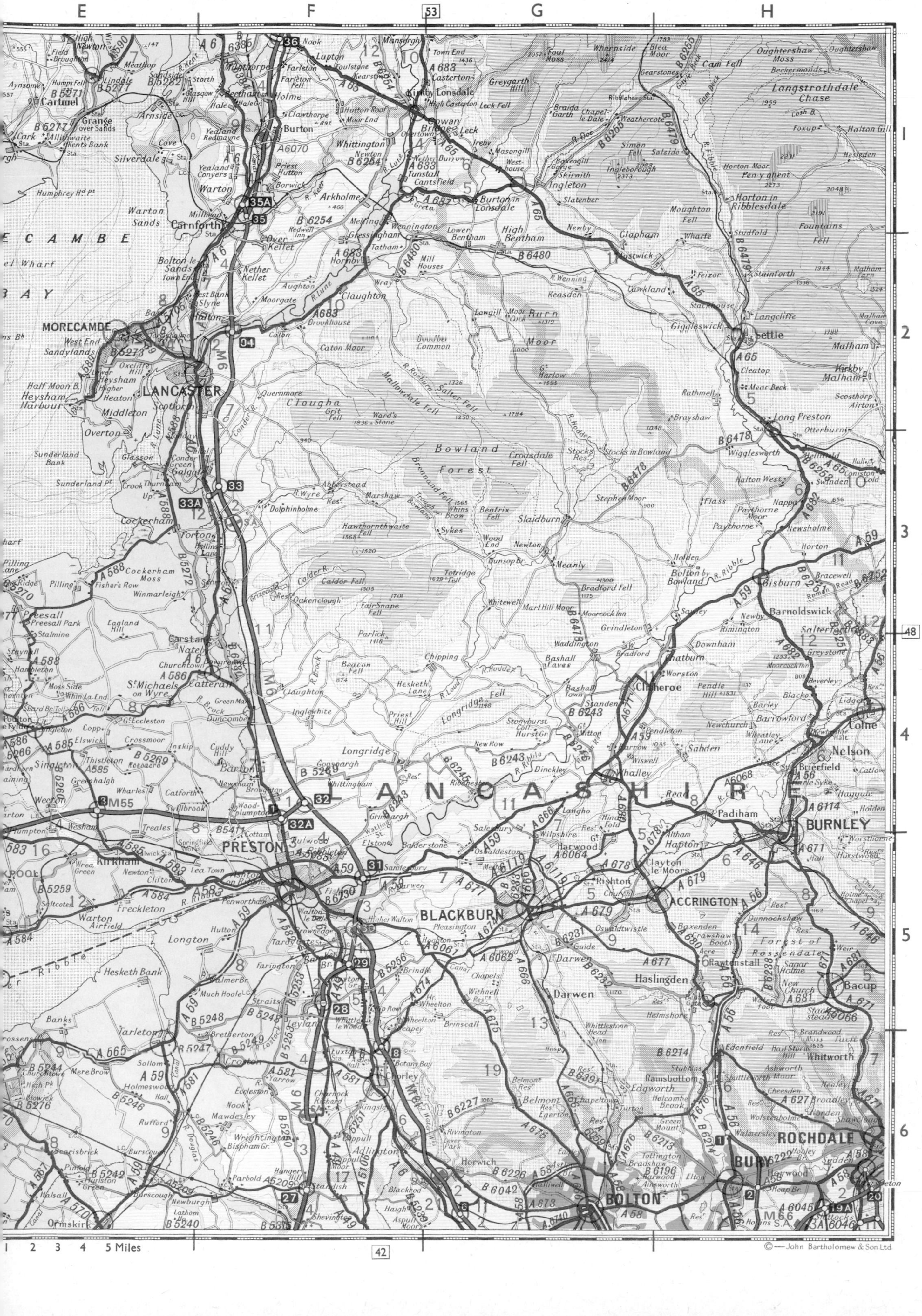

LANCASHIRE

Major places: Grange over Sands, Cartmel, Arnside, Silverdale, Carnforth, Morecambe, Heysham, Lancaster, Kirkby Lonsdale, Ingleton, Clapham, Settle, Long Preston, Garstang, Preston, Longridge, Clitheroe, Whalley, Gisburn, Barnoldswick, Colne, Nelson, Burnley, Blackburn, Accrington, Darwen, Haslingden, Rawtenstall, Bacup, Whitworth, Rochdale, Bury, Bolton, Chorley, Leyland, Ormskirk, Tarleton

Bowland Forest, Forest of Rossendale

Scale: 1 2 3 4 5 Miles

© — John Bartholomew & Son Ltd.

A 53 B C 54 D

NORTH

WEST

LANCASHIRE

Whernside
Foul Moss
Blea Moor
Cam Fell
Oughtershaw Moss
Oughtershaw
Beckermonds
Deepdale
Langstrothdale Chase
Hubberholme
Gray
Buckden
Stake Moss
Kidstone
Horsehouse
Bradley
Arkleside
Woodale
Little Whernside
Masham Moor
Birk Gill
Greygarth Hill
Leck Fell
Braida Garth
Chapel le Dale
Weathercote
Simon Fell
Selside
Ingleborough
Horton Moor
Pen y ghent
Buckden Pike
Scar House Res.
Angram Res.
Nidderdale
Limley
Agill
Burton in Lonsdale
Ireby
Masongill
Westhouse
Ingleton
Slatenber
Ribblehead Sta.
Horton in Ribblesdale
Kirk Gill
Halton Gill
Birks Fell
Litton
Starbotton
Great Whernside
Riggs Moor
Conistone Moor
Nidderdale
Lower Bentham
High Bentham
Clapham
Wharfe
Studfold
Stainforth
Fountains Fell
Malham Tarn
Kettlewell
Conistone
Grassington Moor
Ramsgill
Pateley Bridge
B 6480
Newby
Feizor
Langcliffe
Kirkby Malham
Malham Cove
Hanlith
Kilnsey
Conistone
Grassington
Hebden
Appletreewick
Dry Gill
Greenhow Hill
Guys Cliff
Burn
Moor
Giggleswick
Settle
Cleatop
Malham
Way Gill
Winterburn Res.
Threshfield
Linton
Thorpe
Burnsall
Appletreewick
Padside
Thornthwaite
Bowland Forest
Rathmell
Mear Beck
Scosthorp
Airton
Calton
Hetton
Cracoe
Rylstone
Barden Moor
West End
Long Preston
Otterburn
Winterburn Newfield Hall
Flasby
Eastby
Embsay
Bolton Abbey
Blubberhouses
Wigglesworth
Hellifield
Coniston Cold
Eshton
Gargrave
Thorlby
Halton East
Bolton
Beamsley
Nesfield
Middleton
Halton West
Swinden
Bank Newton
Skipton
Draughton
Addingham
Ilkley
Stephen Moor
Nappa
Newsholme
East Marton
Broughton
Carleton
Elslack
Ravenshaw
Low Bradley
Silsden
Burley in Wharfedale
Bolton by Bowland
Gisburn
Bracewell
Thornton-in-Craven
Earby
Lothersdale
Cononley
Kildwick
Crosshills
Sutton
Steeton
Keighley
Barnoldswick
Greystone
Kelbrook
Cowling
New Road Side
Utley
Riddlesden
East Morton
Bingley
Clitheroe
Downham
Pendle Hill
Barley
Blacko
Foulridge
Laneshaw Bridge
Keighley Moor
Oakworth
Stanbury
Ingrow
Harden
Cullingworth
Wilsden
Shipley
Chatburn
Worston
Wheatley Lane
Colne
Trawden
Forest of Trawden
Haworth
Oxenhope
Leeming
Denholme
Thornton
Allerton
BRADFORD
Clayton
Whalley
Read
Padiham
Brierfield
Nelson
Catlow
Boulsworth Hill
Wadsworth Moor
Denholme Clough
Queensbury
BURNLEY
Holden
Widdop
Heptonstall Moor
High Gate
Hebden Bridge
Illingworth
Holmfield
Northowram
BLACKBURN
Accrington
Baxenden
Crawshaw Booth
Forest of Rossendale
Todmorden
Walsden
Mytholmroyd
Sowerby Bridge
Halifax
Brighouse
Elland
Darwen
Haslingden
Rawtenstall
Bacup
Britannia
Shawforth
Walsden
Lydgate
Luddenden
Norland
Greetland
Stainland
Lindley
Huddersfield
Helmshore
Edenfield
Brandwood Moss
Facit
Whitworth
Wardle
Littleborough
Rishworth
Ripponden
Soyland Moor
Barkisland
Holywell Green
Marsh
Milnsbridge
Golcar
Linthwaite
Belmont
Ramsbottom
Edgworth
Holcombe Brook
Cheesden
Norden
Broadley
Smallbridge
Moss Moor
Slaithwaite
Marsden
Meltham
Horwich
Tottington
Ainsworth
Elton
BURY
ROCHDALE
Milnrow
Shaw
Crompton
BOLTON
Bradshaw
Harwood
Heywood
Sudden
Crompton

The Edinburgh Geographical Institute

BRADFORD Thruways (p99)

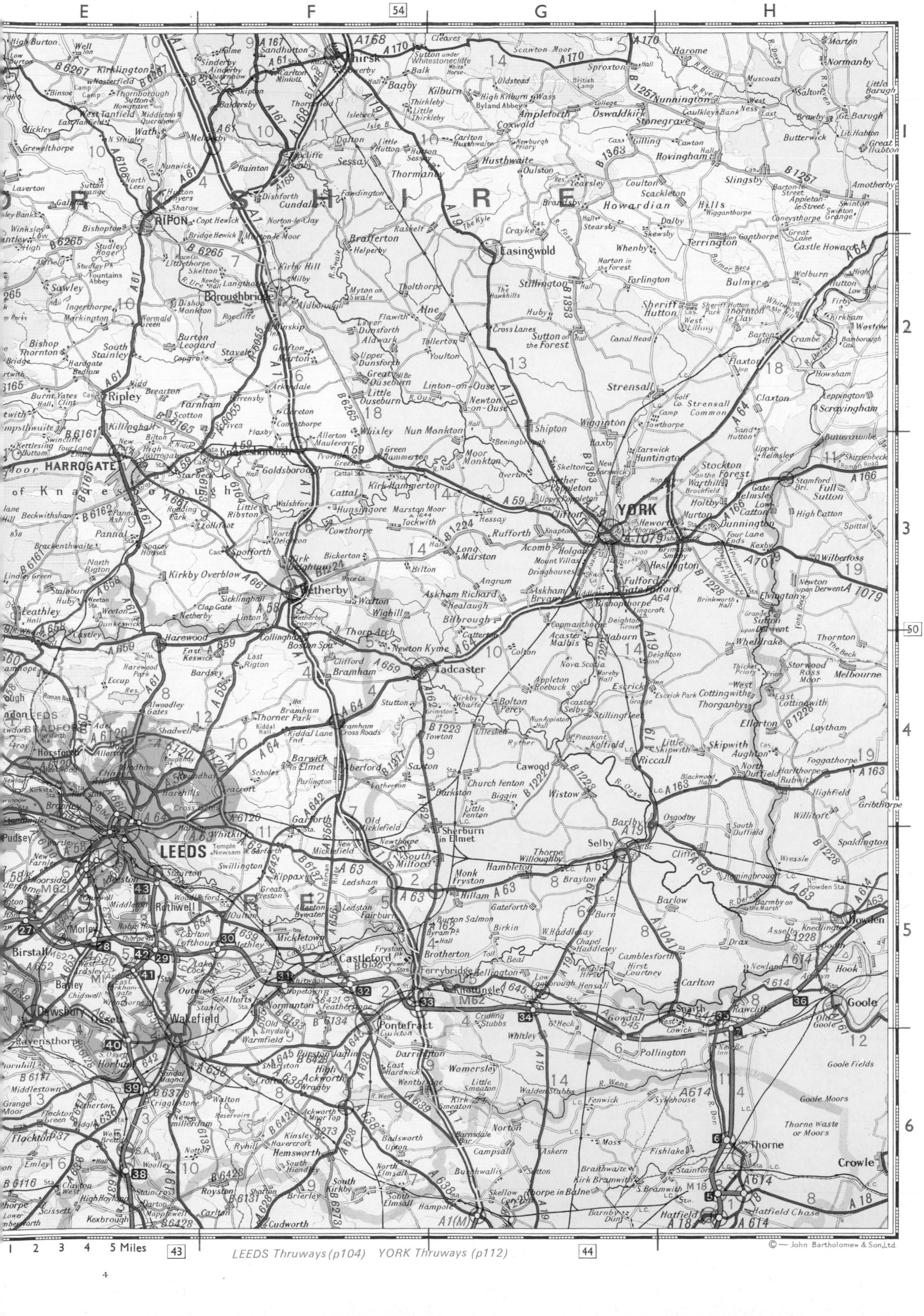

E   F   54   G   H

YORKSHIRE

RIPON
Boroughbridge
Ripley
HARROGATE
Knaresborough
Wetherby
Tadcaster
LEEDS
BRADFORD
Rothwell
Morley
Birstall
Dewsbury
Ravensthorpe
Wakefield
Castleford
Pontefract
Knottingley
Ferrybridge
Easingwold
YORK
Selby
Goole
Thorne
Crowle

Thirsk
Byland Abbey
Coxwald
Ampleforth
Oswaldkirk
Stonegrave
Nunnington
Hovingham
Terrington
Castle Howard
Welburn
Kirkham
Strensall
Huntington
Stockton on the Forest
Dunnington
Wilberfoss
Elvington
Sutton upon Derwent
Melbourne
Skipwith
North Duffield
Bubwith
Howden
Hook
Rawcliffe
Old Goole
Goole Fields
Goole Moors
Thorne Waste or Moors
Hatfield Chase

A1 A19 A64 A59 A61 A167 A168 A170 A166 A1079 A163 A614 A162 A63 A645 A638 M62 M18 A1(M)

LEEDS Thruways (p104)   YORK Thruways (p112)

1 2 3 4 5 Miles   43   44

© — John Bartholomew & Son, Ltd.

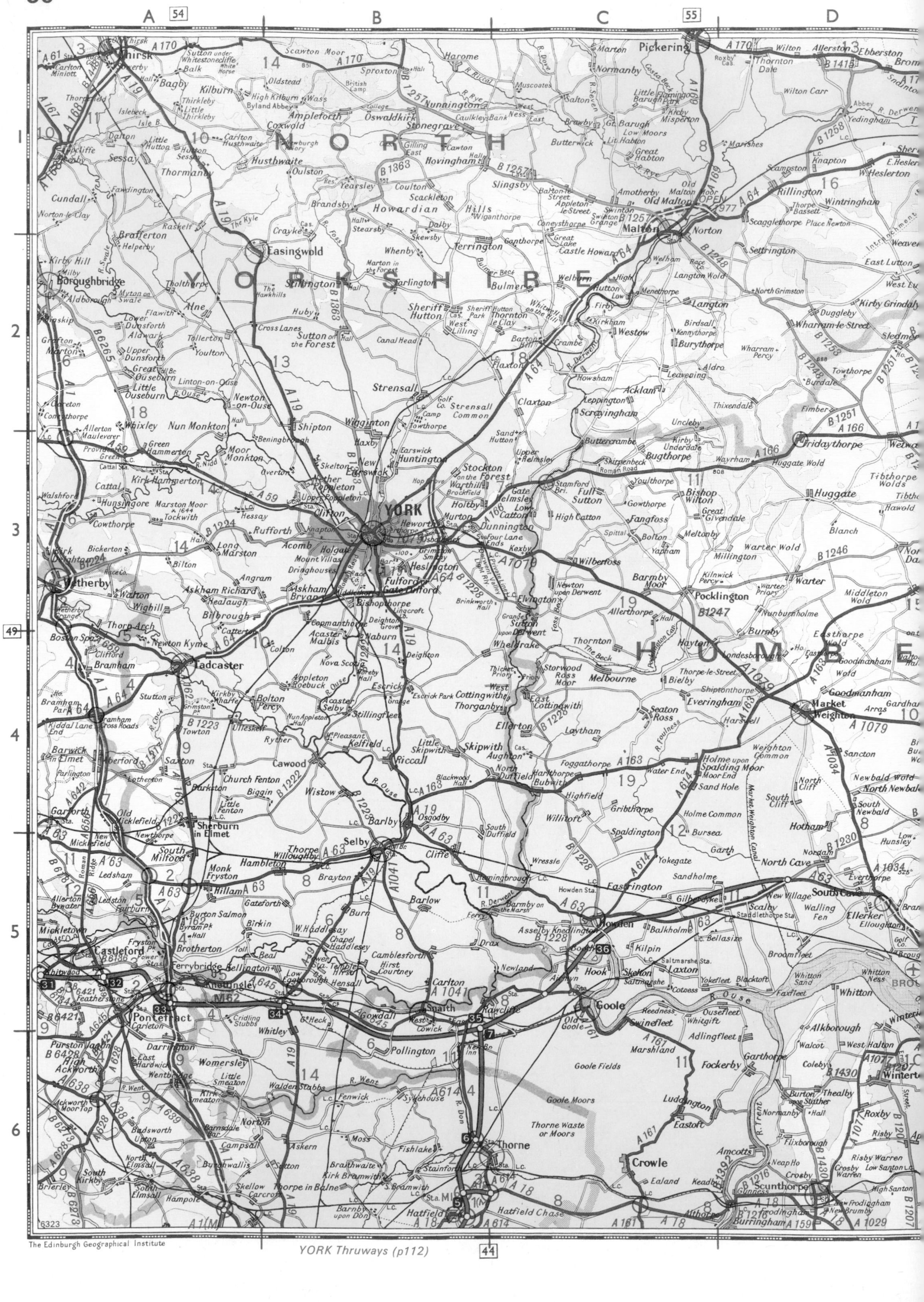

A 54 B C 55 D

NORTH YORKSHIRE

HUMBERSIDE

Thirsk · Pickering · Malton · Old Malton · Norton · Rillington

Easingwold · Boroughbridge · Husthwaite · Coxwold · Ampleforth · Kilburn · Bagby

Helmsley · Hovingham · Slingsby · Howardian Hills · Terrington · Bulmer

Sheriff Hutton · Strensall · Sutton on the Forest · Shipton · Newton-on-Ouse · Whixley · Nun Monkton

Westow · Acklam · Leavening · Burythorpe · Langton · Settrington · East Lutton · Kirby Grindalythe

Wetherby · Tadcaster · **YORK** · Heslington · Fulford · Dunnington · Stamford Bridge · Pocklington

Bishop Wilton · Huggate · Fridaythorpe · Wharram Percy · Thixendale · Warter Wold

Boston Spa · Thorp Arch · Bramham · Newton Kyme · Bolton Percy · Escrick · Elvington · Melbourne

Market Weighton · Goodmanham · Everingham · Seaton Ross · Holme upon Spalding Moor

Garforth · Sherburn in Elmet · Cawood · Riccall · Skipwith · Bubwith · North Duffield · Spaldington

Castleford · Pontefract · Ferrybridge · Knottingley · Selby · Barlby · Hemingbrough · Howden · North Cave · South Cave · Ellerker

Brotherton · Birkin · Hensall · Snaith · Rawcliffe · Goole · Swinefleet · Adlingfleet

Darrington · Womersley · Askern · Thorne · Crowle · Ludington · Eastoft · Luddington

Hatfield · Stainforth · Scunthorpe · Winterton · Alkborough · Burton upon Stather

M62 · M18 · A1(M) · A63 · A64 · A19 · A1079 · A614 · A1041 · A163 · A166 · A170 · A1077

E   F   G   H

1039 · Filey Brigg
Filey
Filey Bay
Hunmanby
Reighton
Speeton
Bempton
Buckton
Flamborough Hd
B 1259
Flamborough
Old Town
Bridlington

B R I D L I N G T O N
B A Y

Hilderthorpe
Carnaby
Burton Agnes
Carnaby Moor
Fraisthorpe
Harpham
Gransmoor
Barmston
Great Kelk · Lissett
Gembling
Foston on the Wolds
Ulrome
Skipsea
Great Driffield
Wansford
Skerne
Church End
Beeford
Nth Frodingham
Dunnington
Bewholme
Atwick
Hempholme
Brandesburton
Seaton
Catwick
Hornsea
Hornsea Mere
Sigglesthorne
Goxhill
Rolston
Mappleton
Gt Hatfield
Gt Cowden
Long Riston
Rise
Withernwick
Beverley
Woodmansey
Wawne
West Newton
Aldbrough
Ellerby
Burton Constable
Flinton
Garton
Cottingham
Skirlaugh
Coniston
Sproatley
Humbleton
Grimston Hall
Hilston
Haltemprice
Willerby
Sutton
Bilton
Wyton
Lelley
Owstwick
Tunstall
Elstronwick
Preston
Burton Pidsea
Roos
Waxholme
HULL
Hedon
Wadworth Hill
Rimswell
Withernsea
Burstwick
West End · East Halsham End
Thorngumbald
Ryhill
Keyingham
Ottringham
Winestead
Hollym
Holmpton
Paull
New Holland
Goxhill
East Halton
Sth End
Patrington
Welwick
Out Newton
Weeton
Barrow Haven
Barton upon Humber
Nth Killingholme
South Killingholme
Immingham Dock
To Amsterdam, Rotterdam & Zeebrugge
Haven Side
B 1445
Skeffling
Easington
Sunk Island
Skeffling Clays
Kilnsea
Horkstow
Saxby Wolds
Saxby All Saints
Bonby
Worlaby
Ulceby
Immingham
Stallingborough
Immingham to Gothenburg
Elsham
Kirmington
Brocklesby
Keelby
GRIMSBY
Spurn Head

H U M B E R   R I V E R

1 2 3 4 5 Miles

HULL Thruways (p104)   45

© — John Bartholomew & Son Ltd.

A   B   59   C   D

1

R. Waver
Cas.   Hayrigg   Kelsick   Oulton   Micklethwaite   Crofton Hall   Thursby   Dalston
Abbey Town   Dundraw   Waverbridge   Wigton   Buckabank   Woodside   Wray
Beckfoot   Highlaws   B 5302   Wheyrigg   B 5308   A 596   A 595   Holme   Burnthwaite
B 5300   Pelutho   Blencogo   B 5302   Waverton   Highmoor   Gatesgill   Monk
Dubmill Pt.   St Cuthberts   Holme   Croft Ho.   Bromfield   Old Carlisle   B 5299   Cas.   Rosey
Mawbray   Arkshaw   Langrigg   High Scales   Red Dial   Warblebank   Broughtonhead
Edderside   Mealo   Allerby   Blennerhasset   Allhallows   Bolton Low Houses   Thackthwaite   M 6
Allonby   Westnewton   12   Aspatria   A 596   Fletchertown   A 596   Brocklebank   Sebergham
Allonby Bay   Hayton   Baggrow   Faulds Brow 1125   B 5299   Caldbeck   Middlescough Hall   Thomas Close
Crosscanonby   R. Ellen   Arkleby   Torpenhow   Whelpo   Parkend   R. Ive   Ivegill   Calthwaite

2

MARYPORT   Dearham   Plumbland   Bothel   A 59   Ireby   Snowhill   Hesket Newmarket   Millhouse   Lamonby   Skelton
Ellenborough   A 594   Parsonby   A 596   High Ireby   Uldale   Caldbeck Fells   Carrock Fell 2174   Hutton Roof   Johnby
Flimby   A 596   Gilcrux   Blindcrake   Binsey 1466   Over Water   Knott 2329   Berrier Hill   Greystoke Cas.   Greystoke
Seaton   Broughton Hall   Tallentire   Bridekirk   Bewaldeth   Bassenthwaite   Gt. Calva 2265   Mosedale   Berrier
WORKINGTON   Brigham   COCKERMOUTH   A 66   Bassenfell   B 5291   Skiddaw 3053   Saddleback or 2847   Mungrisdale   A 66   Motherby   A 66
A 66   Greysouthen   B 5292   Thornthwaite   Wythop Hall   Dodd Fell   Blencathra   Scales Inn   Newbiggin

3

Westfield   Schoose   Stainburn   Eaglesfield   A 66   Lords Seat 1811   Millbeck   Applethwaite   Threlkeld   Great Mell Fell   Little Mell Fell 1657
Harrington   Clifton   Deanscales   High Lorton   Thornthwaite   Latrigg 1203   A 66   Matterdale End   Matterdale   15
B 5296   High Harrington   A 5086   Dean   Lorton Hall   Whinlatter 1043 Pass   Braithwaite   KESWICK   B 5322   Matterdale Common   Dockray
Distington   Branthwaite   Mosser   Mockerkin   Grisedale Pike 2593   Portinscale   Great Dodd 2807   Ulcat Row   ULLSWATER
Gilgarran   Pica   Ullock   Pardshaw   Hopegill Head 2525   Derwent Water   Falcon Crag   Stybarrow Dod 2756   Sandwick
Parton   Moresby   Loweswater   Lamplugh   Brackenthwaite   Causey Pike   Star   A 591   Aira Force   Glenridding   Martindale
WHITEHAVEN   Arlecdon   Rowrah   Loweswater Fell 1878   Grasmoor 2791   Emerald Bank   Helvellyn 3118   Place Fell 2154   Patterdale   Common
Hensingham   Frizington   Kirkland   Crummock Water   Grange   Bowder Stone   Sticks Pass   Angle Tarn

4

St Bees Head   Cleator Moor   B 5294   Crossdale   Buttermere   Derwent Fells   Kings How   Wythburn   Dollywaggon Pike   Brothers Water   Hartsop
Sandwith   B 5345   Cleator   Ennerdale Bridge   Anglers Inn   High Stile 2643   Buttermere Fell   Dale Head 2473   Rosthwaite   Blea Tarn   Ullscarf 2370   Grisedale Tarn   Fairfield   Hayes Water
St Bees   Moor Row   Ennerdale Water   Ennerdale Fell   Steeple 2687   Pillar 2927   Seatoller   Borrowdale Fells   Steel End   Middle Dodd 2106   Kirkstone P. 1476
Rottington   B 5345   Kirk Beck   Lank Rigg 1750   Haycock 2618   Kirk Fell 2631   Great Gable 2949   Glaramara 2560   High White Stones 2500   Rydal Fell   Kirkstone Pass   Ill Bell
Egremont   Winscales   R. Calder   Seatallan 2266   Wasdale Head   Strands   Great End 2984   Allen Crags   Esk House   Langdale Pikes   Stickle Tarn   Grasmere   Wordsworths Cottage

5

Nethertown   Braystones Sta.   Beckermet   Haile   Thornholme   Worm Gill   R. Bleng   Scafell 3162   Scafell Pikes 3210   Bow Fell 2960   Langdale   Bow Fell   Rydal   Wansfell   Applethwaite Common   12
Calder Bridge   Ponsonby   Copeland Forest   Illgill Head 1978   Burnmoor Tarn   Crinkle Crags   Langdale Chapel   Elterwater   Ambleside   Troutbeck
Windscale Works   Wellington   West Water   Whin Rigg 1755   Eskdale Fell   Pike of Blisco 2304   Blea Tarn   Waterhead Hotel   A 591   Troutbeck Br.
Sellafield Works   Calder Hall   R. Irt   Druidical Temples   Boot   Eskdale   Wrynose Pass   Wetherlam 2502   B 5286   High Wray   Wray Cas.
Gosforth   R. Calder   Santon Br.   R. Mite   Eskdale Green Sta.   Hard Knott Pass   Butterilket   Grey Friar 2537   Levers Water   Hawkshead   Windermere   Bowness
Seascale Sta.   B 5344   Holmrook   Gubbergill   Harter Fell 2140   Seathwaite   Coniston   Brantwood   Esthwaite Water   B 5284

6

Drigg   B 5344   Ravenglass and Eskdale (Private Rly.)   Birker Fell   Devoke Water   Ulpha Fell 1336   Dow Crag   Old Man 2633   Grizedale   Far Sawrey   High Dam   Winster
Ravenglass   Muncaster Cas.   R. Esk   Lane End   Seathwaite   Torver   A 5084   Satterthwaite   Grizedale fst.   Graythwaite   Gummers Holme
Corney   Bigert Mire   Ulpha   Dunnerdale Fells   A 593   Haverigg Holme   Force Forge   Thwaite Head Fells   Lake Side   Cartmel Fell   Bowland Bridge
A 595   Stub Place   Tarn Bay   R. Duddon   Croft End   Broughton Mills   Blawith Fells   High Nibthwaite   Rusland   Finsthwaite   Newby Br.   Witherslack
Bootle Sta.   Bootle   Bootle Fell   Hawthwaite   Lower   Rosthwaite   Water Yeat   Low Nibthwaite   Colton   Oxen Pk.   A 590   Staveley
Hyton   Annaside   Black Combe 1969   Duddon Broadgate   White Combe   Lady Hall   Broughton-in-Furness   14   Lowick Green   Booth   B 5092   Backbarrow   Ayside   High Newton
Whitbeck   The Green   Foxfield Sta.   Grizebeck   Chapels   Gawthwaite   A 5092   Penny Br.   Haverthwaite   Low Wood   Humps Fell   Cartmel
Silecroft   The Hill   A 5093   Kirkby-in-Furness Sta.   Beck Side   Broughton Beck   Greenodd   Arrad Foot   B 5278   Field Broughton   Lindale
Kirksanton   A 5093   Duddon Sands   Soutergate   A 590   Grange over Sands
Haverigg   Milton   Askam   Marton   ULVERSTON   Holker   Cark   Allithwaite
Hodbarrow   Ireleth   B 5277   Arn.

C U M B E R L A N D

E   60   F   G   61   H

Cumrew
Dunwhogbt Cas.
(Site of)
Newbiggin
Croglin Fell
Kirkhaugh   18
Whitley Cas.
A 686   16   Monope Moor
B 6294
Hartley Moor
Spartylea   19
Nookton Fell
Hunstanworth   Allergate Ho.
Edmondbyers
B 6306

Holmwrangle
Low Ho.
Croglin
Middle Carrick   2154
Alston   Nenthall
A 689
Cur Shield   Elia Ho.
Allenheads
Bolts Law
Redburn Common
Rookhope
Crawley Side
Muggleswick Common
Skaylock Hill   1340
Cross Rigg

Ainstable
Renwick Fell   1833
Black Fell   2179
Hartside Height   2046   B 6277   A 686
Bayles
Nenthead
Alston Moor
Killhope Moor   A 689
Cornriggs   Burtree Ford   Cowshill
Middlehope Moor
Wearhead
Westgate Dale
Old Park
Eastgate
Stanhope   A 689
Wolsingham Park Moor

Renwick
Kirkoswald
Gamblesby
Fiends Fell   2082
Rotherhope Fell
Garrigill
Ashgill
Burnhope Res.   Burnhope Seat   2452   Yad Moss   2035
St Johns Chapel   Ireshope Moor
Brotherlee
Horsley Ho.
Rogerley Hall   Hill End
Frosterley

Lazonby
Glassonby
Melmerby
Melmerby Fell   2331
Ousby Fell
South Tyne
Chapel Fell   2056
Black Hill   1891
Bollihope Common
Harvey Hill   1046

Long Meg & Her Daughters
Lt. Salkeld   Gt. Salkeld
Green Fell   2429
Cross Fell   2930
Teeshead
West Common   Cow Green Res.
B 6277
Grasshill Common   Langdon Common   22
Harwood
Newbiggin Common
Middleton Common
Carrs Hill   1911
Pawlaw Pike   1599

DURHAM

Langwathby   Skirwith
Kirkland
Milburn Forest
Knock Fell   2604   2832
Dufton Fell
Trout Beck
Crowdundle Beck
Maize Beck
High Force
Cronkley Fell
Holwick
Newbiggin
Monks Moor
Eggleston Common

PENRITH
Edenhall
Culgaith
Blencarn
Milburn
Knock
Dufton Pike   1578
Dufton
Backstone Edge   High Cup Nick   2206
Murton Fell
Caldron Snout
Birkdale
Winch Br.
Holwick Fell
Crossthwaite Common
Mickleton
Middleton in Teesdale
Eggleston   B 6282

Brougham
Clifton
Temple Sowerby
Long Marton
Kirkby Thore
Brampton
Keisley
Hilton Fell   2446
Lune Forest
Fish L.
Lune Moor
Wemmergill Hall
Grains o'th Beck
Grassholme Res.
Hunderthwaite
Romaldkirk   B 6279

DANGER
Burton Fell   Warcop Fell
HILTON ZONE
Mickle Fell   2591   2028
B 6276
Iron Band   1843
Hunderthwaite Moor
Bury
Lartington   B 6277
Cotherstone

APPLEBY
Burrells
Hoff
Murton
Hilton
Burton
Fox Tower
Mickleton Moor
Baldersdale Res.
Cotherstone Moor
Startforth

Maulds Meaburn
Sandford
Warcop   B 6269
Bleatarn
Hillbeck
Brough
Stainmore
A 66
Stainmore Common
Deepdale B.
Bowes Moor
A 67   A 66
Bowes   16

Shap
Crosby Ravensworth
Great Asby
Little Musgrave
Brough Sowerby
Kaber
Argill B.
Stainmore Forest
Bowes Moor
Rey Cross   Camp
Old Spital
God's Br.
Gilmonby
Roman Road

Orton
Raisbeck
Crosby Garrett
Soulby
Winton
Kaber Fell
Ease Gill
Sleightholme Moor
Hope Moor
Stang   1677

Wet Sleddale Res.
Shap Fells
Gt. Yarlside   1937
Greenholme
Tebay
Kelleth
Waitby
Hartley
Kirkby Stephen   Nateby
Bastifell   2024
Taylor Rigg
Tan Hill   1732
Arkengarthdale Moor
Arkengarthdale Moor
Water Crag
Whaw

High Borrow Br.
Breasterdale
Gaisgill
Newbiggin
Coldbeck
Smardale
Stenkrith Br.
Begin Hill   1017
Tailbridge Hill   1796
Lammerside
B 6259   B 6270
Birkdale Common
Stonesdale Moor   1881
Rogan's Seat   2204
Great Pinseat   1914
Langthwaite

Ravenstonedale
Tarn House
Southwaite
Birkdale   Tarn
West Stonesdale
Keld
Kisdon   1636
Melbecks Moor
Calver Hill   1599
Healaugh
Reeth

Langdale Fell
Harter Fell
Artlegarth
Studfold
Wild Boar Fell   2324   2328
High Seat   2257
Hoggarths
Angram
Thwaite
Muker
Gunnerside
Low Row   Feetham   Blades
Grinton
B 6270   Swale

The Calf   2220
Yarlside   2097
Blue Caster
Rawthey Br.
Mallerstang Common
Aisgill
Angram Common
Great Shunner Fell   2340
Swaledale
Hardraw
Summer Lodge
High Oxnop
Oxnop Beck
Whitaside Moor
East Bolton Moor

Sedbergh
Firbank
Howgill
West Fell
Holmes Moss
Moorcock
Cotterdale
Lovely Seat   2213
Cliff Gate
Cotterdale
Northside Common
Askrigg Common
Beldon Beck
Castle Bolton

Millthrop   A 684
Baugh Fell   2216
Clough
Garsdale Sta.
Mossdale
Appersett
Hawes   A 684
Gayle
Hardrow Force   Sedbusk
Askrigg   Newbiggin
Nappa Hall   Woodhall   Carperby
Low Bolton

Killington Res.
B 6256
Middleton
Rash
Garsdale   East Fell
Garsdale Ch.
Mossdale Moor
Widdale Fell   1922
Buttersett
Bainbridge   A 684   Aysgarth
North Cote
West Burton

Dent
Cowgill
Dent Sta.
Lea Yeat
Rise Hill   1825
Widdale Beck
Wether Fell   2015
Countersett
Semer Water
Stalling Busk
Thoralby
Newbiggin   B 6160

NORTH
YORKSHIRE

Middleton Fell   1999
Calf Top
Deepdale
Crag Hill   2250   2039
Redshaw Moss
Dodd Fell   2189
Fleet Moss
Birdale Beck
Stake Fell
Bishopdale Beck
Bradley   Brown Haw   Woodale

Barbon
Mansergh
Town End   1436
Whernside   2414
Blea Moor
Cam Fell
Gearstones
Oughtershaw Moss   Oughtershaw
Beckermonds
Deepdale
Langstrothdale Chase
Cray
Hubberholme
Buckden Pike   2302

Kirkby Lonsdale
High Casterton
Leck Fell
Greygarth Hill
Ribblehead Sta.
Gauber
Braida Garth
Chapel-le-Dale   Weathercote
Foul Moss   2052
Cosh B.
Foxup
Halton Gill
Kirk Gill
Buckden   Birks Fell   2001
Cray   1772
R. Nidd

Whittington
Cowan Br.
B 6254
Leck
A 65
B 6480
R. Lune
B 6255
R. Doe
R. Greta
Cam Beck
R. Wharfe
R. Ure
B 6160

1   2   3   4   5 Miles

48

© — John Bartholomew & Son Ltd.

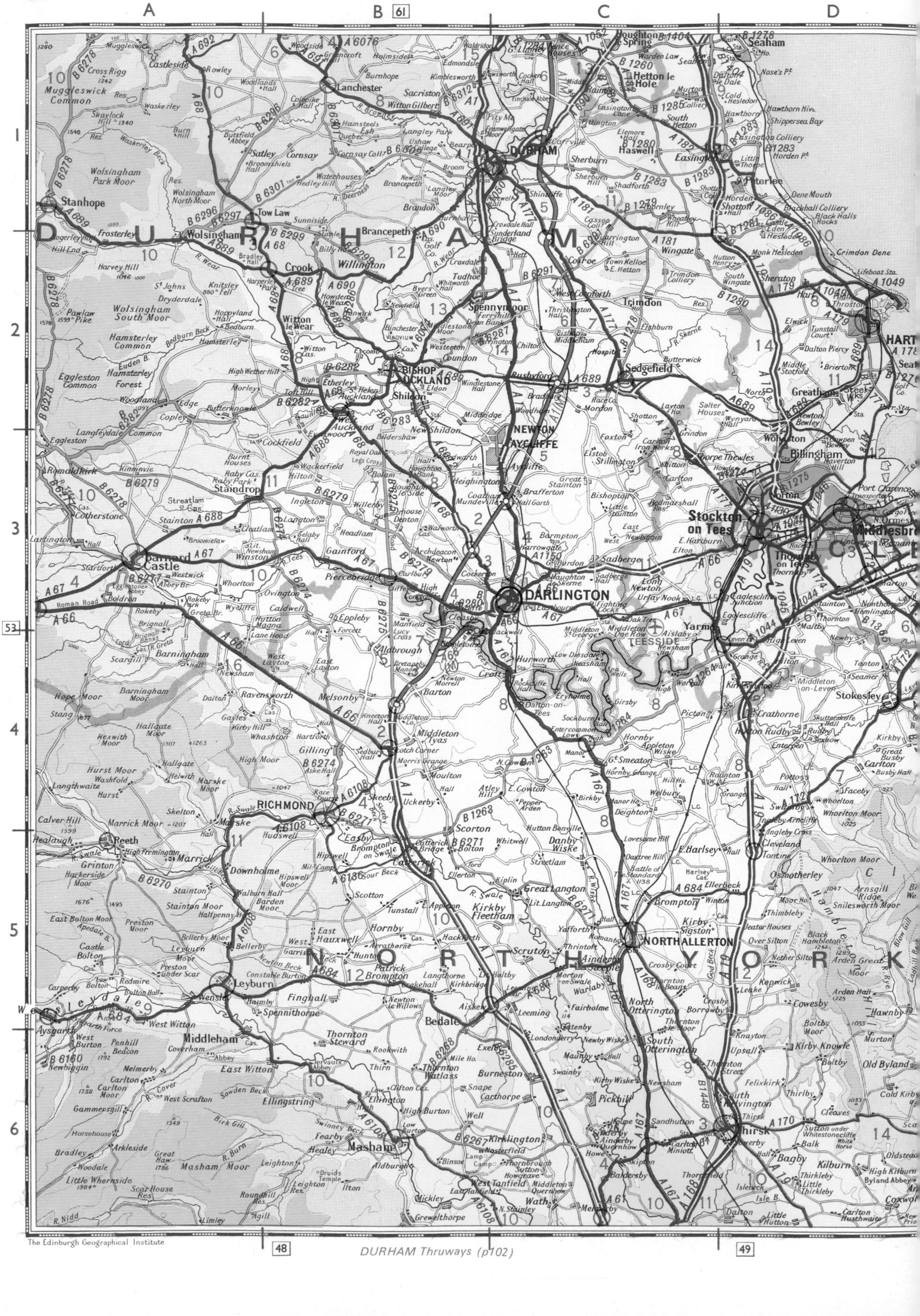

A   B   61   C   D

DURHAM

NORTH YORK

Stanhope
Wolsingham
Tow Law
Crook
Willington
Brancepeth
Lanchester
DURHAM
Haswell
Easington
Peterlee
Seaham
HARTLEPOOL
Bishop Auckland
Shildon
Spennymoor
Sedgefield
Trimdon
Newton Aycliffe
Billingham
Stockton on Tees
Middlesbrough
Barnard Castle
Staindrop
Darlington
Stokesley
Richmond
Reeth
Leyburn
Middleham
Northallerton
Bedale
Masham
Thirsk

A1   A66   A67   A68   A688   A689   A690   A691   A167   A19   A170   A171

53

48   DURHAM Thruways (p102)   49

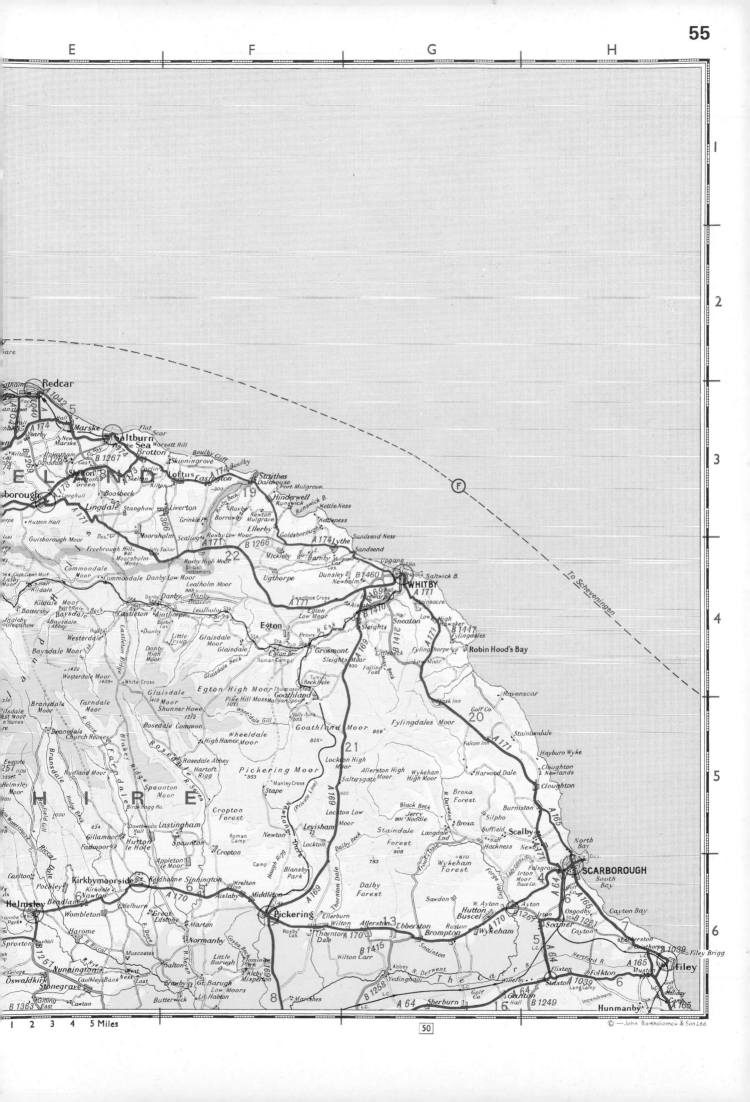

E   F   G   H

1

2

Redcar

To Scheveningen

Marske
Saltburn by the Sea
Brotton
Skinningrove
Loftus
Staithes
Dalehouse
Port Mulgrave
Hinderwell
Runswick B.
Kettle Ness
Kettleness

Skelton
Hutton Green
Kilton
Easington
Boosbeck
Liverton
Newton Mulgrave
Ellerby
Goldsborough
Sandsend Ness

ELAND

borough

Lingdale
Stanghow
Grinkle
Roxby Low Moor
Mickleby
Barnby
Sandsend

Guisborough Moor
Moorsholm
Scaling
A171
B1266
Lythe
Upgang

3

Freebrough Hills
Moorsholm Moor
Roxby High Moor
British Settlement
B1460
Dunsley
Newholm
WHITBY
Saltwick B.

Commondale
Danby Low Moor
Ugthorpe
A171
Ruswarp
Stainsacre

Hutton Hall
Commondale
Lealholm Moor

Kildale
Danby
Danby Beacon
Egton Low Moor
Aislaby
B1410
Sneaton
Low High Hawsker
B1447
Fylingdales
Robin Hood's Bay

Kildale Moor
Castleton
Ainthorpe
Lealholm Sta.
Egton
Grosmont
Sleights
Littlebeck
Fylingthorpe
Low Moor

4

Baysdale
Westerdale
Little Fryup
Glaisdale Moor
Glaisdale
Egton Br.
Roman Camps
Sleights Moor
Falling Foss

Baysdale Moor
Danby High Moor
Glaisdale beck
Tunm'l Beck Hole
Goathland
Mallyan Spout
Fylingdales Moor
Flask Inn
Ravenscar

Farndale Moor
Glaisdale
White Cross
Egton High Moor
Thomasonfoss
Pike Hill Moss
Shunner Howe
Wheeldale Moor
Goathland Moor
Falcon Inn
Staindale
Hayburn Wyke

5

Bransdale Moor
Rosedale Common
Wheeldale Gill
Pickering Moor
Lockton High Moor
Allerston High Moor
Wykeham High Moor
Harwood Dale
Cloughton Newlands
Cloughton

Rosedale Abbey
Hartoft Rigg
Manley Cross
Stape
Saltersgate
Broxa Forest
Burniston
A165

Lastingham
Spaunton Moor
Birch Hagg Ho.
Cropton Forest
Lockton Low Moor
Black Beck
Jerry Noddle
Broxa
Silpho
Suffield
Scalby

Gillamoor
Fadmoor
Spaunton
Appleton le Moor
Newton
Lockton
Levisham
Staindale Forest
Langdale End
Hackness
Newby

6

Kirkbymoorside
Keldholme
Sinnington
Wrelton
Middleton
Blansby Park
Dalby Forest
Wykeham Forest
Sawdon
W. Ayton
Hutton Buscel
Scarborough
North Bay
South Bay

Helmsley
Beadlam
Nawton
A170
Aislaby
Pickering
Thornton Dale
Ellerburn
Wilton
Allerston
Ebberston
Brompton
Wykeham
E. Ayton
B1267
Seamer
Cayton Bay

Harome
Normanby
Marton
Roxby Cas.
Thornton Dale
A170
Wilton Carr
Snainton
Osgodby
Cayton
A64
A165

Wombleton
Welburn
Great Edstone
Little Baugh
Misperton
B1416
Abbey
R. Derwent
Flixton
Hertford R.
Folkton
A165
Filey

Sproxton
Nunnington
Harome
R. Riccal
Salton
West Ness
Kirby Misperton
Wilton
Yedingham
Willerby
Staxton
A64
Muston

Stonegrave
Oswaldkirk
Gilling East
Caulkleys Bank
Carlton
Brawby
Barugh
Marishes
B1258
B1249
A64
Sherburn
Staxton
Hunmanby
Holiday Camp

B1363
B1257

1 2 3 4 5 Miles

© —John Bartholomew & Son, Ltd.

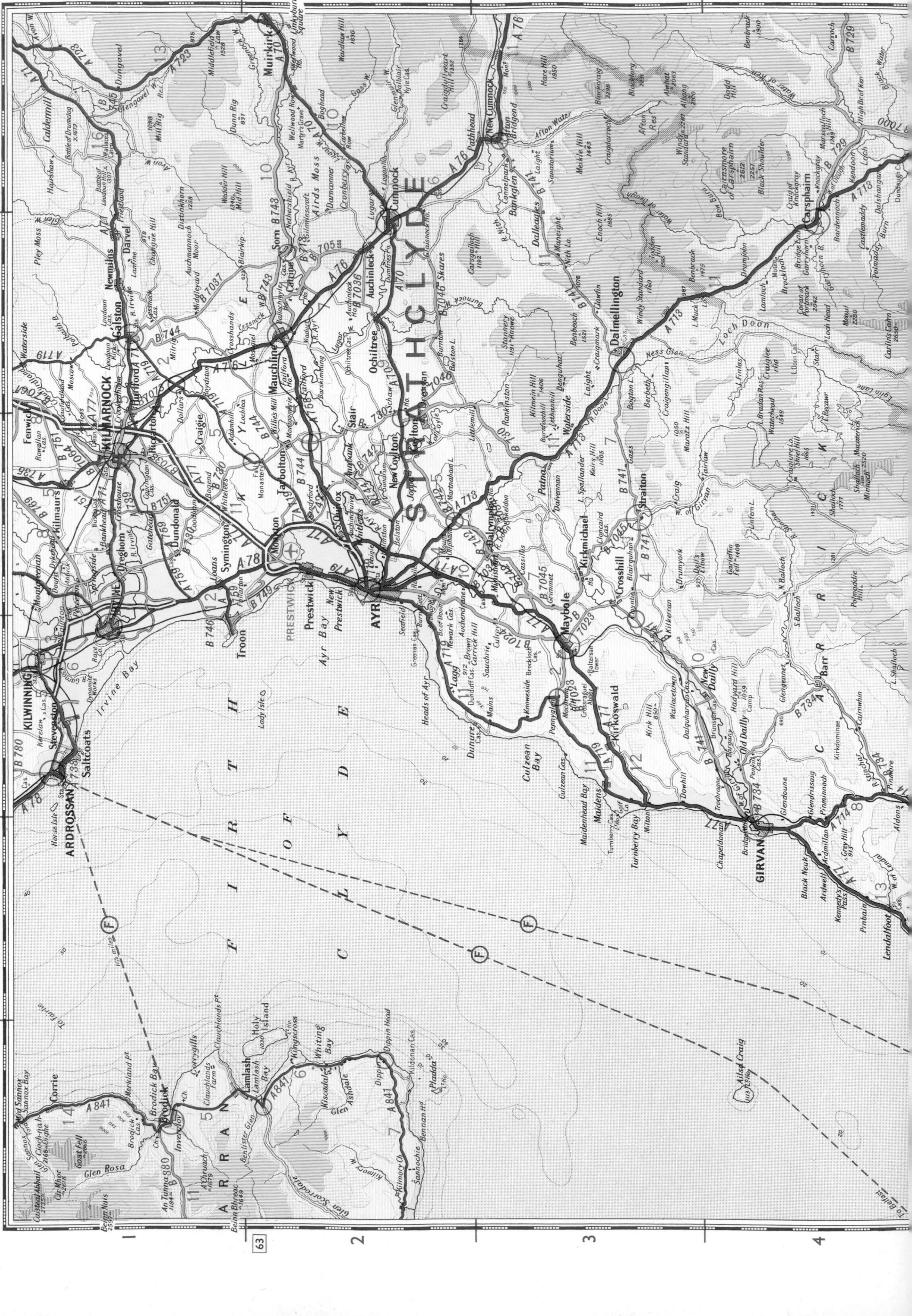

56

STRATHCLYDE

Muirkirk
New Cumnock
Carsphairn
Cumnock
Auchinleck
Darvel
Newmilns
Galston
Catrine
Mauchline
Ochiltree
Dalmellington
Kilmarnock
Stair
Straiton
Fenwick
Craigie
Patna
Kirkmichael
Crosshill
Symington
Tarbolton
Dundonald
Maybole
Troon
New Dailly
Barr
Prestwick
New Prestwick
AYR
Kirkoswald
Girvan
Kilwinning
Stevenston
Saltcoats
ARDROSSAN

CLYDE

FIRTH OF CLYDE

Culzean Bay
Maidenhead Bay
Turnberry Bay

Corrie
Brodick
Lamlash
Kingscross
Whiting Bay
Holy Island
Ailsa Craig

ARRAN

Ayr Bay
Irvine Bay

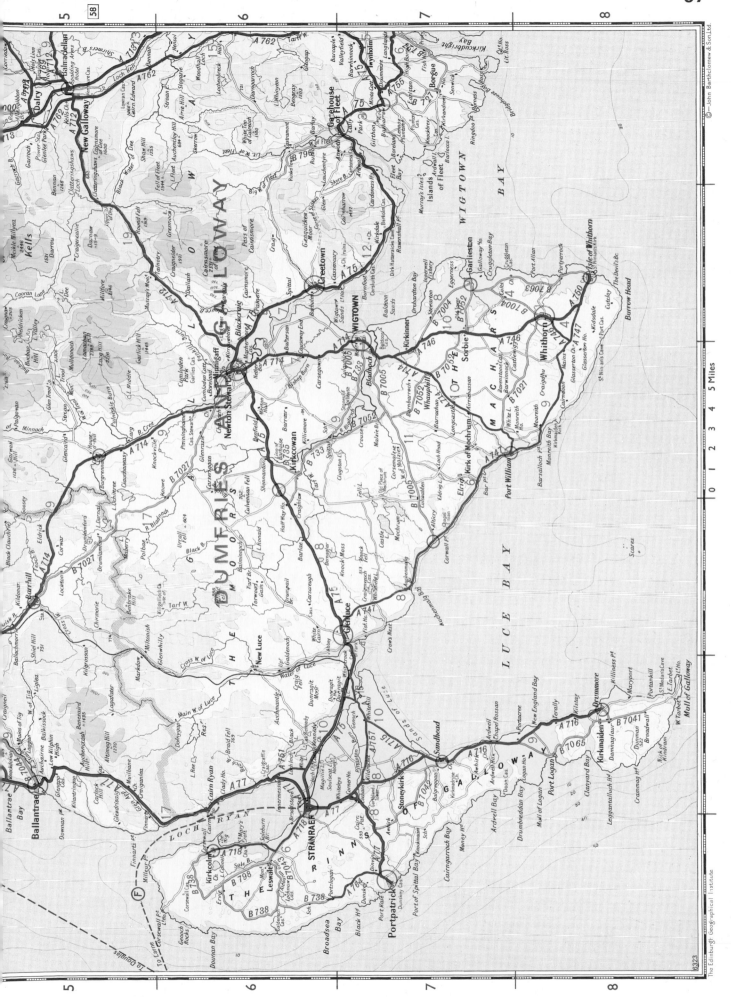

The Edinburgh Geographical Institute

A 64 B C 65 D

The Edinburgh Geographical Institute

Grid references (left margin): 1, 56, 2, 3, 4, 5, 57, 6

Major places and labels:

Dalrymple, Patna, Kirkmichael, Crosshill, Straiton, Dalmellington, Waterside, Carsphairn, New Cumnock, Afton Bridgend, Bankglen, Connelpark, Kirkconnel, Sanquhar, Crawickmill, Wanlockhead, Leadhills, Penpont, Tynron, Moniaive, Dalry, Balmaclellan, New Galloway, Corsock, Crocketford, Springholm, Kirkpatrick Durham, Parton, Crossmichael, Laurieston, Castle Douglas, Dalbeattie, Palnackie, Kirkgunzeon, Haugh of Urr, Newton Stewart, Minnigaff, Blackcraig, Creetown, Wigtown, Bladnoch, Kirkcowan, Kirkinner, Sorbie, Garlieston, Whauphill, Kirk of Mochrum, Eldrig, Port William, Gatehouse of Fleet, Anwoth, Ringford, Twynholm, Tongland, Kirkcudbright, Borgue, Dundrennan, Auchencairn, Palnure, Spittal

Hills and features:
Merrick 2764, Corserine 2668, Rinns of Kells, Meikle Millyea 2446, Cairnsmore of Carsphairn 2612, Cairnsmore of Fleet 2331, Shalloch on Minnoch 2520, Windy Standard, Benbrack, Colt Hill, Cruffell, Wether Hill, Loch Doon, Loch Ken, Clatteringshaws Loch, Loch Dee, Water of Deugh, Water of Ken, Water of Fleet, River Nith, River Dee, River Cree, River Doon

Roads: A713, A76, A702, A712, A75, A714, A746, A711, A762, B741, B729, B7000, B794, B795, B736, B727, B7052, B7005

WIGTOWN BAY

DUMFRIES (D U M F R I)
KIRKCUDBRIGHT
WIGTOWN
MACHARS

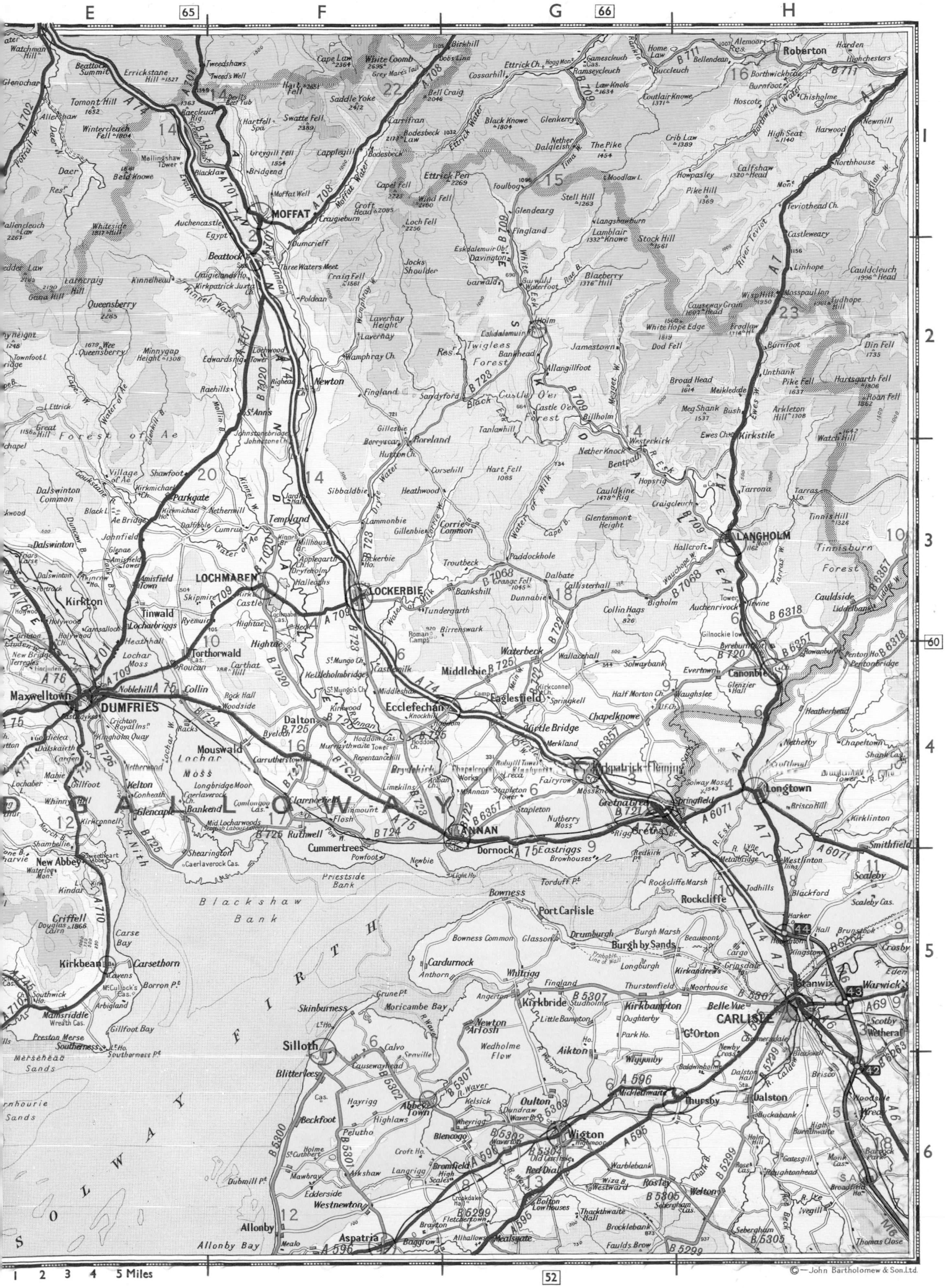

E · 65 · F · G · 66 · H

Roberton

MOFFAT

Beattock

LANGHOLM

LOCHMABEN

LOCKERBIE

DUMFRIES

Maxwelltown

Ecclefechan

Annan

Canonbie

Longtown

Gretna Green

Springfield

Dornock

Eastriggs

Rockcliffe

Port Carlisle

Burgh by Sands

CARLISLE

Wetheral

Dalston

Thursby

Wigton

Silloth

Allonby

Aspatria

Kirkbean

New Abbey

Southerness

S O L W A Y   F I R T H

Blackshaw Bank

D · G A L L O W A Y

Forest of Ae

Tinnisburn Forest

1 2 3 4 5 Miles

© — John Bartholomew & Son Ltd.

· 52 ·

· 60 ·

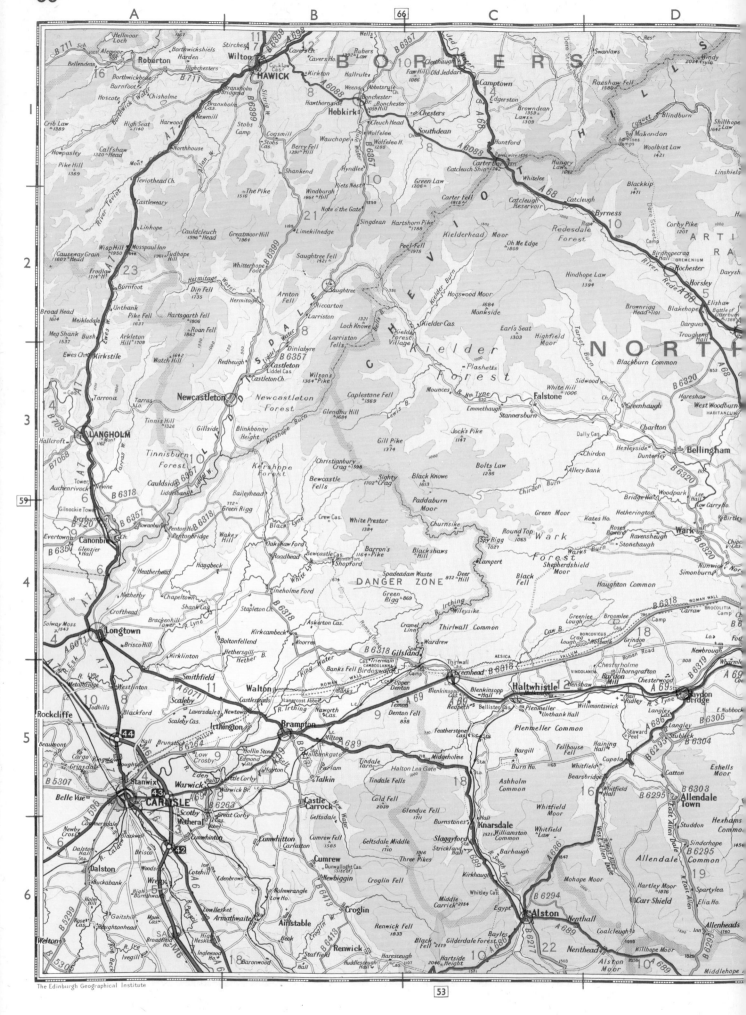

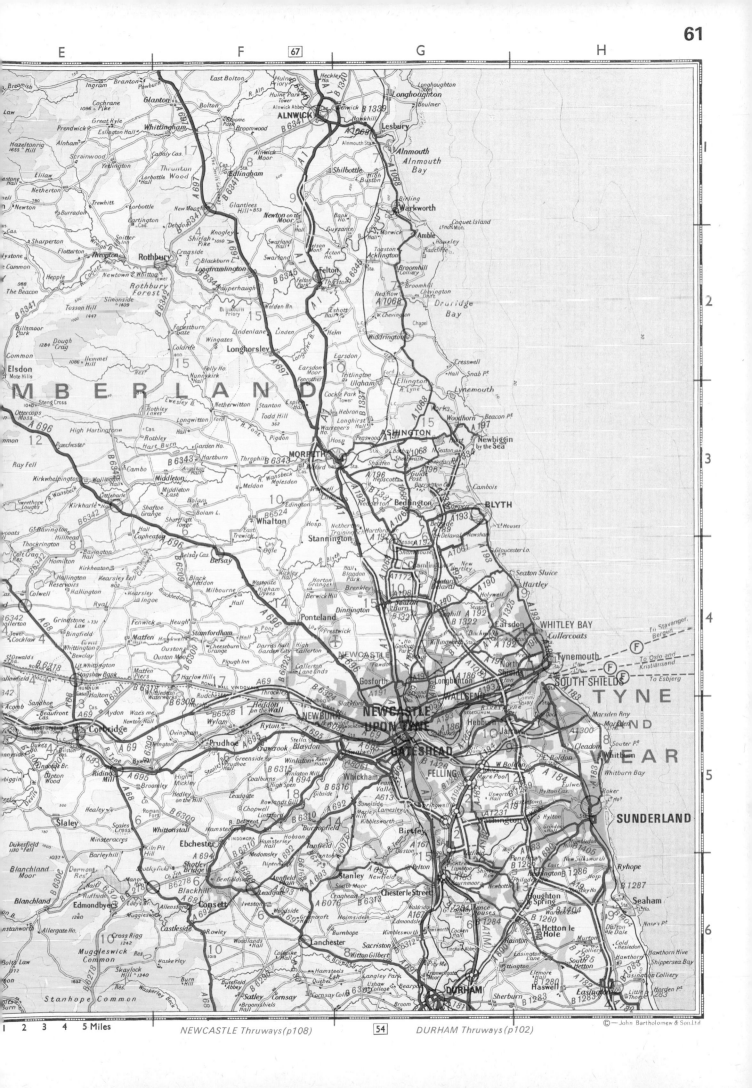

A   B   69   C   D

1

JURA

Creag nam
fiadh Mor
Lagg
Glenbatrick
Rubh'a'Chrois-aoinidh
Rubh'Aird na Sgitheich
Rubha'Mhàil
Light Ho.
Rubha Bholsa
Brèin Phort
Port Domhnuill Chruinn
Blod nan Sgarbh
Nave Island
Na Peileirean
Cha.
Ardnave Pt.
Gortantaoid
Carraig Bhàn
Ardnave
Ton Mhòr
Tayovullin
Killinallan
Gortantaoid
Beinn Bhreac
937
Eilean Mòr
Sanaigmore
Leckgruinart
Crois Mhòr
Bun-an-uillt
Rubha Lamanais
Smaull
Ballinaby
Coille
Loch
Gorm
Aoradh
Brainel
Craigens
Lyrabus
B 8018
Machir
Bay
Rockside
Kilchoman
Gartmain
Kilchiaran B.
Gearach
Carn
Beinn
Tart a Mhill
758
Carn
Cottage
Kelsay
Nereabolls
Lossit B.
Rubha na Faing
E. Ellister
Portnahaven
Orsay
Rinns Point
Port Wemyss

Scrinadle
1439
Beinn Bhreac
1660
Beinn Tarsuinn
1306
Gate House
Achamore
Jura Forest
Beinn an Òir
2571
Paps of Jura
Beinn Shiantaidh
2477
Port Doir a' Chrorain
Eilean Mòr
Kilmory Isle
Corsr Eilean
Lan t-Siob
Gleann Asdale
An Dùnan
Point of Knap
Sròn Gharbh
L'Ho.
Stotfi
Miller's R.
Small
Isles
Kilberry
Head
Keppoch Pt.
Rubha na Traille
Rubha Cru

Port Askaig
Feolinferry
Dubh Bheinn
1737
Craighouse
Cabrach
Ardfin
Jura Ho.
Brosdale
Island

2

Bowmore
Bridgend
Ballygrant
Port Charlotte
Gartbreck
Laggan
A 847
B 8016
A 846
ISLAY

F

Gigha
W. Tarbert Bay
E. Tarbert Bay
Tarbert
Ardaily
Ardminish
Ardminish B.
Craro I.
Gròb Bagh
Gigalum
Cara
Mull of Cara
Cleit Dhubh

3

Port Ellen
Laggan Bay
ISLAY (PORT ELLEN)
Machrie R.
Machrie Hotel
Golf Lo.
Kintra
Leorin
Leorin Lochs
Kildalton Ho.
Lagavulin
Ardbeg
Laphroaig
Texa

The Oa
Maol Buidhe
542
Carnmore
The Oa
Lower Killeyan
Loch Kinnabus
Mull of Oa
Ard Achadh
Port Chubaird
Ballychatrigan
Rubha nan Leacan

4

Glenbar
Abbey
A 83

5

Machrihanish Bay
MACHRIHANISH
Machrihanish
Westport
Ballivain
Dalivaddy
Chiscan
Drumlemble

6

RATHLIN ISLAND
Church B.
447

Killypole
Cnoc Moy
Earadale Pt.
The Slate
Killellan
Rubha Dùin Bhàin
Largybaan
Cnoc Reamhar
Cnoc Odhar
A' Chruach
Beinn na Lice
1405
Garveld
Mull of Kintyre
South Point
Light Ho.
Borgadelmore Pt.

E   F   70   G   H

L. Errol · Srôndoire · Srondoire · Achavraich · B 802 A · A 83 · Faur-Bheinne · Cruach a'Phubuill 1564 · Clachbreck · Ballyaurgan · Cnoc a'Bharaille · Sliabh Gaoil 1580 · Meall Mór 1840 · Rudha Beag · Kilfinan B · Kilfinan · Otter B 8000 · Drum Point · Craig · Springfield · Ormidale L · Ardbeg · Invervegain · Bishop's Seat 1651 · Dunloskin · GOUROCK · Kirn · Prince's Pier

Achaglachgach · Cnoc a'Bhaille · Cruach a'Bharaille · Erines · Meall Mór · Artilligan Cott. · B 8000 · Drum F.ll · Acharosson · Fearnach · Troustan · 1658 · Beinn Bhreac · Glen Morag · DUNOON · A 885 · A 815 · Castle Levan · A 8 · A 770 · GREENOCK

Dubh Chreag 1574 · Meall Reamhar 1080 · Auchalick B · Auchalick · Ardmarnock · Millhouse · Kilmichael · West Buttock's · Colintraive · Coustonn · Inverchaplain · Corlarach Hill · Kilmacolm · Buthkollidar · A 8 · Lurg Moor · L. Thom · Greenock Water Wks. · Gryfe Res.

Tarbert · A 8015 · W. Tarbert · L. Tarbert · TIGHNABRUAICH · Kames · Blair's Ferry · Glenmore · Kames Hill 875 · Ardmaleish · Toward Cas. · Knockdow · Achafour · Achavoulin · Beinn Ruadh 1057 · Dunan · Lunderston Bay · Ardgowan · INVERKIP · A 78 · Leap Moor · Corkney Top 1175 · 1448

Escart · Stonefield · Barmore · Buic B. · Asgog L. · Derybruich · Kilbride · Kames Cas. · Kames B. · Drumachloy · Port Bannatyne · Ardbeg · Bogany Pt. · WEMYSS BAY · Skelmorlie · A 78 · Knockencorsan · Hydro. · Duchall Moor · Black Fell

Cruach an t-Sorchain · Corranbuie 1125 · Achadacaie 1236 · Cnoc a'Bhaille shios 1385 · Kilbride B. · Ardlamont · ROTHESAY · A 844 · B 878 · Ascog · Toward Pt. · Skelmorlie Cas. · LARGS · Meigle Bay · S. Fillans · Hill of Stake 1711

Mindarruhh · Dunmore · Kennacraig · Whitehouse · Coire nan Capull 1095 · Glenskible · Ardlamont B. · Ardlamont Pt. · Camas na Ceardaich · Up. Ardroscadale · Craigmore · Ardbeg · Ardyne · Greenan · Straad Cott. · Bell B. · Fintry Bay · Kelburne · Rowantree 1404 · Slaty Law 1584

Cruach Doire Leithe · Rudha Lagganroaig · Gartavaich · Gartnacloch · Garvorne · Skipness · Claonaig · Rockfield · A 841 · Kilbride · Blindman's · Etterick Bay · Loch · Ardscalpsie · Ambrismore · A 844 · Meikle Kilmory · Ardscalpsie Pt. · Piperhall · GREAT CUMBRAE · MILLPORT · Fairlie Roads · Noddsdale · Black Law · Irish Law

Drimnaleck · Clachan · L. Ciaran · Eascairt · B 842 · Port Fada · Toitdubh · Crossaig · A 83 · Skipness Pt. · SOUND OF BUTE · Kingarth · Kilchattan B. · Kilchattan · B 881 · Garroch Hd. · Little Cumbrae Island · Gull Pt. · Portencross · West Kilbride · Seamill · Burnside · B 780 · DRAKEMIRE · DALRY · B 780

Talatoll · L. Garasdale · Coul Bay · Cock of Arran · Newton · Lochranza · Catacol Bay · Cnoc Reamhar · Craw (N. Thundergay) · S. Thundergay · Beinn Bhreac 2333 · Beinn Tarsuinn · Caisteal Abhail 2735 · Mid Sannox · Sannox Bay · Corrie · Ann's Lodge · Horse Isle · Kerelaw · STEVENSTON · A 78

Narachan Hill 935 · Cnoc Reamhar 866 · Creagmhor · Deucheran Hill 1091 · Sunadale · Garrachcroit Bagh · Grogport · Barmollack · Pirnmill · Whitefarland Pt. · Beinn Bharrain 2345 · Beinn Bhreac · L. Tanna · Cir Mhor 2618 · Goat Fell 2866 · Glen Sannox · Cioch na h-Oighe 2168 · Merkland Pt. · ARDROSSAN · A 738 · SALTCOATS · A 78

Cruach nan Gabhar · Dippen · Beinn an Tuirc 1491 · Diollaid Mhór 1124 · Arinanuan · Beinn Bhreac 1398 · Carradale · Dougrie Pt. · Dougrie · Iorsa Water · Glen Iorsa · Beinn Nuis 2697 · Beinn Tarsuinn 2706 · Glen Rosa · Brodick Cas. · Brodick Bay · BRODICK · Invercloy · FIRTH OF CLYDE

Saddell Abbey · Saddell Bay · Bunlarie · 1338 · Whitestone · Rhonadale · Auchencar · Chap. · Machrie Bay · Machrie · Glaister · A'Chruach 1679 · Ard Bheinn 1678 · Corrygills · Corrygills Pt. · Clauchlands Farm · Clauchlands Pt. · Lady Isle

Ugadale Pt. · Ballochgair · Ardnacross Bay · Lussa Water · Ardacross · Peninver · Tormore · King's Caves · Machrie · B 880 · Ballymichael · Beinn Bhreac 1649 · Benlister Glen · LAMLASH · Lamlash Bay · Holy Island

Davaar I. · Davarr · Torbeg · Shiskine · Shedog Inn · BLACKWATERFOOT · Drumadoon Bay · Kilpatrick · Brown Head · Glen Scorradale · Kilmory W. · Kiscadale · Glen Ashdale · WHITING BAY · Kingscross · A 841

Sound · New Orleans · Feochaig · Polliwilline · Corriecravie · Castle Hill · Sliddery · Lagg Inn · Shannochie · Bennan Hd. · Kilmory Ch. · Kildonan Cas. · Pladda · A 841 · Dippin · Dippin Head

To Belfast · To Douglas (Summer only) · Dunure · Culzean Bay · Culzean Cas. · Maidenhead Bay · Pennyglen · Maidens · Turnberry Bay · Turnberry Cas. · KIRKOSWALD · A 77 · Kirk Hill 850 · Dowhill · Dalquharran Cas.

Sheep I. · Sanda

ARRAN

KILBRANNAN SOUND

1   2   3   4   5 Miles

© —John Bartholomew & Son Ltd.

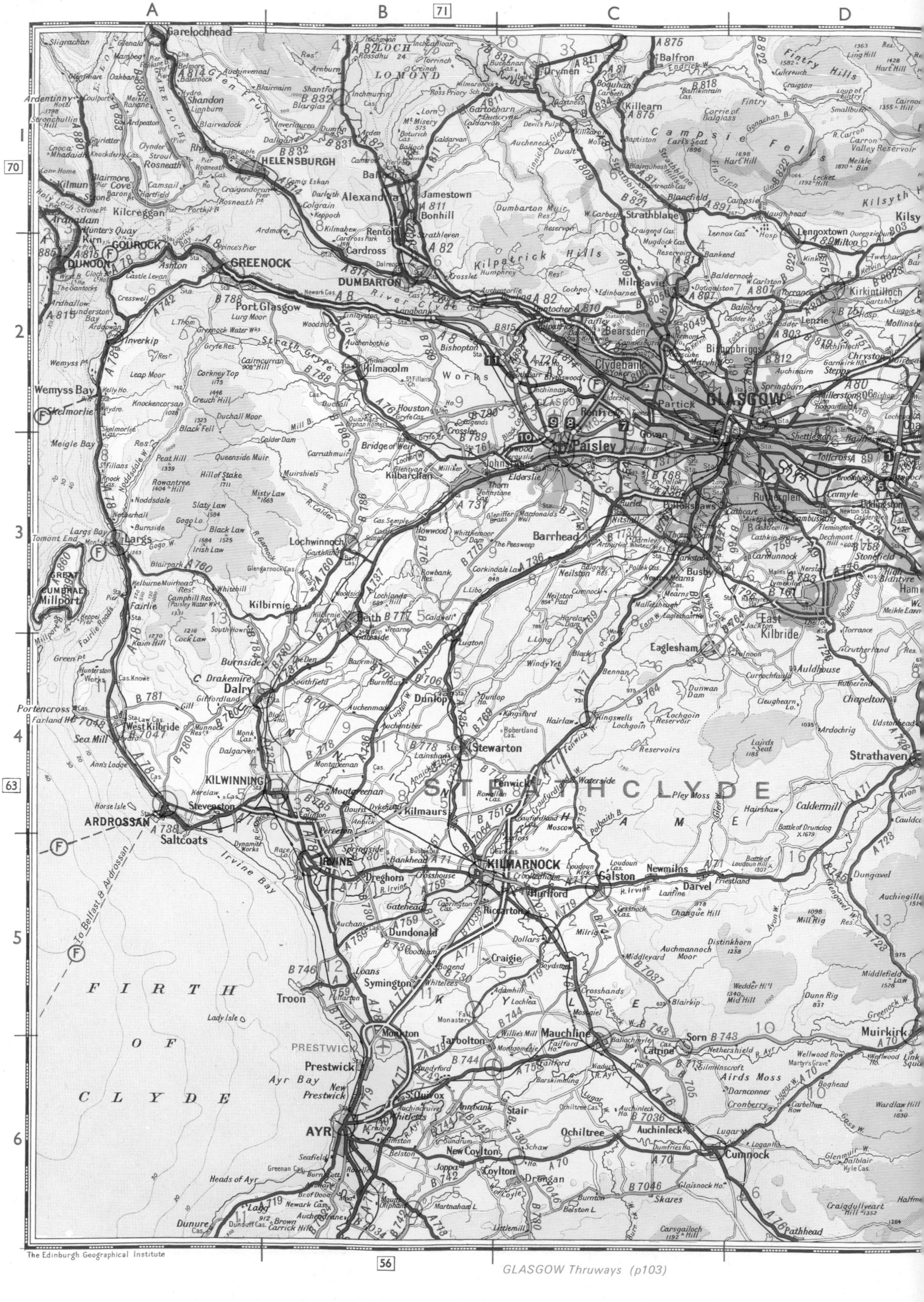

71

70

LOCH LOMOND

Garelochhead

Sligrachan

HELENSBURGH

Alexandria
Bonhill
Jamestown
Renton
Cardross

GOUROCK
GREENOCK
DUNOON

DUMBARTON

Port Glasgow

Kilpatrick Hills

Campsie Fells

Balfron
Killearn
Strathblane

Milngavie
Bearsden
Clydebank

Kirkintilloch
Lenzie
Bishopbriggs

GLASGOW

Inverkip

Wemyss Bay
Skelmorlie

Kilmacolm

Houston

Bridge of Weir
Kilbarchan

Renfrew
Govan
PAISLEY
Johnstone
Elderslie

Partick

Rutherglen
Cambuslang

Largs

Lochwinnoch

Barrhead
Neilston
Busby

Eaglesham

East Kilbride

Strathaven

GREAT CUMBRAE
Millport

Kilbirnie
Beith

Dalry
Drakemire

Dunlop

Stewarton

Fenwick

S T R A T H C L Y D E

West Kilbride

Kilwinning
Stevenston

Kilmaurs

ARDROSSAN
Saltcoats

IRVINE
Dreghorn
Crosshouse

KILMARNOCK
Galston
Newmilns
Darvel

Muirkirk

Dundonald

Troon

Symington
Loans

Monkton

Tarbolton
Mauchline
Sorn
Catrine

PRESTWICK
Prestwick

AYR

New Prestwick

Annbank
Stair
Ochiltree
Auchinleck

Coylton
Drongan

Cumnock

FIRTH
OF
CLYDE

Dunure

GLASGOW Thruways (p103)

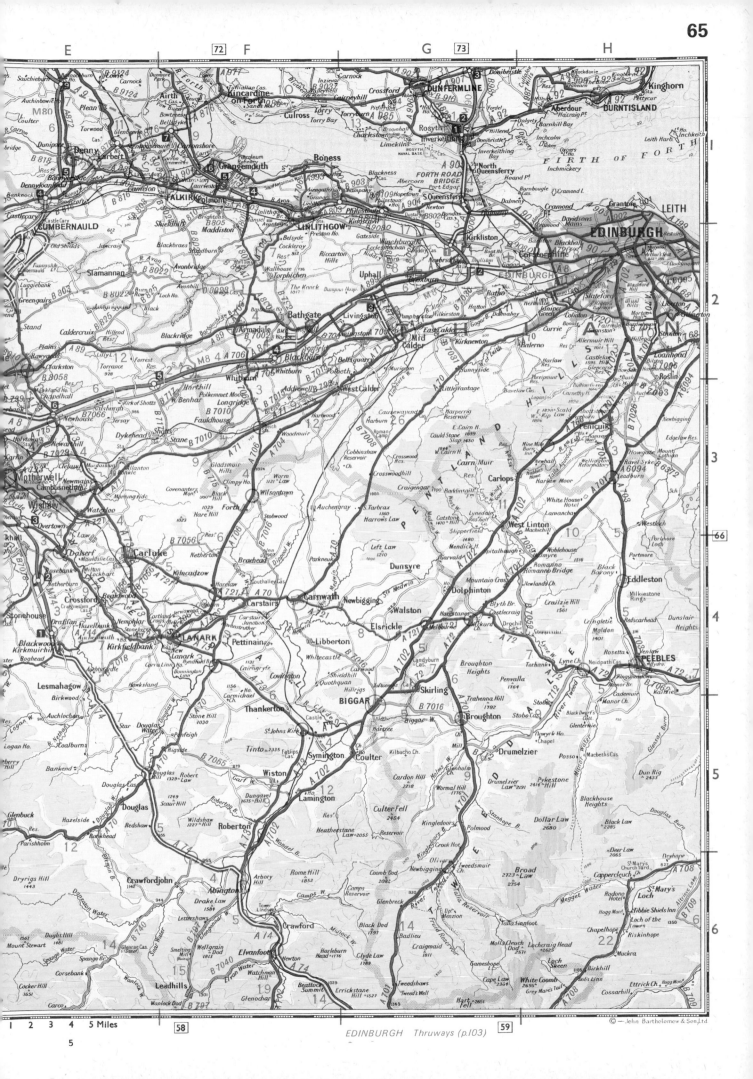

© — John Bartholomew & Son, Ltd.

A B 73 C D

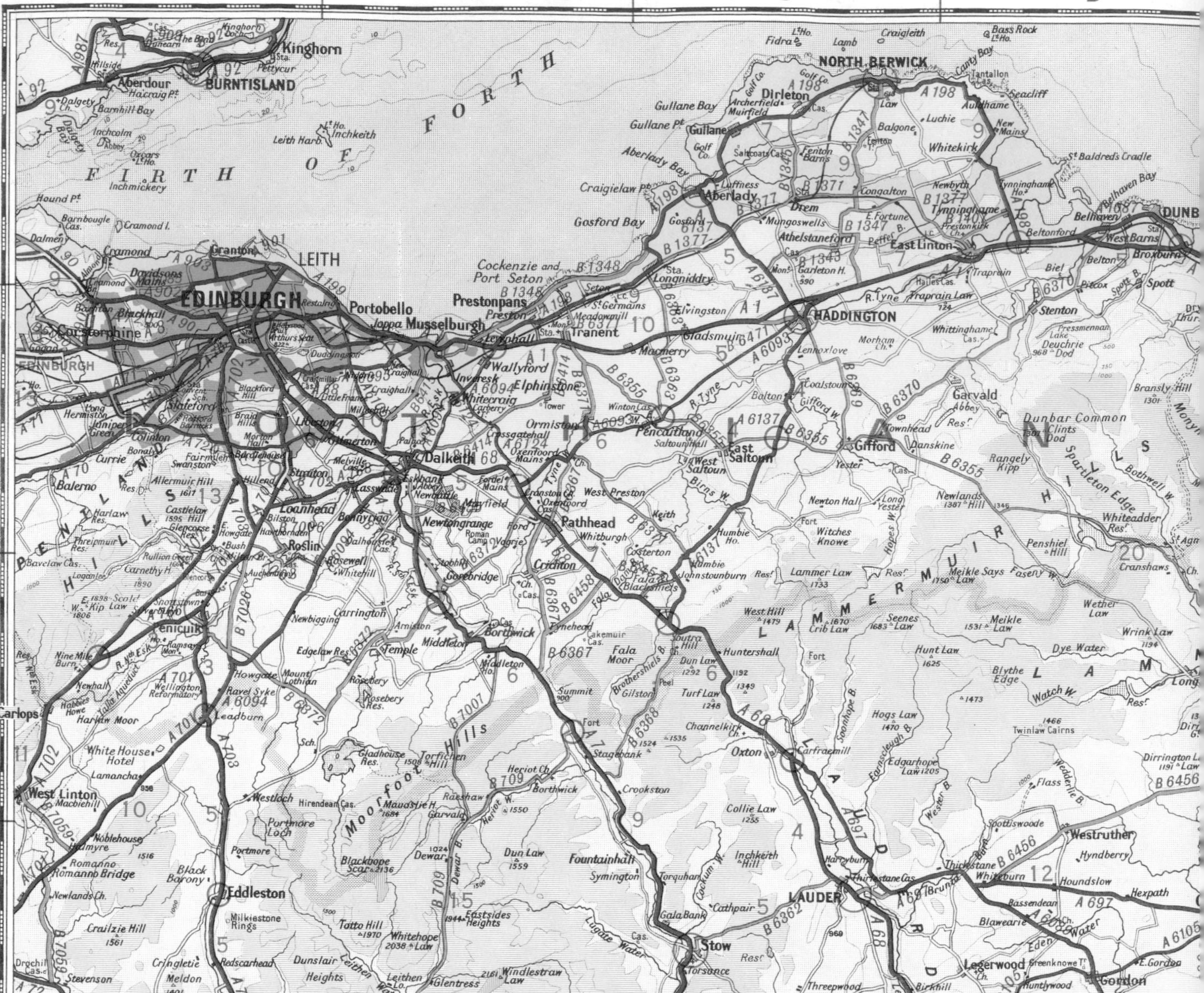

FIRTH OF FORTH

Kinghorn
Pettycur
BURNTISLAND
Aberdour
Inchkeith
Inchcolm
Inchmickery

NORTH BERWICK
A 198
Dirleton
Gullane
Tantallon
Bass Rock
Muirfield
Gullane Bay
Aberlady Bay
ABERLADY
Drem
Whitekirk
East Linton
DUNBAR

Cramond
Granton
LEITH
EDINBURGH
Portobello
Joppa Musselburgh
Prestonpans
Port Seton
Cockenzie and
Longniddry
Tranent
HADDINGTON

Corstorphine
Slateford
Wallyford
Inveresk
Elphinstone
Ormiston
Pencaitland
East Saltoun
West Saltoun
Gifford
Garvald
Dunbar Common

Currie
Balerno
Juniper Green
Colinton
Dalkeith
Bonnyrigg
Lasswade
Loanhead
Roslin
Newtongrange
Rathhead
Crichton
Humbie
Lammer Law
LAMMERMUIR HILLS

PENTLAND HILLS
Penicuik
Carlops
WEST LINTON
Romanno Bridge
Eddleston
Leadburn
Temple
MOORFOOT HILLS
Heriot
Stow
Oxton
LAUDER
Legerwood
Gordon
Westruther

PEEBLES
Innerleithen Walkerburn
Traquair
Cardrona
Clovenfords
GALASHIELS
MELROSE
Earlston
Smailholm
Maxton
Roxburgh

ETTRICK FOREST
Yarrow
SELKIRK
Bowden
Lilliesleaf
Ancrum
JEDBURGH
Bedrule

St Mary's Loch
Tibbie Shiels Inn
Cappercleuch
Ettrickbridge end
Ashkirk
Minto
Denholm

Broad Law
2754
Dollar Law
2680
White Coomb
2695
Grey Mare's Tail
Ettrick
Roberton
WILTON
HAWICK
A 6088

The Edinburgh Geographical Institute

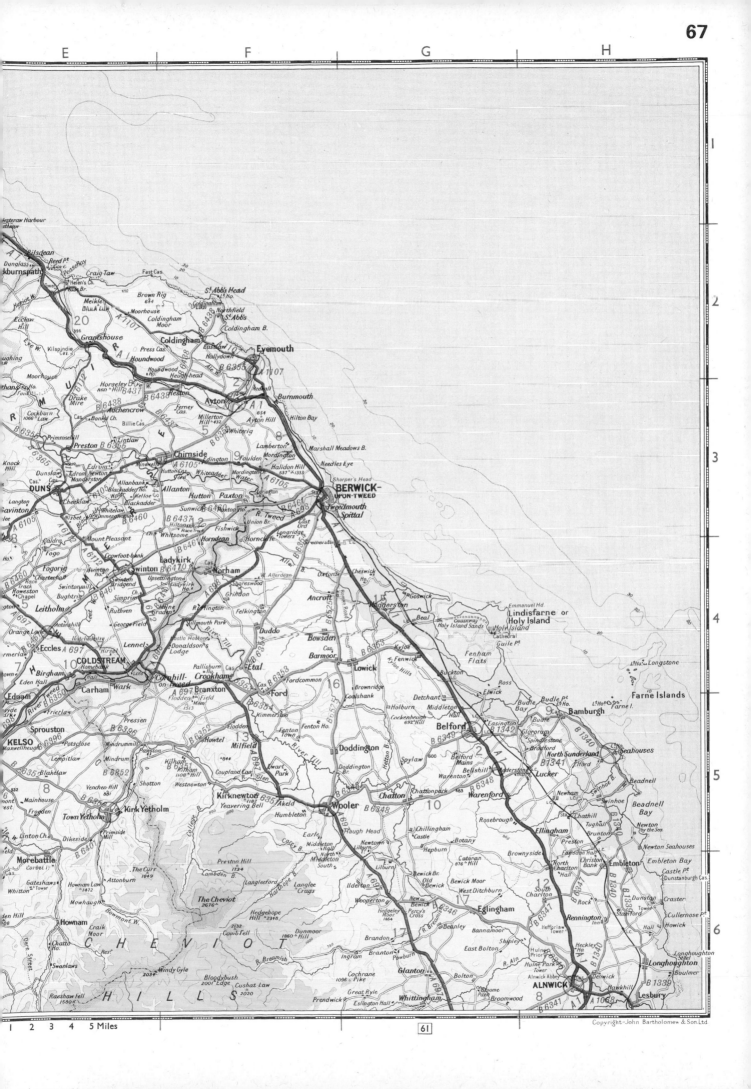

E   F   G   H

1

2

3

4

5

6

kateraw Harbour
thour

Dunglass
kburnspath
Bilsdean
Reed Pt.
Pease Bay
Helen's Ch.
Tweed
Craig Taw
Fast Cas.
Brown Rig
614
St Abb's Head
Lt. Ho.
Northfield
St Abbs
Coldingham B.
Eyemouth
Burnmouth
Redhall
Hilton Bay
Ayton Hill
432
Whiterig
Marshall Meadows B.
Needles Eye
Sharper's Head
BERWICK-
UPON-TWEED
Tweedmouth
Spittal
East
Ord

Heriot W.
Ecclaw
Hill
Eye W.
Kilspindie
Cas.
Grantshouse
996
MUIR
A1107
Moorhouse
Coldingham
Moor
Coldingham
Houndwood
Houndwood
Ho.
Heughhead
Horseley
Hill 6437
W.
Reston
Ayton
A1
B6355
B6438
B6438
Hallydown
Eastlano

Moorhouse
thans Ho.
ughing
Drake
Mire
Cockburn
1066 Law
Cas.
Bonkyl Ch.
Billie Cas.
Millerton
Hill 432
Whiterig
Lamberton
Mordington
Halidon Hill
537 1333

Knock
Hill
Dunslaw
Cas.
Edrom Newton
Manderston
Chirnside
Edington
Faulden
Mordington
Water
A6105
A6105
Whiteadder

DUNS
Langton
Cheeklaw
Whitelaw
Blackadder Ho.
Blackadder
Hutton
Paxton
Sunwick
Paxton Vic.
R. Tweed

avinton
lee
A6105
Nisbet
Blackadder
Kelloe
Allanton
B6460
B6437
Hilton
Swinton Ho.
Swinton
Bridgend
Ladykirk
Ho.
B6470
Norham
Ladykirk
A698
Shoreswood
Allerdean
Oxford
Cheswick
Goswick

A6112
Mount Pleasant
Crowfoot-bank
Simprim
Grindon
Felkington
Ancroft
Haggerston
Beal
Holy Island Sands
Lindisfarne or
Holy Island

B6460
Caldra
Fogo
Fogorig
Swinton
Race
Track
Rowston
Chapel
Ruthven
George Field
Tillmouth Park
River Till
Duddo
Bowsden
Cas.
Barmoor
Kyloe
Fenwick
Tice Hills
Bucktor
Emmanuel Hd.
Causeway
Holy Island
Cathedral
Guile Pt.
Fenham
Flats

5
Leitholm
Antonshill
Orange Lane
B6461
Hirsel
Lennel
Donaldson's
Lodge
Castle Heaton
Etal
Fordcommon
Lowick
B6358
B6365
Ross
Elwick
Farne Islands
Longstone

COLDSTREAM
Eccles A697
Birgham
Eden Hall
Carham
Wark
Cornhill-
on-Tweed
Crookham
Branxton
Flodden
Field
1513
Ford
Holburn
Detchant
Middleton
Budle
Bay
Bamburgh
Farne I.
Budle Pt.

Edman
B6350
River Tweed
B6396
Pressen
Kimmerston
Fenton
Tower
Fenton Ho.
Cockenheugh
692 Hall
Easington
Lt. Ho.
Belford
B1342
Glororum
Bradford
Spindlestone

KELSO
Maxwellheugh
Potsclose
Lempitlaw
B6396
Mindrummill
B6352
Paxton
Mindrum
Howtel
Milfield
Howburn
Doddington
Doddington
Br.
Spylaw
600
Belford
Mains
Bellshill
Warenton
B6349
North Sunderland
B1341
Elford
Lucker

Sprouston
Blakelaw
B6352
Venchen Hill
681
Kilham
1108 Hill
Ewart
Park
Shotton
Westnewton
R. Glen
Kirknewton
B635
Akeld
Wooler
B6348
Chatton
Chattonpark
483
Warenford
10
Newham
Seahouses
Swinhoe
Beadnell

8
Mainhouse
Frogden
B6352
Town Yetholm
Kirk Yetholm
Yeavering Bell
Humbleton
Haugh Head
A69
Earle
Middleton
High
Middleton
South
Newtown
Lilburn
Chillingham
Castle
Hepburn
Botany
Roseborough
Chatmill
Preston
Brunton
Newton
by-the-Sea

Morebattle
Corbet
Gateshaws
Tower
Mowhaugh
Bownam Law
1472
Hownam
B6401
Dikeside
Primside
Mill
The Curr
1849
Hownam Law
Attonburn
Preston Hill
1124
Lambden B.
Langleeford
Langlee
Crags
Ilderton
Wooperton
Lilburn
Bewick Br.
Old
Bewick
Bewick Moor
West Ditchburn
Brownyside
North Charlton
Hall
Christon
Bank
Embleton
Embleton Bay
Castle Pt.
Dunstanburgh Cas.

Whitton
Chatto Ho.
CHEVIOT
Raeshaw Fell
1580
Swanlaws
Windy Gyle
2034
Bloodybush
2001 Edge
Cushat Law
2020
The Cheviot
2676
Comb Fell
2132
Dunmoor
Hill
1860
Hedgehope
Hill 2348
Broomie
Hedgeley
Moor
1464
New
Bewick
Percy's
Cross
Brandon
Ingram
Branton
Powburn
R. Breamish
Beanley
Bannamoor
Shipley
East Bolton
Eglingham
Heffer law
Tower
North
Charlton
South
Charlton
12
Rock
B6347
Rennington
Inn
Dunston
Tower
Stamford
Craster
Cullernose Pt.
Howick

HILLS
Dere Street
Kale W.
Hownam
Craik
Moor
Bownam W.
Cochrane
Pike
Great Ryle
Prendwick
Eslington Hall
Whittingham
Glanton
Bolton
Broome
Park
Broomwood
Hulne Park
Tower
Alnwick Abbey
ALNWICK
B6341
A1
A1068
Hulne
Priory
Lesbury
Hawkhill
Longhoughton
Boulmer
B1339

SOUND OF ARISAIG

NORTH MORAR
L. Nevis
SOUTH MORAR
Loch Morar
ARISAIG
A 830

LOCHAILORT

MOIDART
A 861
Kinlochmoidart

SUNART
Strontian River
A 861
A 884
B 8043

MORVERN
A 884

Salen
Loch Sunart
A 861

ARDNAMURCHAN
Ardnamurchan Pt.
Ben Hiant
B 8007

Sanna Point
Sanna Bay

RUM
Askival
Ainshval
Ruinsival

EIGG
Sgurr of Eigg

SOUND OF EIGG

MUCK
Camas Mor

SOUND OF RUM

TOBERMORY
A 848
Quinish Point

AROS
Loch Frisa
Salen
A 849
LOCH TUATH

Loch Aline
Lochaline

MULL

Gometra

Calgary Bay

COLL
Arinagour
B 8070
B 8071

To Lochboisdale

To Castlebay

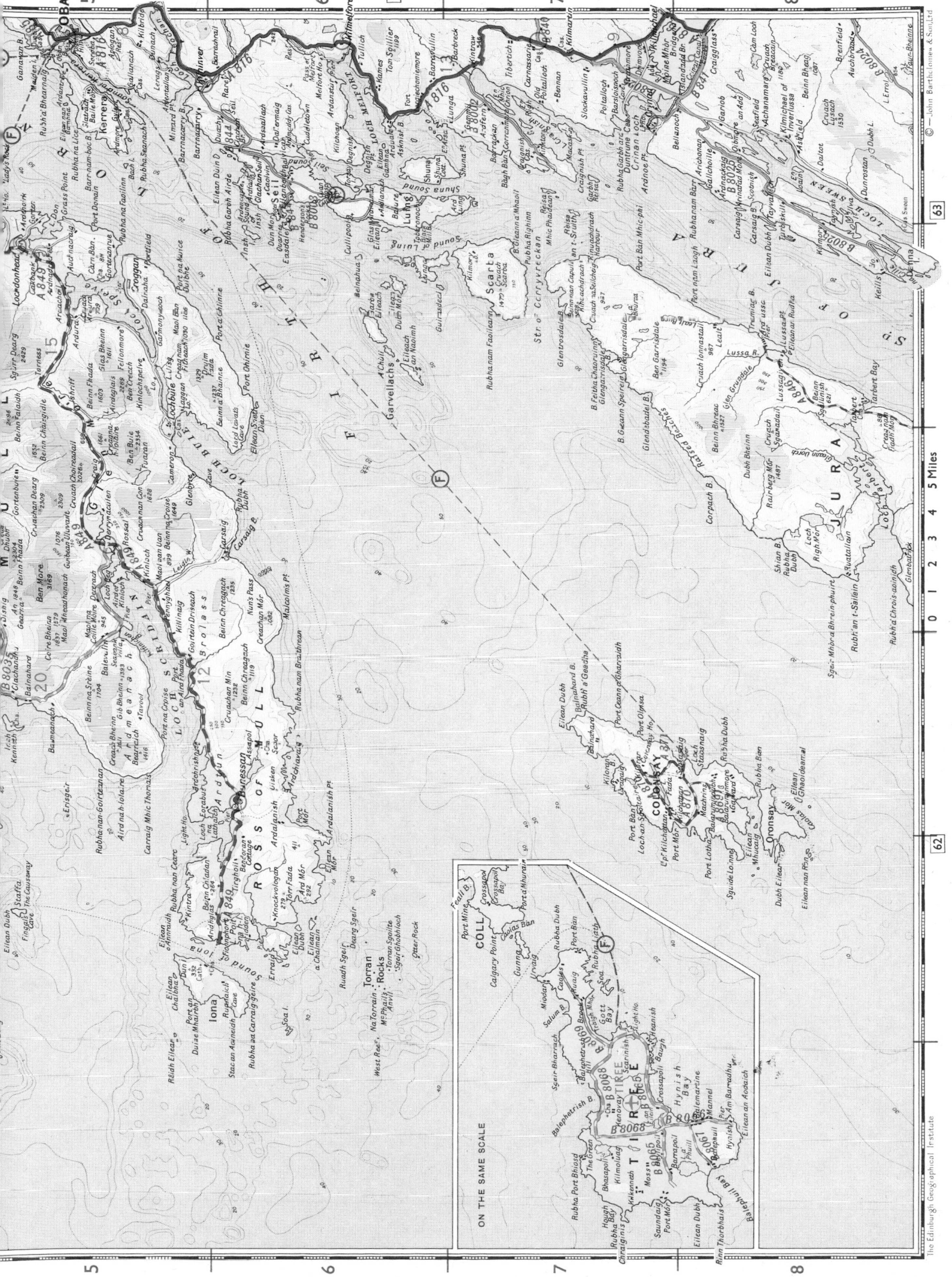

OBAN

MULL

KERRERA

SEIL

LUING

FIRTH OF LORN

JURA

COLONSAY

ORONSAY

ROSS OF MULL

IONA

Staffa

Fingal's Cave

Garvellachs

LOCH MELFORT

Kilmartin

Crinan

Ardfern

SOUND OF JURA

LOCH SWEEN

TIREE

COLL

ON THE SAME SCALE

Hynish Bay

Gott Bay

Calgary Point

Torran Rocks

Na Torran

West Reef

5 Miles

0 1 2 3 4 5

A   B   74   C   D

MORVERN

LYNN OF LORN

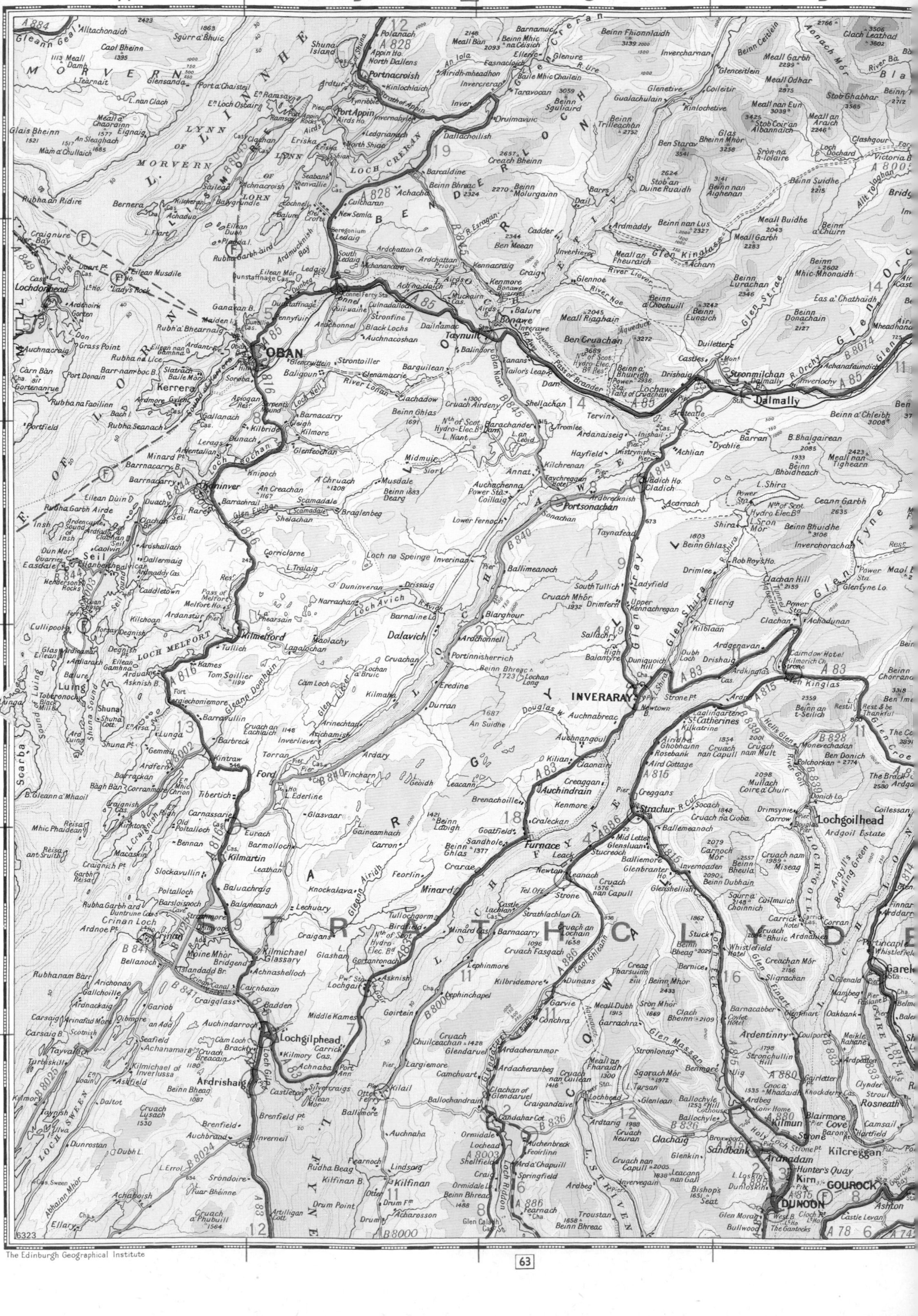

LYNN OF MORVERN

Portnacroish
Port Appin
Appin Ho.
Ballachulish

Craignure Bay
Lochdonhead

OBAN
Kerrera
Dunstaffnage Cas.
Connel Ferry

Taynuilt
Bonawe
Ben Cruachan 3689
Pass of Brander
Dalmally
Stronmilchan

Kilninver
Kilmelford
Kames
Luing
Scarba

Kilmartin
Ford
Kilmichael Glassary

INVERARAY
Furnace
Minard
Strachur
Auchindrain
Lochgoilhead

Lochgilphead
Ardrishaig
Crinan Loch
Crinan Canal

NORTH

STRATHCLYDE

Kilfinan
Tighnabruaich

Kilmun
Sandbank
DUNOON
GOUROCK
Kilcreggan

LOCH FYNE

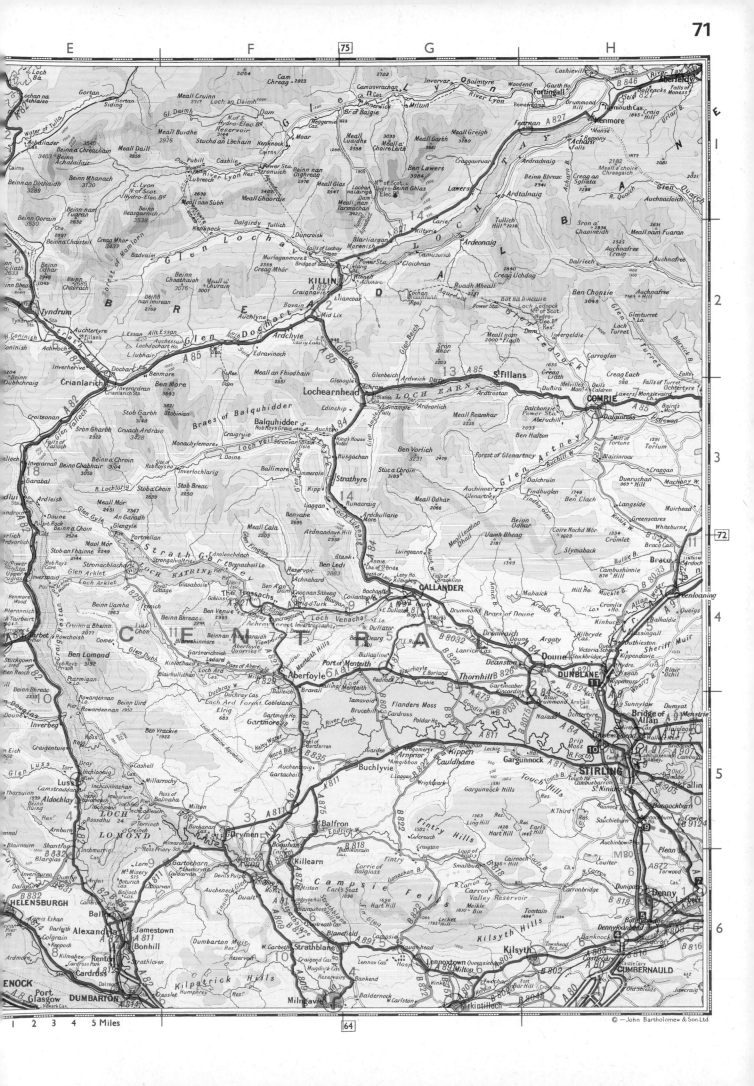

1 2 3 4 5 Miles

A   B   C   D

Map of Central Scotland

Major places and features:

DUNKELD, Birnam, Bankfoot, Methven, CRIEFF, Muthill, Auchterarder, Dunning, Aberuthven, Blackford, Gleneagles, Dollar, Tillicoultry, Alva, ALLOA, Clackmannan, Kincardine-on-Forth, Culross, BONESS, LINLITHGOW, Grangemouth, FALKIRK, Denny, Larbert, CUMBERNAULD, Kilsyth, Kirkintilloch, Milngavie, Strathblane, Killearn, Balfron, Buchlyvie, Aberfoyle, Port of Menteith, Thornhill, Doune, DUNBLANE, STIRLING, St Ninians, Bannockburn, Bonnybridge, Kippen, Gargunnock, CALLANDER, Strathyre, Lochearnhead, Balquhidder, KILLIN, St Fillans, COMRIE, Crieff.

Lochs and rivers: Loch Tay, Loch Earn, Loch Lubnaig, Loch Venachar, Loch Katrine, River Forth, River Lyon, River Almond, River Earn, River Carron, River Devon, Loch Turret.

Hills/mountains: Ben Lawers 3984, Ben Vorlich 3231, Ben Ledi 2883, Ben Chonzie, Ben Cleuch 2363, Meall Garbh, Meall Greigh, Ben Lomond area.

Roads: A9, A82, A84, A85, A827, A826, A811, A873, A91, A907, A905, A872, A803, A80, B818, B822, B8032, B8031, B8075, B8063, B827, A875.

The Edinburgh Geographical Institute

A B 80 C D

Brochs
Màm nan Uranan · Gleann Beag · Balvraid
Beinn a'Chapuill 2421 · Sgùrr a'Gharg Gharaidh 2076 · Torrlaoighseach · 3505 · GLEN SHIEL · Sgùrra Ciste Dhuibhe 3406 · R. Shiel · Sgùrr a'Bhealaich Dheirg · A'Chralaig 3673 · Sgùrr nan Conbhairean · Ceannacroc Forest · Beinn an t-Sìdhein 1622 · Dundreggan Lo. · A 887 · Lagganbane · Torgyle · Dalchreichart · Dalchreichart Br. · Tomorasky · Wade's Military Rd.
Meall Buidhe 1594 · Ben Screel 2536 · The Saddle 3092 · 3314 · Sgùrr na Sgine 3098 · Creag nan Damh 3012 · 3294 · Cluanie Br. · Carn nam Feuaich 2396 · Power Sta. · Ceannacroc Lo. · Ceannacroc Br. · Power Sta. · Inchnacardoch Forest · Fort A.
Arnisdale · Beinn a'Chlachach · Gleandubhlochain · GLEN CLUANIE · L. Cluanie · Reservoir · Dam · Moriston · Bun Loyne · Ceann a'Mhàim · Carn Raonuill · Invervigar Br.
Druim Fada 2014 · Loch Hourn · Kinloch Hourn · Skiary · Runival · Aonach air Chrith 3350 · Maol Chinn-dearg 3102 · 2655 · Bunloinne Forest · Beinneun Forest · Meall Dubh · Br. of Oich · Aberchalder
LOCH HOURN · OYDART · Barrisdale Bay · Carn Màiri · Gleann Cosaidh · Loch Quoich · Gleouraich 3396 · Spidean Mialach 3268 · Druim na h-Achlaise · Glenquoich Forest · Glenquoich Lo. · Tomdoun Hotel · Inchlaggan · Greenfield · Loch Garry · Bolinn Hill · Dam · Invergarry Hotel · Glengarry Ho.
Ladhar Bheinn 3343 · Sgùrr a'Chlaidheimh · Kinlochquoich · N. of S. Hydro-Elec. · Gairich 3015 · Gearr Garry · Darvorgil · Glas Bheinn 1825 · Ben Tee 2685 · Leac Ladaidh · Leagan(?) · South Laggan · Laggan Locks
Luinne Bheinn 3107 · Ben Aden 2905 · Sgùrr Mòr 3290 · Sgùrran Fhuarain 3250 · GLEN KINGIE · R. Kingie · nan Sgud · Sgùrr Mhùrlagain 2885 · Meall Tarsuinn 2063 · Glengarry Forest · A'Choire Ghlais · Leacann Doire Bainneir
Meall Buidhe · Sgùrr Mòr 3410 · Sgùrr na Ciche 3410 · Druim a'Chuirn · Kinbreack · Sgùrr Chòinnich 2450 · Meall Coire nan Saobhaidh 2636 · Stob a'Choire Ghairbh · Turret Br.
Carnoch · Sgùrr nan Coireachan 3125 · Sgùrr Thuilm · Fraoch Bheinn 2808 · Caonich · Beinn Chraoibh · Glas Bheinn · Meall Coire Lochain 2971
N. MORAR · Kylesmorar · Sgùrr Breac · Sgùrr na h-Aide 2818 · GLEN DESSARRY · Glendessarry · Murlaggan · LOCH ARKAIG · Ardachvie · Mile Dorcha · Clunes · Glas Bheinn · Leana Mhòr
L. MORAR · Finiskaig · Carn Mòr 2718 · Glen Pean · Kinlocharkaig · Mullach Coire nan Geur-oirean · Locheil Forest · Inver Mallie · Achnasaul · Achnacarry · Invergloy · New Br. · Leana Mhòr
S. MORAR · Meoble · An Stac 2350 · Druim a'Chuirn · Sgùrr nan Coireachan · Sgùrr Thuilm 3160 · Gulvain 3238 · Beinn Bhàn 2522 · Glenfintaig Ho. · Glenfintaig Lo. · Coire Ceirsle Hill · Rathliesbeg · Bohenie
Loch Beoraid · Kinlochbeoraid · Streap 2988 · Sròn Liath · 2533 · Meall a'Phubuill · Druim Gleann Laoigh 2285 · Achnanellan · Glen Loy · Moy · Br. of Mucomir · Commando Memorial · Spean Br. · Tirandrish
Arieniskill · Sgùrr Mhuidhe · GLEN FINNAN · Nah-Uamhachan 2099 · Gleann Fionnlighe · Druim Fada · Stob a'Ghrianain · Strone · Muirsheartich · Kilmonivaig Ch. · Sta. · Roy Br. · Achluachrach
RANNOCH · Sgùrr na Paite · Glenfinnan Sta. · A 830 · Kinlocheil · Gleann Suileag · Gl. Laragain · Crùim Leacainn · Invergarry · Tom an Teine · Beinn Chlianaig 2343
Beinn Odhar Mhòr · Meall a'Bhàinne · Drumfern · A 861 · Garvan · LOCH EIL · Dulisky · Blaich · Achaphubuil · Caol · Banavie · Alltan Loin · Parallel Roads · Leanachan Forest
Croit Bheinn · Beinn Odhar Bheag · Meall Mòr · Sgòr Craobh a'Chaoruinn · Meall nan Damh · Sròn an t-Sluichd · Ceann Cael 1600 · Camus nagaul · Trislaig · Inverlochy Cas. · Aonach Mòr 4012 · Stob Choire Claurigh · Stob Ban
Glenaladale · Meall nan Creag Leac · Conaglen · Stob Coire a'Chearcaill 2527 · Achaphubuil · Aluminium Works · Ben Nevis · FORT WILLIAM · Carn Mòr Dearg · Aonach Beag 4060 · Stob Coire Easain
Gaskan · Scamodale · Meall Mòr · Corrlarach · Gorten an Chladaich · Ben Nevis 4406 · Blarmachfoldach · Polldubh · Binnein Mòr · Sgùrr Eilde Mòr · L. Eilde
Gorstanworran · Besourie · Druim Leathad nam Fias · Conaglen · Coruanan · Achriabhach · Steall · Binnein Beag · Glas Bheinn
Pollach · L. Doilet · Kinlochan · Carn na Nathrach · Tighnacomaire · Aryhoulan · Inverscaddle · Mamore Forest · Stob Ban 3274 · Sgòran Fhuarain 1998 · L. Eilde
SUNART · Bellsgrove L. · Sgùrr a'Chaoruinn · GLEN GOUR · ARDGOUR · Beinn Bhàn · Corrychurrachan · Mullach nan Coirean 3077 · Kinlochmore · Meall na Duibhe
Scotstown · Sgùrr nan Cnamh · Tigh Ghlinnegabhair · Sallachan · Ardgour Hotel · Glenachulish · Laing Mòr · Kinlochleven · Aluminium Works · BLACKWATER RES.
Anaheilt · Druimnantoran · Glen Leamhain · Clovullin · Corran · Onich · North Ballachulish · Callert · Garbh Bheinn · River Leven
A 861 · Strontian · Achnalea · Gearradh · Sallachan Pt. · Ballachulish Pier · Loch Leven · Kinlochmore · Caolasnacon · Garbh Bheinn
L. Sunart · Ardnastang · Inversanda · GLEN TARBERT · Inversanda · Ballachulish · A 82 · Bridge of Coe · Pap of Glencoe · Beinn Bheag · Devil's Staircase · Black Corries
Achleek · A 884 · Glas Bheinn · Meall a'Choirein Luachraich · Ardsheal · Kentallen · BALLACHULISH · E. Laroch · Achnacon · GLEN COE · Ossian's Cave · Altnafeadh · Kingshouse
Taobh Dubh · Fuar Bheinn · Rudha Mòr · Dalnatrat · Sgòr Dhearg 3362 · Sgòr Dhonuill · Meall Mòr · Aonach Eagach 3173 · Clachaig · Bidean nam Bian 3766 · Buachaille Etive Mòr 3345
Creach Bheinn · Kilmalieu · Back Settlement · Cuil Bay · Acharra · GLEN DUROR · Fraochaidh · Salachail · Meall Lighiche 2225 · Sgòr na h-Ulaidh · Dalness · Sròn na Creise · Clach Leathad
Beinn Mheadhoin · Kingairloch · Camasnacroise · Glenalmadale · Keil · Lurignich · Polanach · Barnamuc · Beinn Fhionnlaidh 3139 · Invercharnan · Clach Leathad 3602 · Lochan na Stainge
Caol Bheinn · Port a'Chaisteil · Shuna Island · Appin Ho. · North Dallens · Meall Bàn · Ellerig · Glenure · R. Ure · Glenetive · Meall Garbh · Bà Br.
Glensanda · Eignaig · Portnacroish · Kinlochlaich · Airdhmheadhon · Taravocan · Beinn Sgulaird 3059 · Gualachulain · Kinlochetive · Stob a'Choire Odhair · Black Mount
MORVERN · Port Appin · Airds Ho. · Ledgnianach · North Shian · Inver · Druimavuic · Beinn Trilleachan 2752 · Ben Starav 3541 · Sròn na h-Iolaire · Clashgour Forest
LYNN OF LORN · Eriska · Ballachoilish · A 828 · LOCH CRERAN · Barcaldine · Creach Bheinn 2624 · Glas Bheinn Mhòr 3258 · Sròn na Creise · Victoria Br. · A 8005

70 · The Edinburgh Geographical Institute

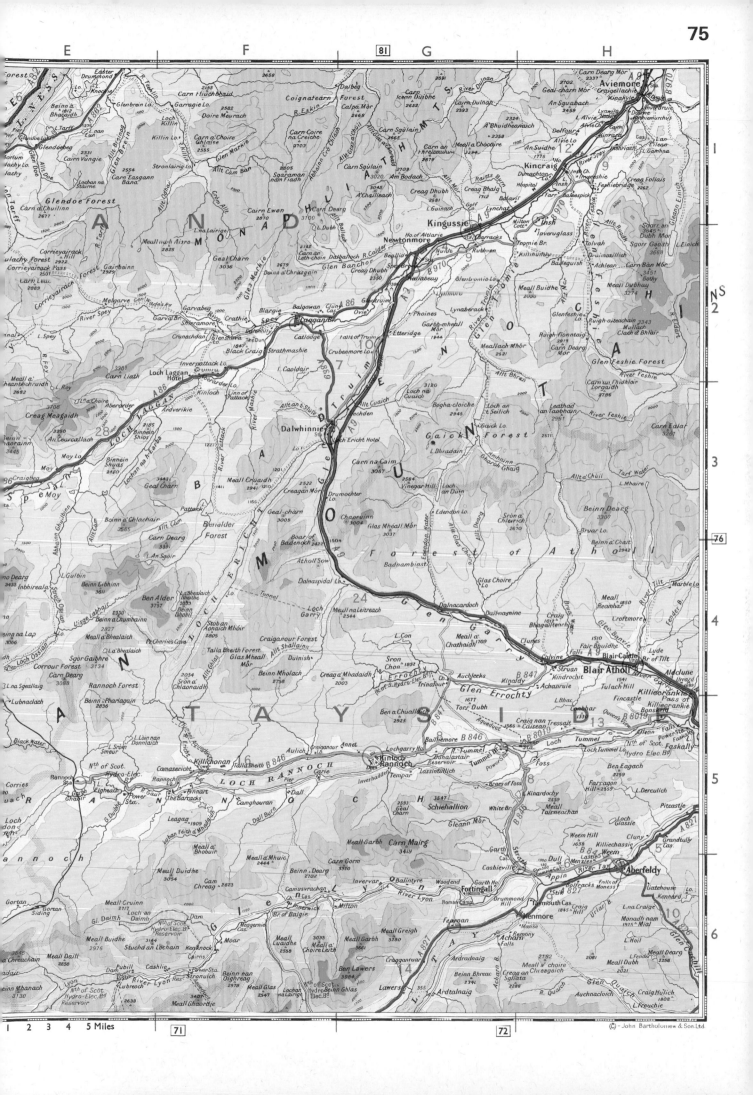

A   B   C   D

81 82 75

CAIRNGORM MOUNTAINS

Aviemore
Craigellachie
Kinakyle
Coylumbridge
Queen's
Meall a' Bhuachaille 2654
Revoan
Carn Bheadhair 2656
Craig Vegin 2328
Carn Ealasaid 2597
Geal Charn 2207
Inverernan
Allargue
Greenbank
River Don
Loganmore
Coyle Bridge
Cergart
Corgarff
Cock Bridge
Mona Gowan 2456
Morven 2456
Lynwilg
Doune
Rothiemurchus
Morlich
Glenmore Lodge
An Lurg 2463
Forest of Glenavon
L. Builg
Brown Cow Hill 2721
Corndavon Lo.
Carn a' Bhacain
Candacraig
Milton of Tullich
Ballater
Alvie
Insheriach
Rothiemurchus
Forest
Bynack More 3574
River Avon
Big Garvoun 2431
Inchrory
Daldownie
Carn Ealar
Gairnshiel
Glengairn Ch.
Dalfad
Coilacriech
Craig of Bunzeach

CAIRNGORM MOUNTAINS
Cairn Gorm 4084
L. Avon
Shelter Stone 3878
Beinn Mheadhoin 3880
Beinn a' Chaoruinn 3553
North Top 3924
Ben Avon 3843
Carn Eas 3556
Culardoch 2953
Bridgend of Bush
Duchrie
Gairnshiel
Torbeg
Braenaloin
Balmoral Castle
Easter Balmoral
Invergelder
Abergeldie
Clachanturn
Strathgirnock
Birkhall
Glenmuick

Braeriach 4248
Sgor Gaoith 3668
Meall Dubhag 3274
Cairn Toul 4241
Ben Macdui 4296
Cairn Gorm of Derry
Beinn Bhreac 3051
The Devils Point 3294
Carn Crom 2847
Beinn a' Bhuird South Top 3860
Carn Liath 3036
Invercauld Forest
Meall Gorm 2029
Invercauld
Braemar
Ballochbuie Forest
Gelder Shiel
Danzig Shiel
Creagan nan Gall 1969
Auchcholzie
Cairn Leuchan 2293

Balmoral Forest
Coc Carn Beag 2789
Lochnagar 3789
Cairn Taggart
White Mounth
Broad Cairn 3268
Glas-allt Shiel
Black Hill of Mark 2531
Fasheilach
Spittal of Glenmuick
L. Muick

Achlean
Carn Ban Mor 3451
Bothy
Ruigh aiteachain 3343
Mullach Clach a' Bhlair
Glen Feshie Forest
Carn an Fhidhleir Lorgaidh 2786
R. Feshie
Beinn Dearg 3307

Monadh Mor 3651
Beinn Bhrotain 3795
Sgor Mor 2666
Carn Geldie
Geldie Burn 2039
Geldie Lo.
Bynack Lo.
Carn Liath 2676
Glen Ey Forest
Colonels Bed
Newbigging
Baddoch
An Socach 3059
Carn Bhac 3015
Iutharn Mhor 3424
Beinn Iutharn Bheag 3096
L. nan Eun
The Cairnwell 3059
Carn a' Gheoidh
Carn Aosda 3003
Cairn of Claise 3484
Glas Maol 3502
Monega Hill 2917
Shielin
Mayar 3043
Driesh 3105
Hill of Strone 2778
Clova
Glen Clova

Tarf Water
L. Mhairc
An Sligearnach 2577
Bedford Mem. Bridge
Falar Lo.
Glas Tulaichean 3445
Rhidorroch
Carn Ait 2824
Tulchan Lo.
Monamenach 2649
Mid Hill
Hunt Hill 2407
Cairn of Barns 2129
Mount Blair
Driesh

Beinn Dearg 3307
Tarf Water 2942
L. Tilt
River Tilt
Beinn a' Ghlo 3675
L. Loch
Forest Lar
Beinn a' Ghlo 3505
Marble Lo.
Meall Reamhar 1850
Croftmore
Ben Gulabin 2641
Spittal of Glenshee
Glenlochsie Lo.
Glenshee
L. Shechernich
Glen Beag
Carn an Daimh 2449
Badendun Hill 2429
Cairn Dournie 2066
Glenprosen
B 955
Balnaboth

Blair Castle
Blair Atholl
Tulach Hill 1541
Fincastle
Bonskeid
Killiecrankie
Pass of Killiecrankie
Craigower
Ben Vrackie 2757
Tarvie
Stralodh Ho.
Glen Brerachan
Dalnacardoch
Kindrogan
Enochdhu
Balvarran
Ashintully
Kirkmichael
Finegand
Dalnaglar
Forter Cas.
Folda
Glenisla
Kirkton of Glenisla
Alrick
Mount Blair 2441
Cray
Dalrulzian
Knockton
Hare Cairn 1632
Longdrum
Cat Law 2196
The Crandart
Glenmarkie Lo.
Tomnup

Queen's
B 8019
L. Tummel
Faskally
Pitlochry
Moulin
A 924
Faire Mhor 1592
Loch Broom
Creag Dhubh 2042
Creag a' Mhadaidh 1414
Loch Broom
Creag na h-Iolaire 1468
Ballinluig
Merklands Ho.
Balmyle
Ballintuim
Persie
Bleaton Hallet
Forest of Alyth
Druim Dearg
Creigh Hill
Balintore
Dykend
B 951
Kirkton of Kingoldrum
Westmuir
Bridgend of Lintrathen
Ben Eagach 2259
Portnacraig
Power Sta.
Dunfallandy
Lochbroom
Strath Ardle
Ashmore
Woodhill
Blackcraig Hill 1842
Cally Ho.
Tullymurdoch
Balduff Hill 1394
Reekie Linn
Loch of Lintrathen
Craig
Airlie Cas.
Kirkton of Airlie
Lindertis
Craigton

Aberfeldy
Logierait
Ballinluig
Grandtully Cas.
Balnaguard
Cluny
Grandtully Ho.
L. Skiaich
Dalguise
Dowally
Rotmell
Butterstone
Kinnaird
Deuchary Hill 1670
Benachally
Rochallie
Glenericht
Cochrage Muir
Craighall
Alyth
New Alyth
Bamff
Ruthven
Balhary
Jordanstone
Dean Water
Castleton
Glamis

Pitcastle
L. Glassie
L. na Craige 1408
Kennard
Monadh nam 1915
L. Hoil
Meall Dubh 2021
Meall Dearg 2258
Dalmarnock
Craiglush
Craigie Barns
Dunkeld
Birnam
Birnam Hill 1324
Craig Liath 1359
Waterloo
Rumbling Br.
Trochry
Rohallion
Butterstone
Loch of Butterstone
Achalader
Williamsburgh
Kinloch
Blairgowrie
Rattray
Rosemount
Kinloch
Keillor
Meigle
Newtyle
Eassie and Nevay
Charleston

Craiglush
L. of Lowes
Kincairney
Snaigow
Newtyle Ho.
Thornton
Spittalfield
Caputh
Murthly
Delvine
Kirkton of Lethendy
Tower
Stenton
Caputh
R. Tay
Kinclaven
Meiklour
Woodside
Burrelton
Coupar Angus
Hettins
Kinpurney Hill 1134
Ardler
Auchterhouse Hill
Kirkton of Auchterhouse

Craig Hulich 1808
L. Freuchie
Ballinloan
Kinloch
Creag Liath 1359
Waterloo
Ballathie
Lintrose
Pitcur
Lundie
Thriepley
Kirkton of Auchterhouse

The Edinburgh Geographical Institute

72 73

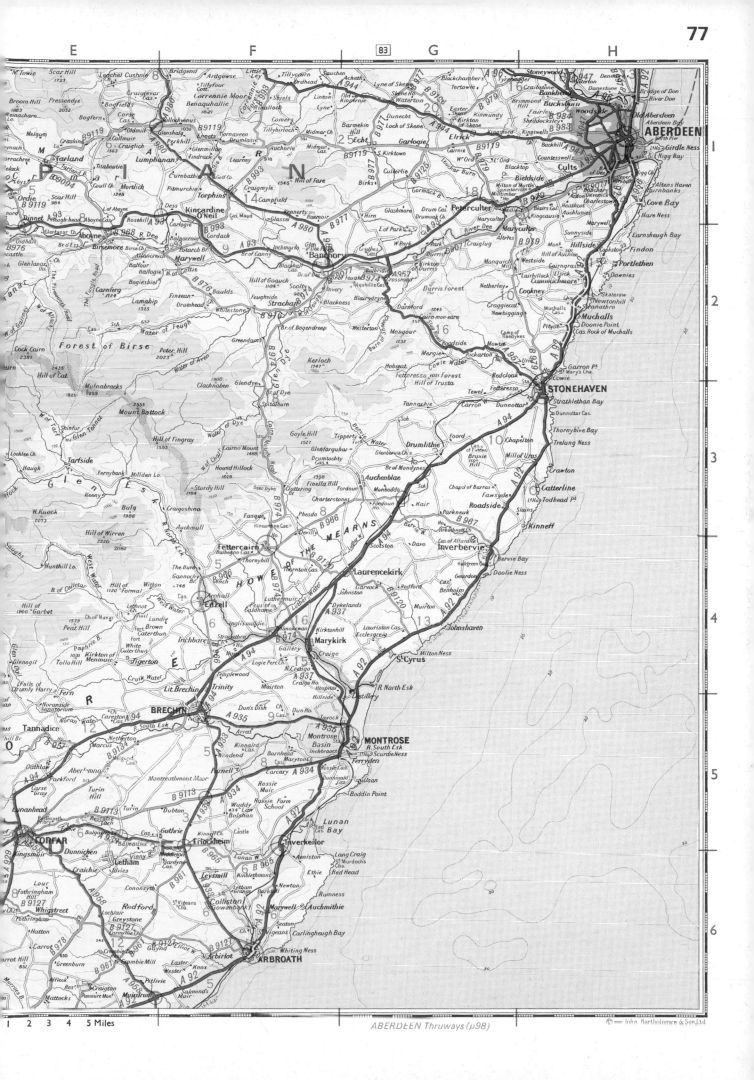

LEWIS
HARRIS
Shiant Islands
Eilean Trodday
Ascrib Islands
LOCH SNIZORT
LOCH DUNVEGAN
TROTTERNISH
Score Bay
Uig
Staffin
The Storr
RONA
SOUND OF RAASAY
LOCH TORRIDON
GAIR LOCH
Gairloch
LOCH EWE
Poolewe
Isle of Ewe
Rubha Reidh
Shieldaig
Applecross Forest
Loch Dunvegan
Dunvegan
Waternish
Scalpay
To Tarbert
To Lochmaddy
Greenstone Pt.
Flodigarry
Kilmaluag
Red Point
Beinn Alligin
UPPER LOCH TORRIDON
Loch Pooltiel

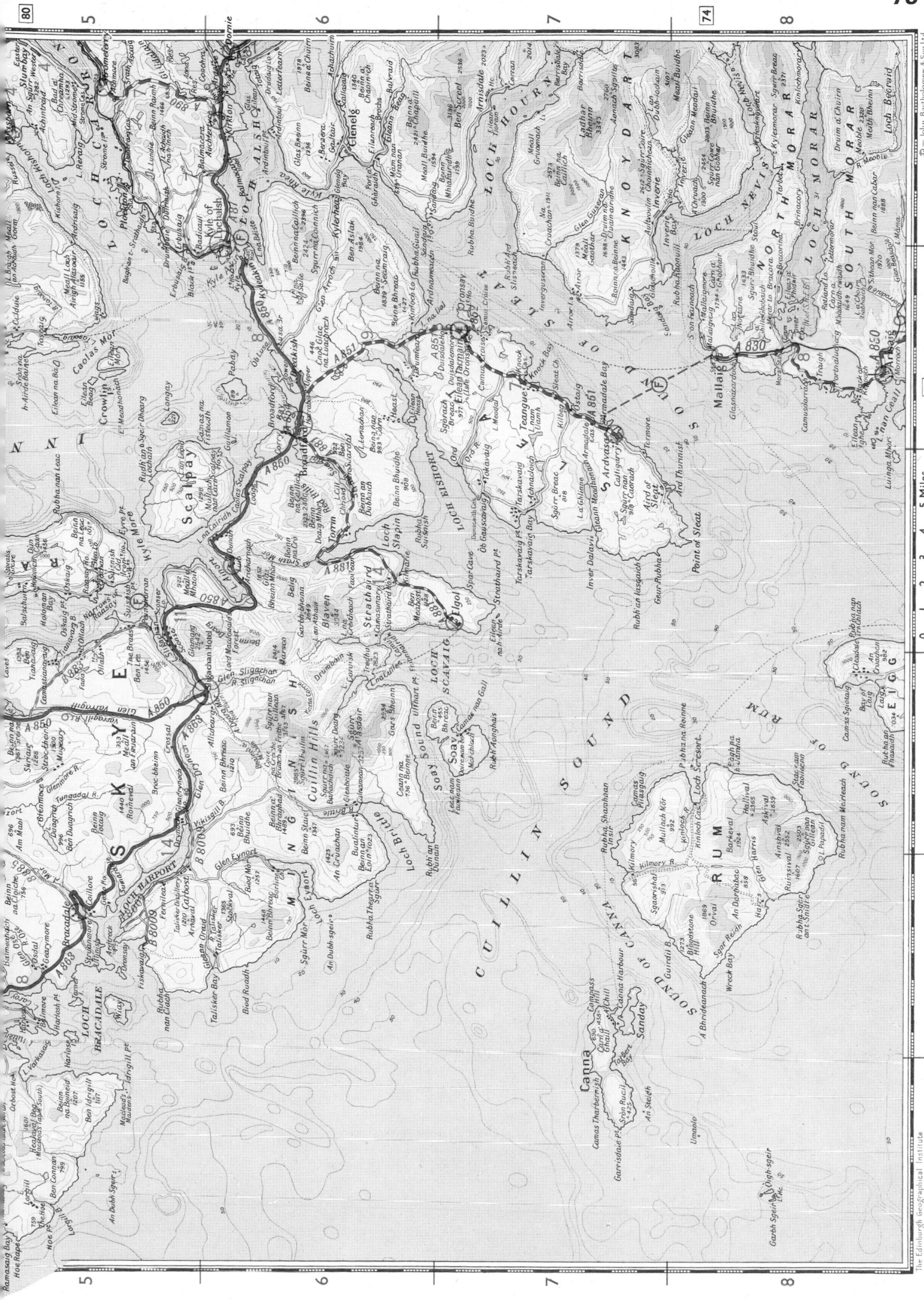

SKYE

CUILLIN SOUND

SOUND OF RUM

RUM

CANNA

SOUND OF CANNA

EIGG

LOCH HOURN

KNOYDART

NORTH MORAR

SOUTH MORAR

LOCH NEVIS

LOCH MORAR

Mallaig

LOCH ALSH

Kyle of Lochalsh

Broadford

Scalpay

LOCH HARPORT

Cuillin Hills

MINGINISH

LOCH BRACADALE

LOCH SCAVAIG

Strathaird

Elgol

© —John Bartholomew & Son Ltd.

0 1 2 3 4 5 Miles

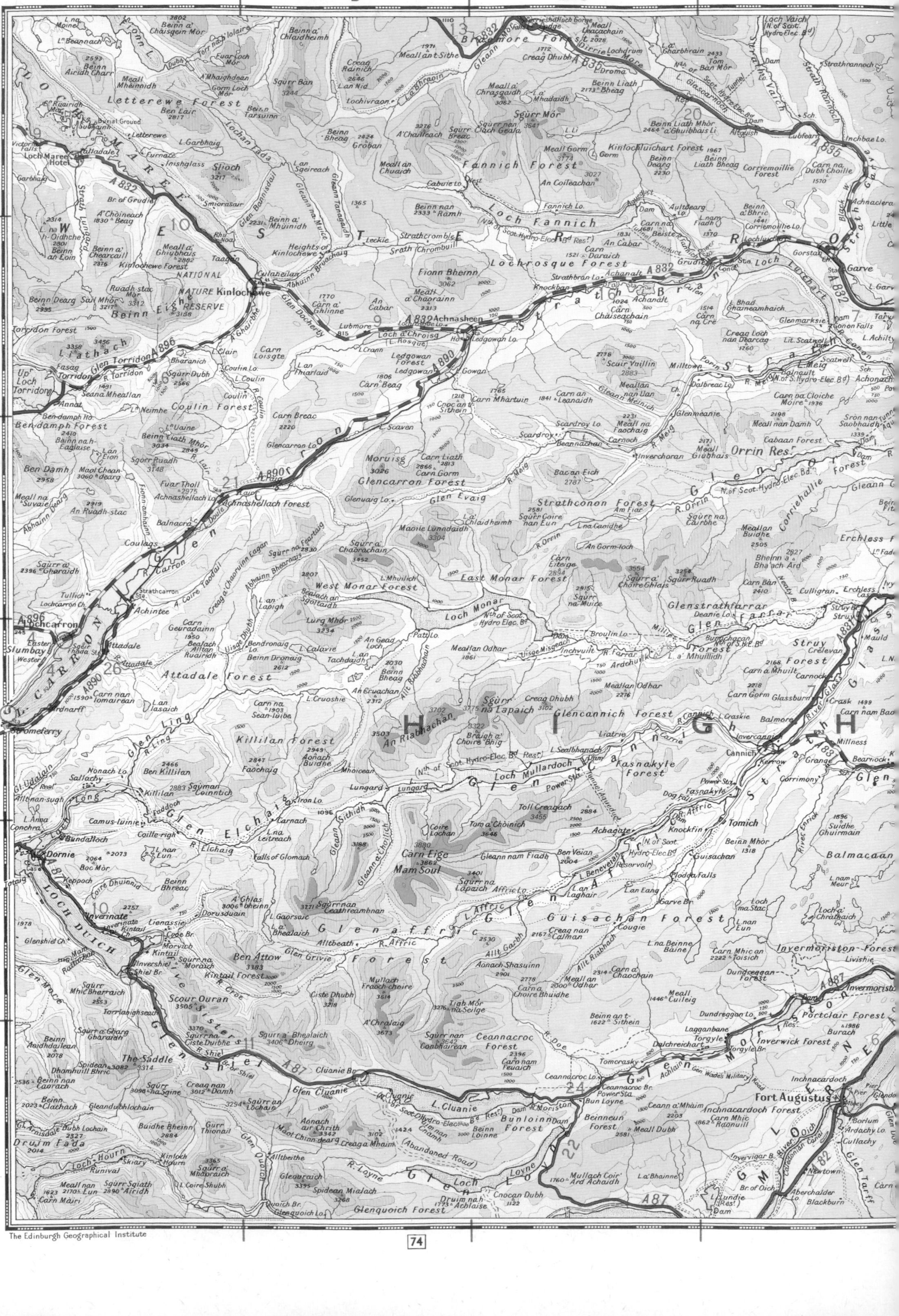

A   B   85 C   D

1

78

2

3

4

5

79

6

74

LETTEREWE FOREST
Loch Maree Hotel
Loch Maree
Kinlochewe
NATURE RESERVE
Beinn Eighe
Torridon Forest
Glen Torridon
A896
Upr Loch Torridon
Ben-damph Forest
Coulin Forest
Ben Damh
Slioch
West
Fannich Forest
Loch Fannich
Lochrosque Forest
Achnasheen
A832
Strath Bran
Ledgowan Forest
Ledgowan
Cabaan Forest
Orrin Res.
Strathconon Forest
Glencarron Forest
Glen Carron
Glen Orrin
Corriehallie Forest
Erchless F
Achnashellach Forest
Coulags
Strathcarron
Lochcarron
Achintee
Attadale
Attadale Forest
West Monar Forest
East Monar Forest
Loch Monar
Glenstrathfarrar
Glen
Struy Forest
Strathconon
Glencannich Forest
Killilan Forest
Ben Killilan
Glencannich
Fasnakyle Forest
Cannich
An Riabhachan
Sgurr na Lapaich
Mam Soul
Carn Eige
Glen Affric
Guisachan Forest
Tomich
Glen Elchaig
Falls of Glomach
Dornie
Loch Duich
Invermoriston Forest
Kintail
Kintail Forest
Glen Affric Forest
Glenaffric Forest
Scour Ouran
The Saddle
Glen Shiel
A87
Glen Cluanie
Loch Cluanie
Ceannacroc Forest
Fort Augustus
Inchnacardoch Forest
Inverwick Forest
Portclair Forest
Loch Hourn
Glen Quoich
Glenquoich Forest
Glen Loyne
Loch Loyne
Bunloinn Forest

The Edinburgh Geographical Institute

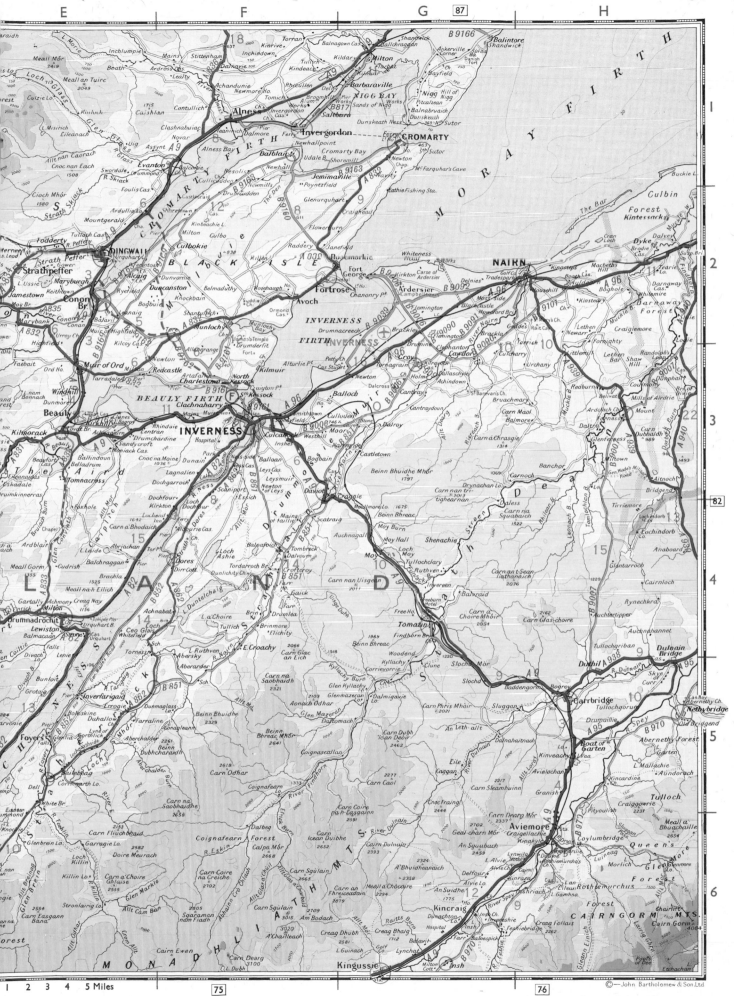

©—John Bartholomew & Son Ltd.

87

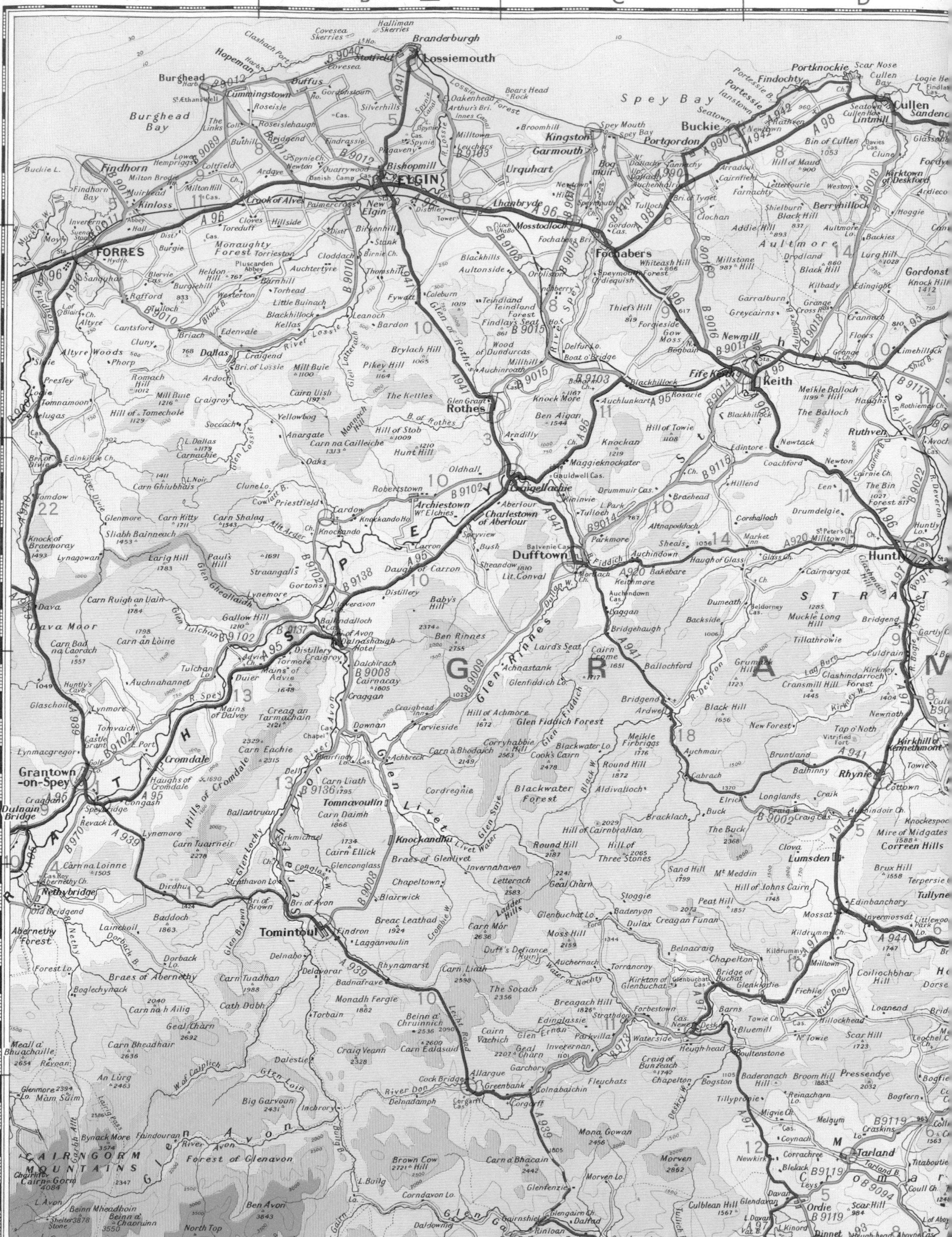

81

76

The Edinburgh Geographical Institute

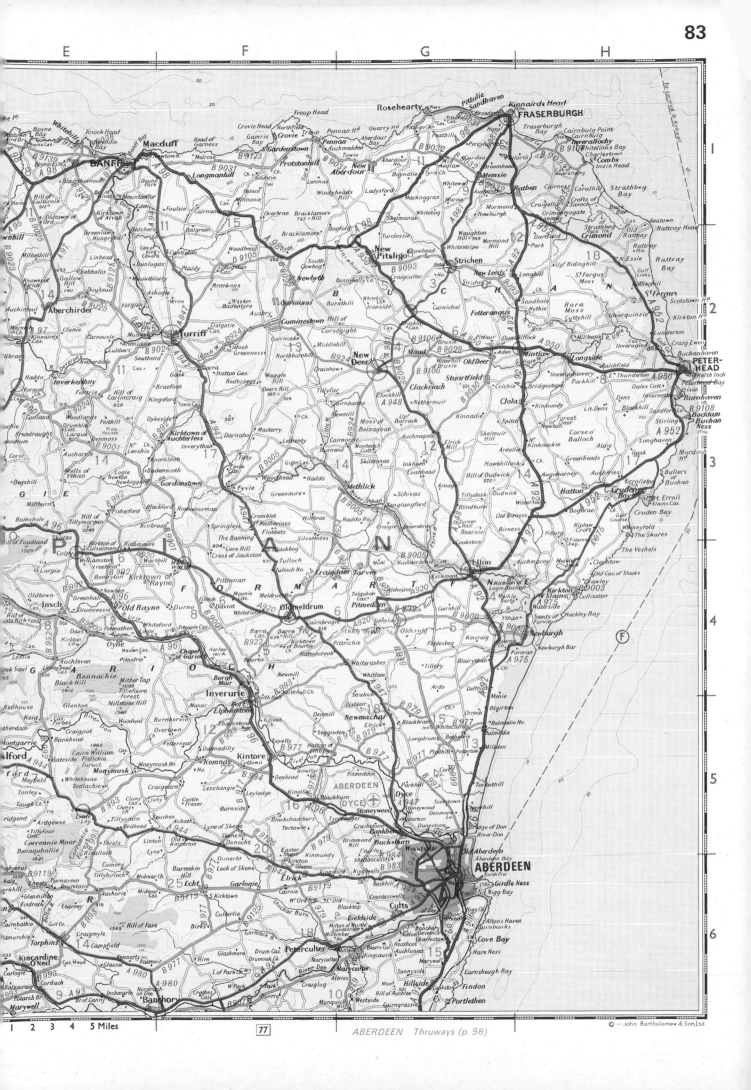

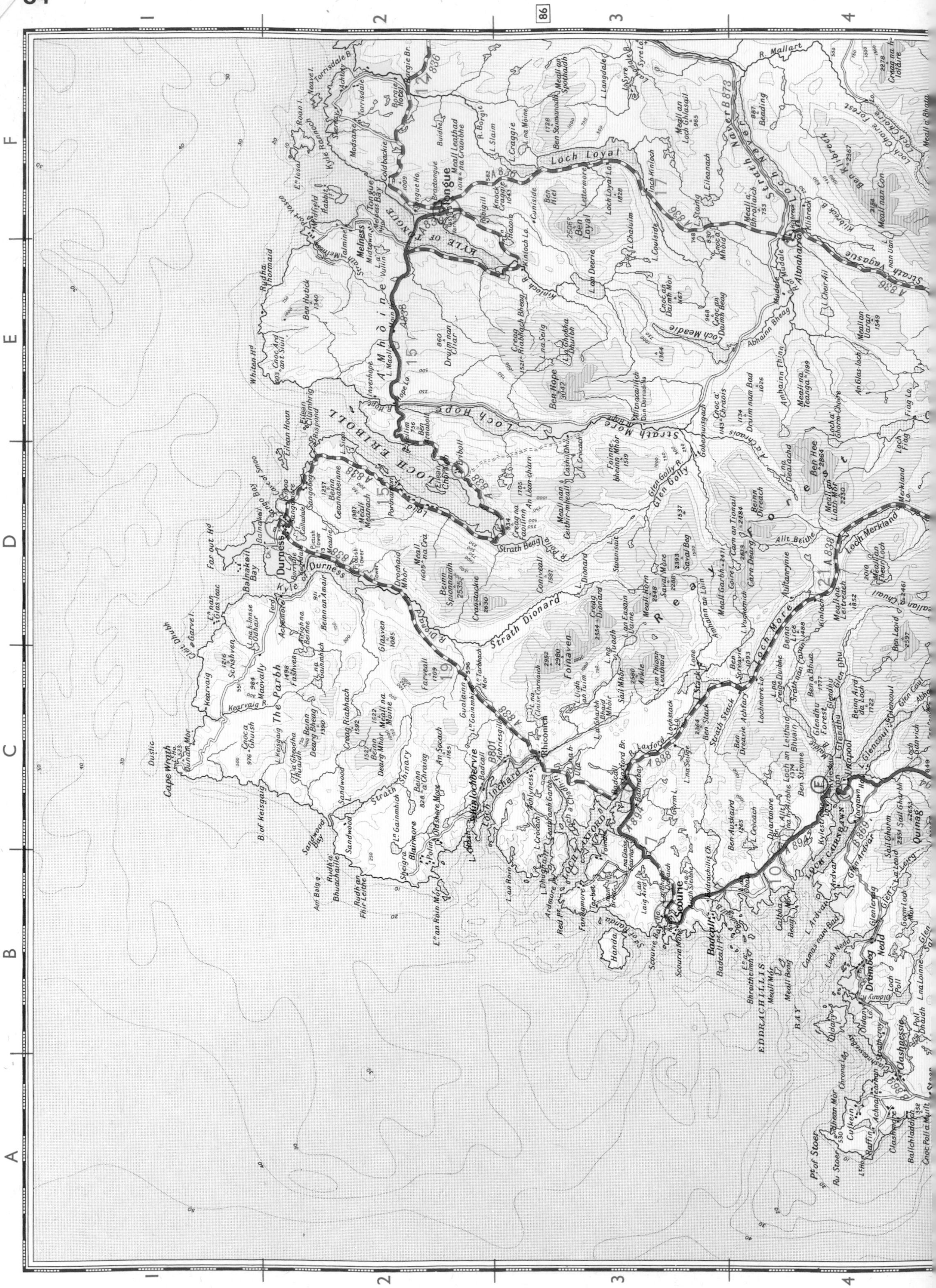

86

F

E

D

C

B

A

1   2   3   4

Torrisdale B.
Kyle of Tongue
Loch Loyal
R. Naver
Strath Naver
Ben Hutig
Whiten Hd.
Melness
Tongue
Ben Loyal
Ben Hiel
A' Mhòine
Loch Hope
Ben Hope 3042
Strath More
Eilean Hoan
Loch Eriboll
Durness
Kyle of Durness
Balnakeil Bay
Loch Merkland
Cape Wrath
The Parbh
Strath Dionard
Foinaven
Kearvaig
Rhiconich
Loch Inchard
Kinlochbervie
Loch More
Strath Stack
Scourie
Badcall
Handa
EDDRACHILLIS BAY
Pt. of Stoer
Ru Stoer
Clashnessie
Drumbeg
Loch Nedd
Quinag
Kylesku
Loch Cairnbawn
Strath Oykel

Kyle of Tongue   836

0 1 2 3 4 5 Miles

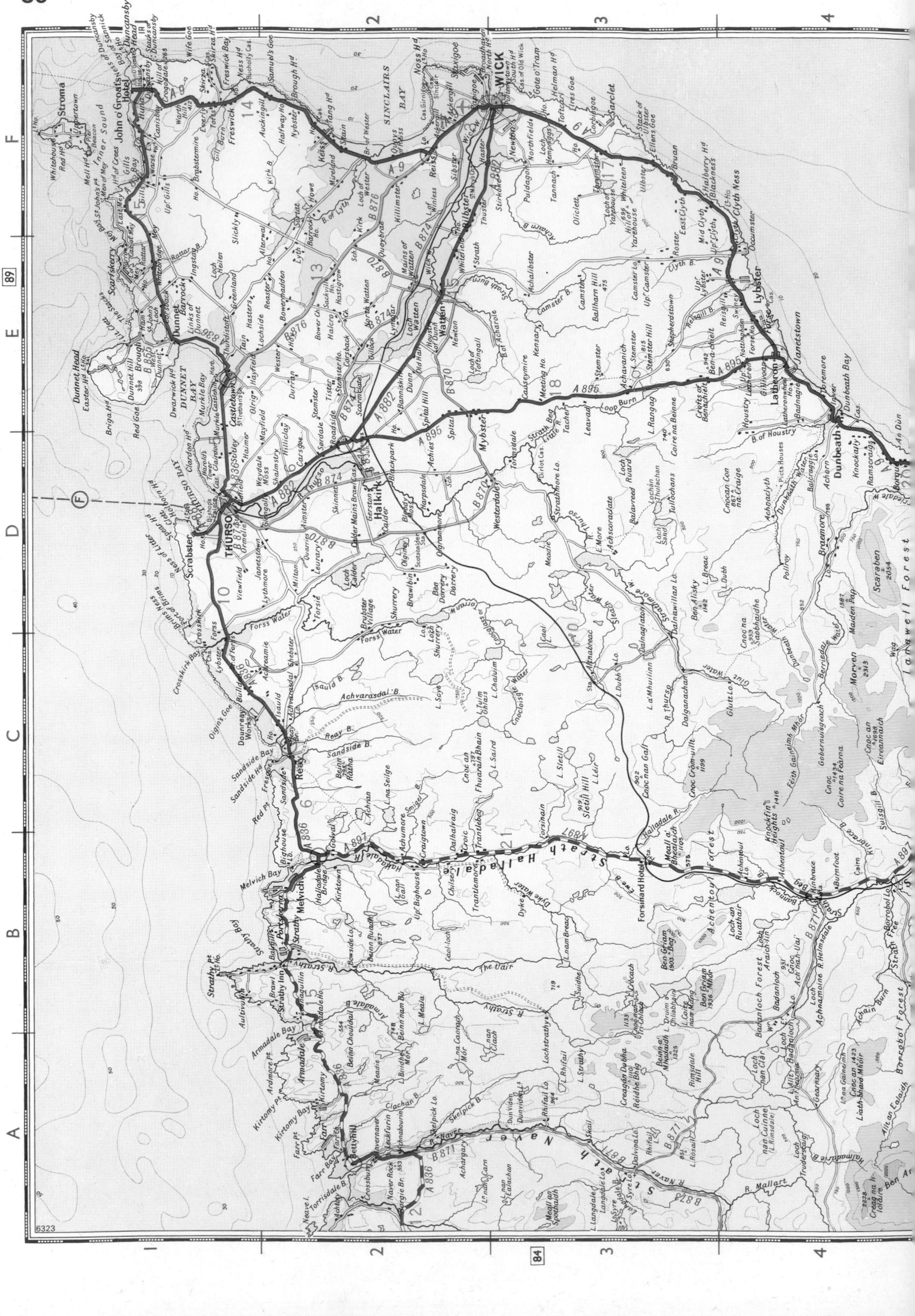

WICK

THURSO

John o'Groats

Dunnet

Castletown

Halkirk

Watten

Lybster

Latheron

Dunbeath

Scrabster

Reay

Melvich

Portskerra

Strathy

Bettyhill

Stroma

Dunnet Head

Strath Halladale

Tanavell Forest

Morven

A 9

B 876

B 874

A 882

A 895

B 870

B 871

A 897

A 836

SINCLAIR'S BAY

DUNNET BAY

THURSO BAY

Dunbeath Bay

89

84

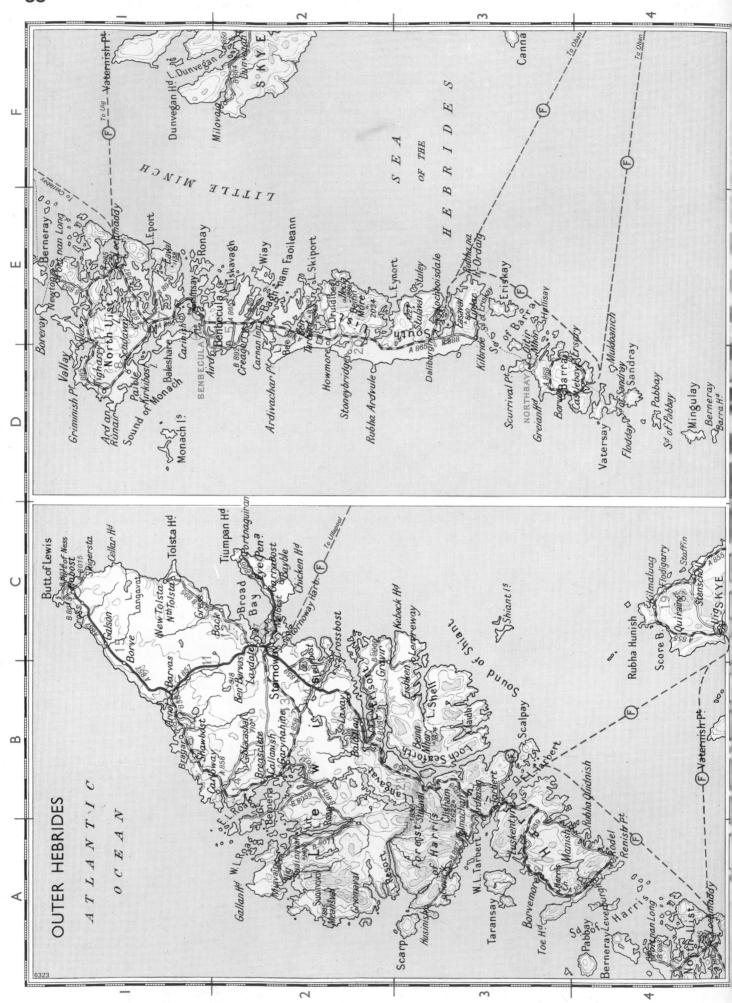

OUTER HEBRIDES

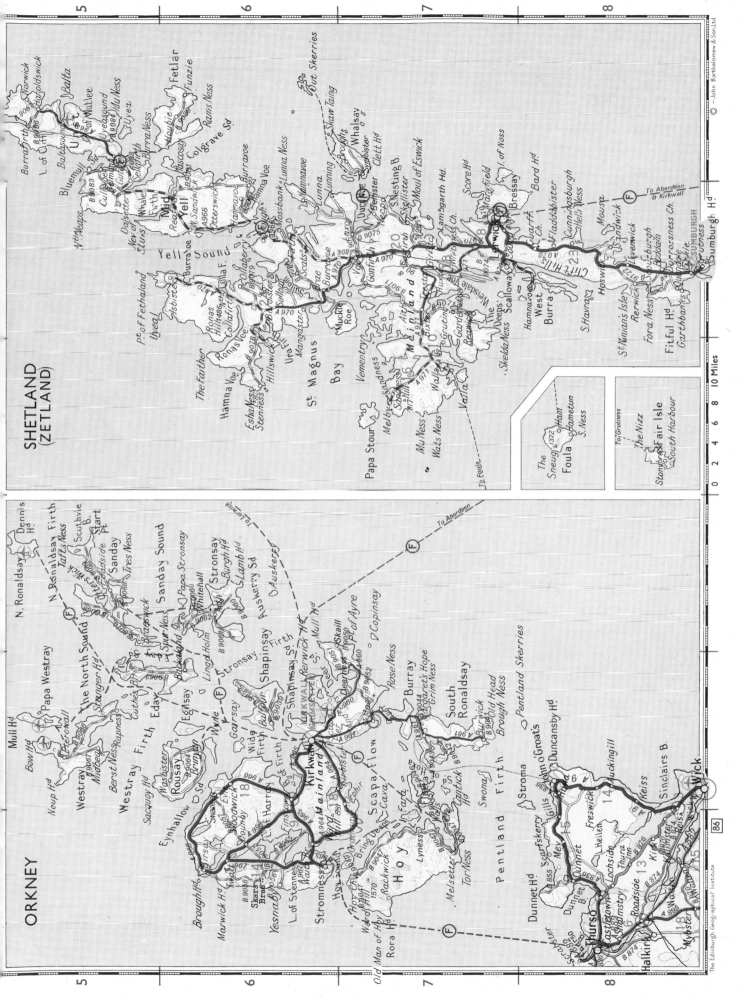

SHETLAND (ZETLAND)

ORKNEY

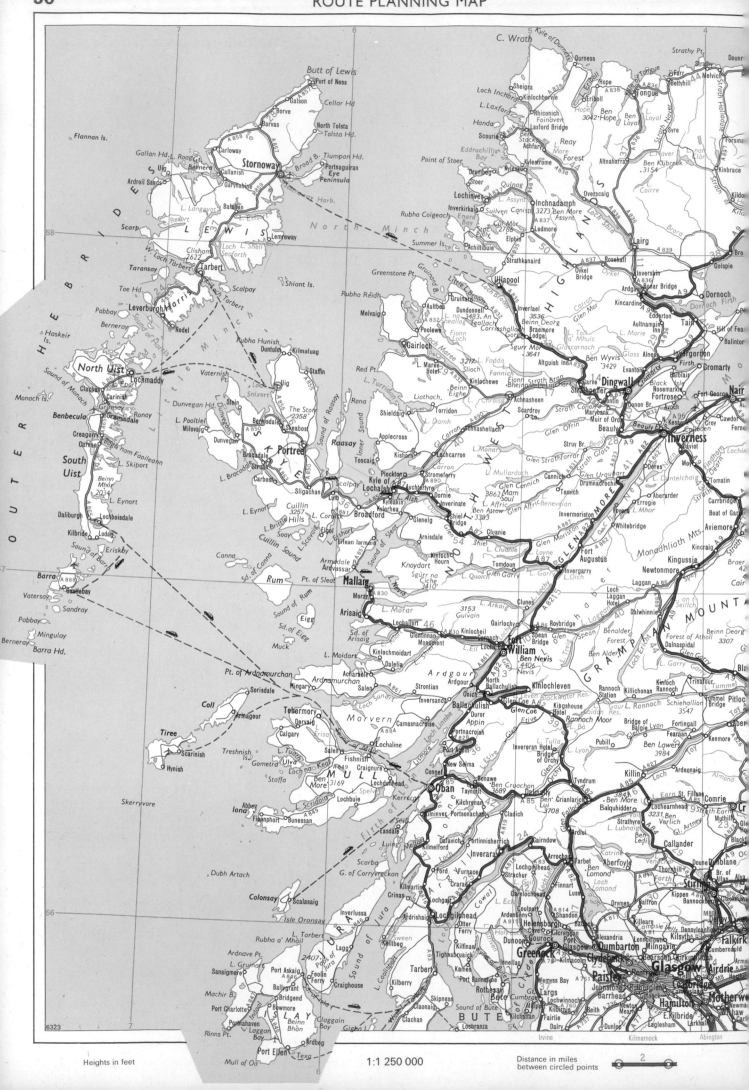

Heights in feet

1:1 250 000

Distance in miles between circled points

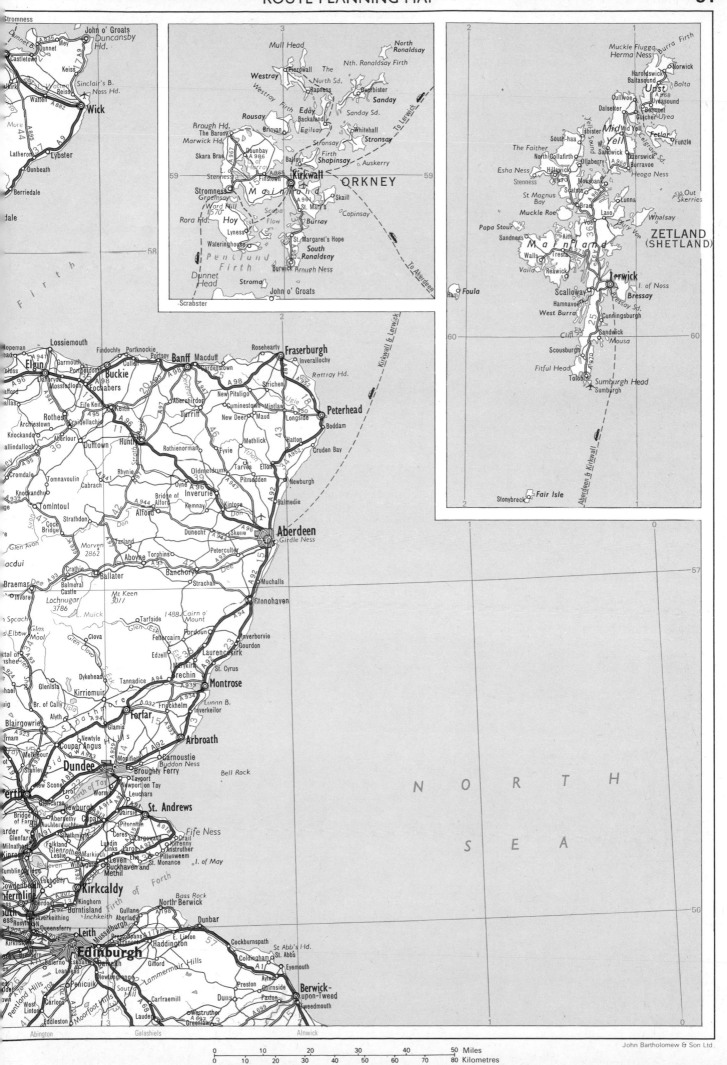

ORKNEY

ZETLAND
(SHETLAND)

N O R T H

S E A

| 0 | 10 | 20 | 30 | 40 | 50 Miles |
| 0 | 10 20 | 30 40 | 50 60 | 70 | 80 Kilometres |

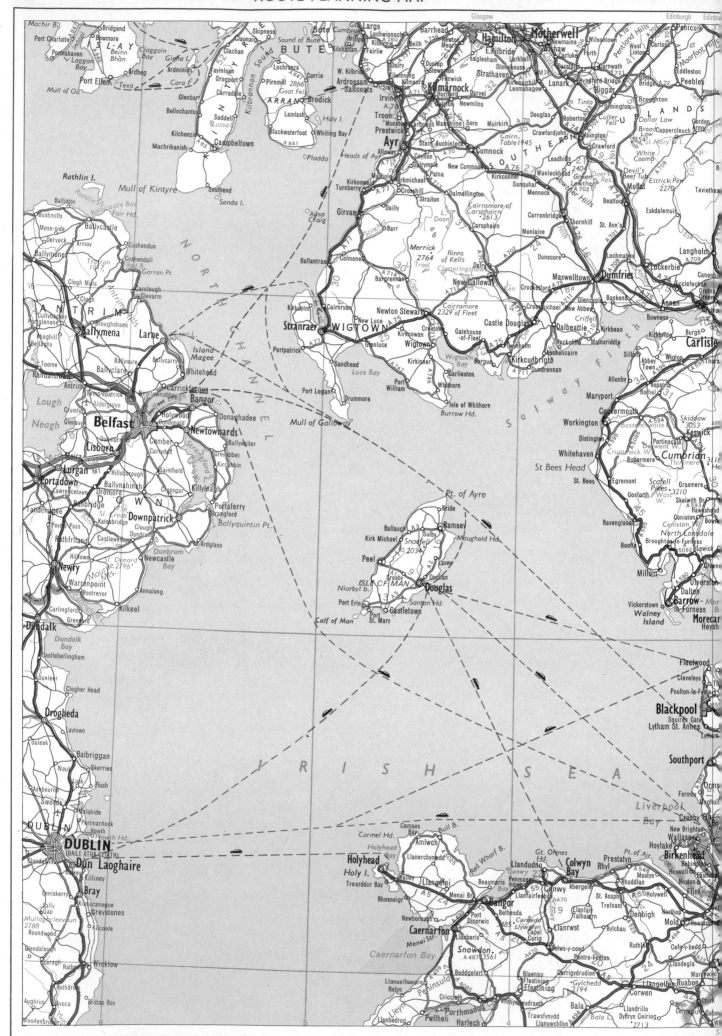

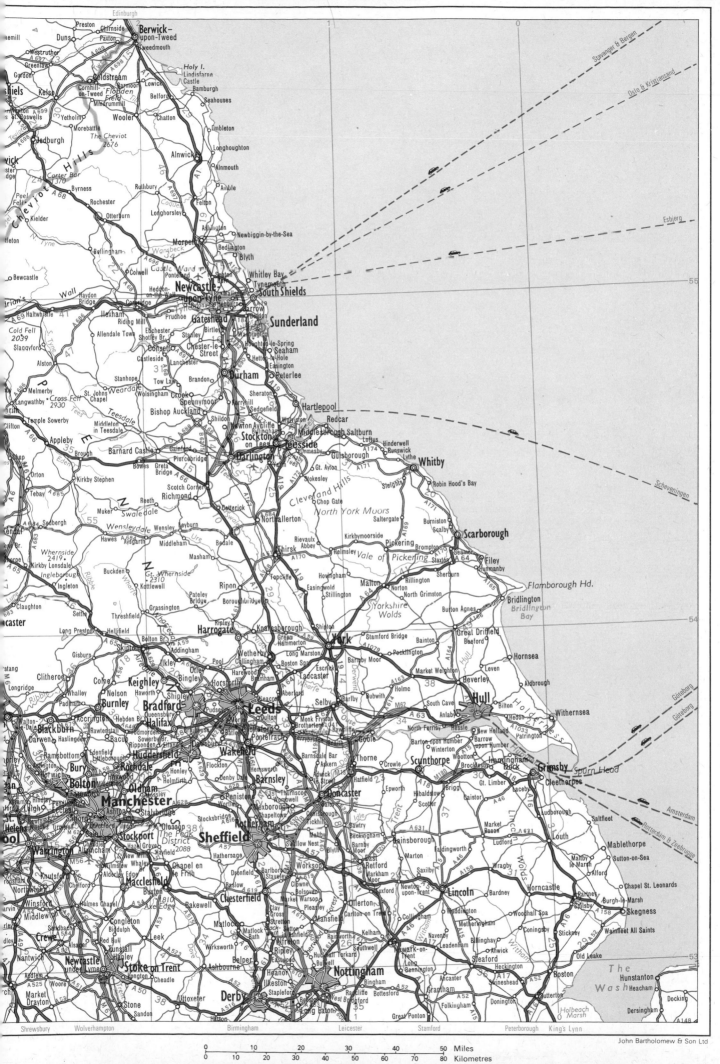

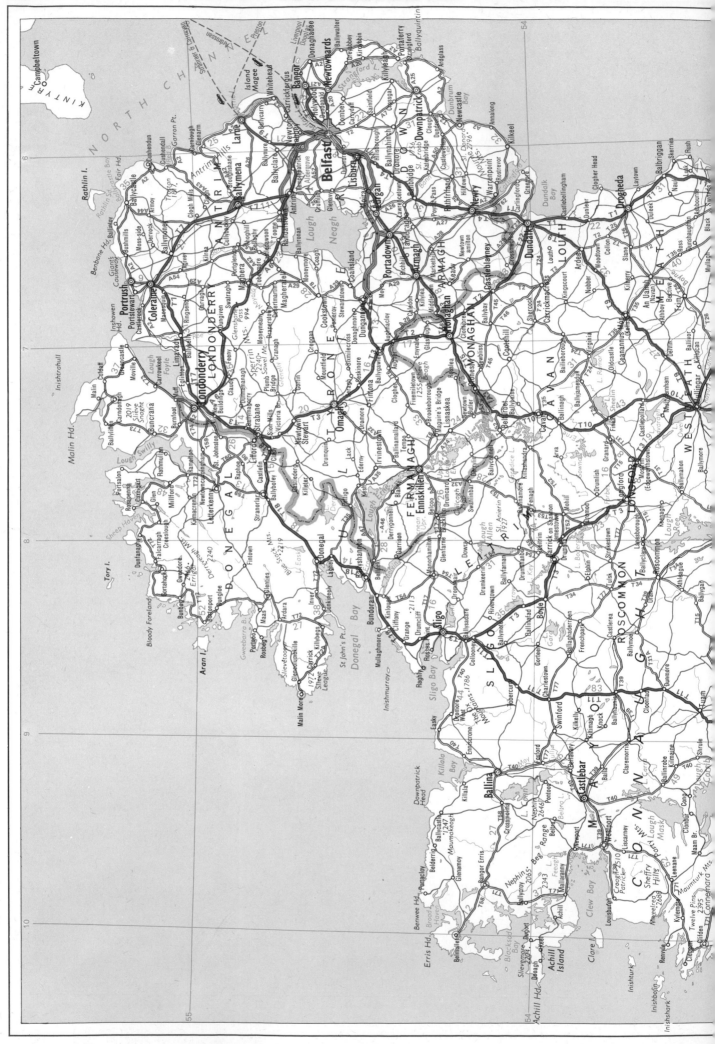

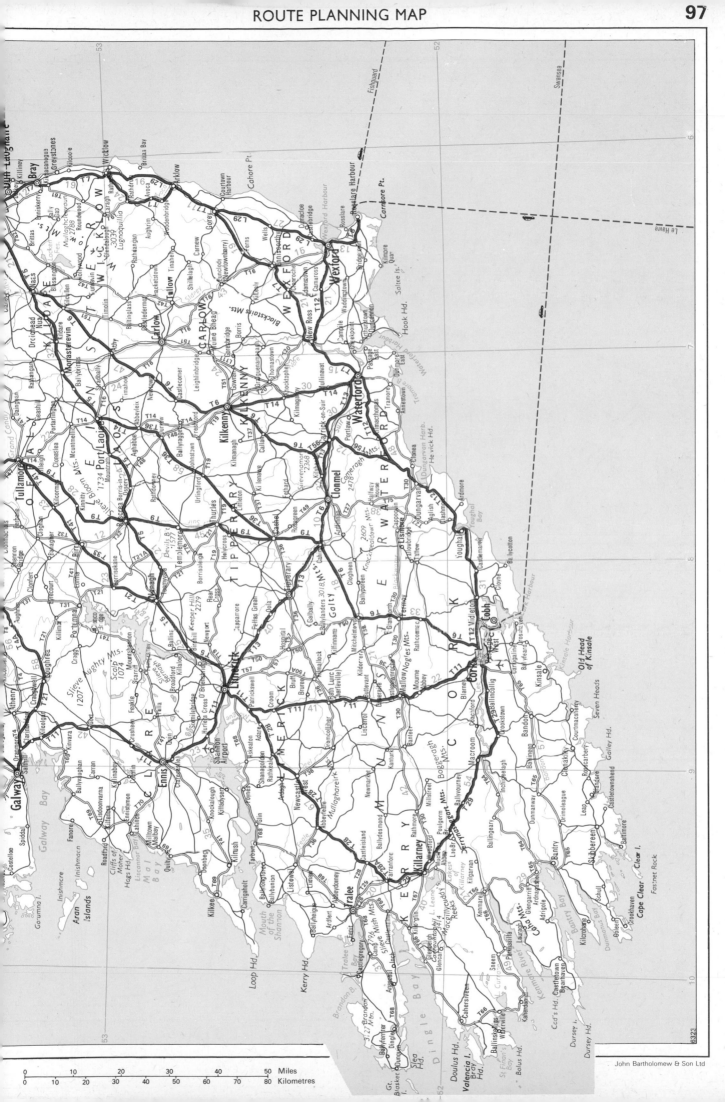

John Bartholomew & Son Ltd

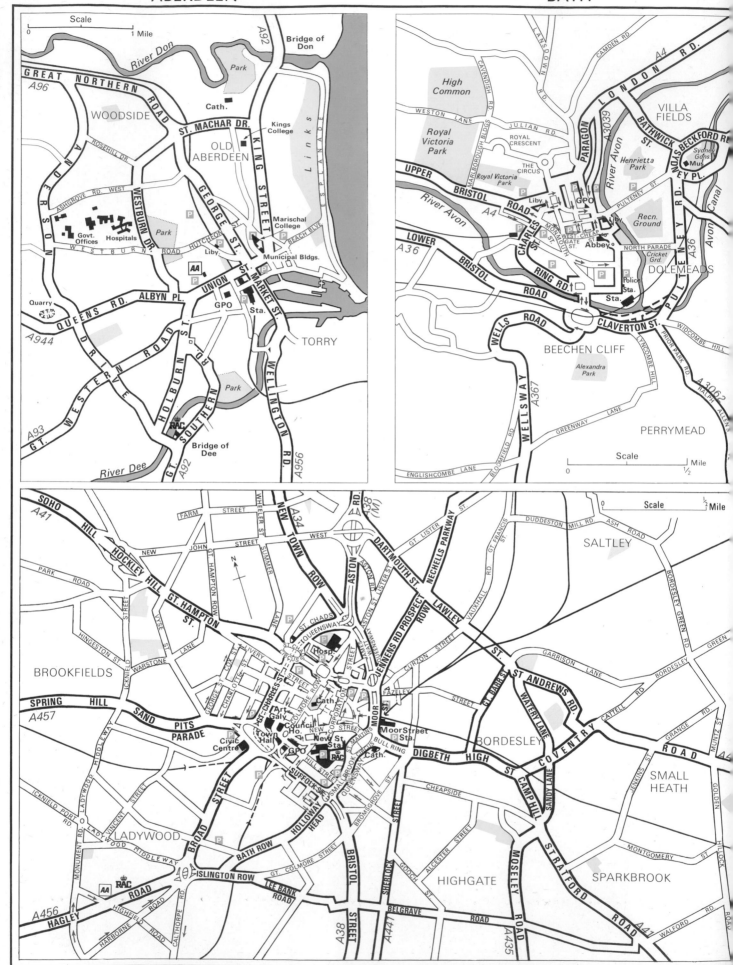

ABERDEEN

Scale
0   1 Mile

River Don
Bridge of Don
A92
Park
GREAT NORTHERN ROAD
A96
Cath.
WOODSIDE
ROSEHILL DR.
ST. MACHAR DR.
Kings College
OLD ABERDEEN
KING STREET
Links
ANDERSON
ASHGROVE RD. WEST
WESTBURN DR.
Govt. Offices
Hospitals
GEORGE ST.
HUTCHEON
WESTBURN ROAD
Park
Liby.
Marischal College
BEACH BLVD
Municipal Bldgs.
ESPLANADE
AA
UNION ST.
MARKET ST.
GPO
Sta.
TORRY
Quarry
QUEENS RD.
ALBYN PL.
HOLBURN ST.
WESTERN ROAD
DRIVE
A944
SOUTHERN RD.
WELLINGTON RD.
A9556
Park
A93
GT.
A92
RAC
Bridge of Dee
River Dee

BATH

LANSDOWN
CAMDEN RD.
A4 RD.
High Common
CAVENDISH RD.
WESTON LANE
JULIAN RD.
MARLBOROUGH BLDGS.
Royal Victoria Park
ROYAL CRESCENT
THE CIRCUS
PARAGON
A3039
VILLA FIELDS
BATHWICK ST.
NICHOLAS
BECKFORD RD.
Sydney Gdns.
Mus.
PULTENEY PL.
River Avon
Henrietta Park
UPPER BRISTOL ROAD
Royal Victoria Park
Liby.
GPO
River Avon
A4
PULTENEY RD.
Recn. Ground
LOWER BRISTOL ROAD
A36
CHARLES ST.
MONMOUTH ST.
WEST. CHEAP
GATE ST.
Liby.
Abbey
NORTH PARADE
Cricket Grd.
A36
DOLEMEADS
RING RD.
Police Sta.
Sta.
WELLS ROAD
CLAVERTON ST.
WIDCOMBE HILL
BEECHEN CLIFF
PRIOR PARK RD.
LYNCOMBE HILL
A3062
RALPH ALLEN'S
WELLSWAY
A367
Alexandra Park
PERRYMEAD
GREENWAY LANE
BLOOMFIELD RD.
ENGLISHCOMBE LANE
Scale
0   ½ Mile

BIRMINGHAM

Scale
0   ½ Mile

SOHO HILL
A41
HOCKLEY HILL
PARK ROAD
FARM STREET
WHEELER ST.
NEW TOWN ROW
A34
GT. LISTER ST.
DUDDESTON MILL RD.
ASH ROAD
SALTLEY
NEW JOHN STREET WEST
GT. HAMPTON ROW
SUMMER LANE
ASTON RD.
A38 (M)
DARTMOUTH ST.
NECHELLS PARKWAY
GT. FRANCIS ST.
BORDESLEY GREEN RD.
GREEN
GT. HAMPTON ST.
VYSE ST.
HINGESTON ST.
WARSTONE LANE
ICKNIELD ST.
ST. CHADS QUEENSWAY
ASTON ST.
JENNENS RD.
PROSPECT ROW
LAWLEY ST.
VAUXHALL RD.
GARRISON LANE
BORDESLEY GREEN
BROOKFIELDS
Hosp.
CURZON ST.
FAZELEY ST.
GT. BARR ST.
ST. ANDREWS RD.
WATERY LANE
CATTELL RD.
GRANGE RD.
SPRING HILL
A457
SAND PITS PARADE
GEORGE ST.
CHARLOTTE ST.
LIVERY ST.
GT. CHARLES ST.
COLMORE ROW
Cath.
Art Gall.
Council Ho.
MOOR ST.
MoorStreet Sta.
BORDESLEY
COVENTRY ROAD
SMALL HEATH
LADYWOOD MIDDLEWAY
Civic Centre
Town Hall
New St. Sta.
GPO
RAC
NEW ST.
BULL RING
Cath.
DIGBETH
HIGH ST.
CAMP HILL
SANDY LANE
JENKINS ST.
ICKNIELD PORT RD.
LADYWOOD MIDDLEWAY
VINCENT ST.
SUFFOLK ST.
SMALLBROOK
QUEENSWAY
CHEAPSIDE
MOSELEY ROAD
STRATFORD ROAD
GOLDEN
BROAD STREET
HOLLOWAY HEAD
BROMSGROVE ST.
BRISTOL STREET
ALCESTER STREET
HIGHGATE
MONTGOMERY ST.
HILOCK
LADYWOOD
BATH ROW
LEE BANK ROAD
HIGHGATE
SPARKBROOK
AA
RAC
ISLINGTON ROW
GT. COLMORE STREET
GOOCH ST.
SHERLOCK ST.
A441
A435
A456
HAGLEY ROAD
HARBORNE RD.
CALTHORPE RD.
A38
BELGRAVE ROAD
WALFORD RD.
A41

One-way Streets →

Car Parks P

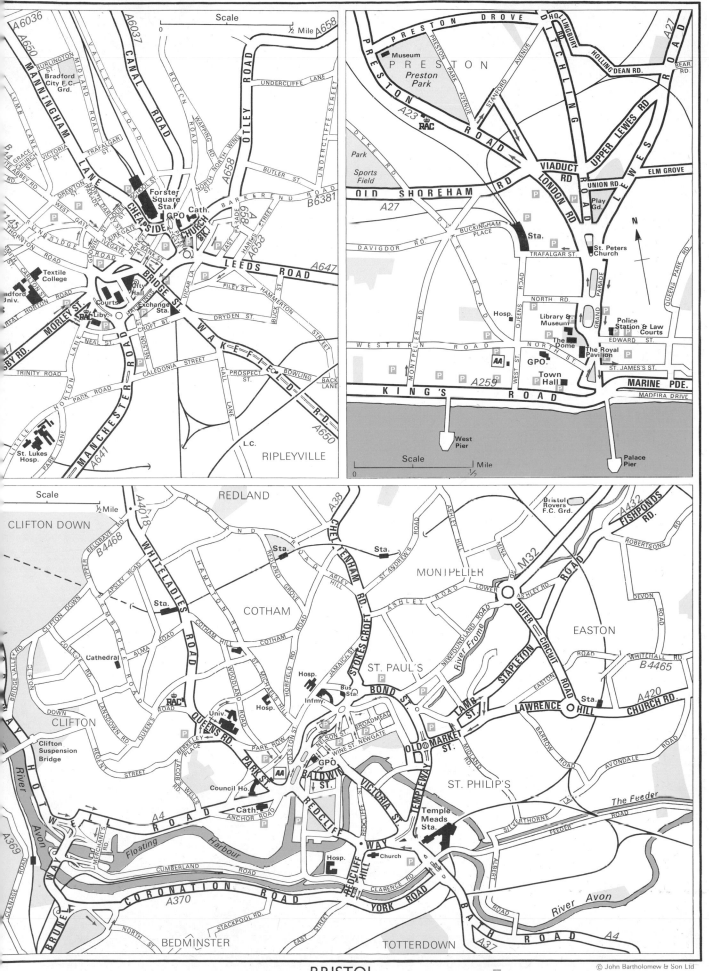

BRADFORD

Scale
0   ½ Mile

A6036
A6037
A650
MANNINGHAM LANE
CANAL ROAD
VALLEY ROAD
MIDLAND ROAD
BOLTON ROAD
WAPING RD.
BURLINGTON ST.
Bradford City F.C. Grd.
LUMB LANE
GRACE ST.
CHURCH
ABBEY RD.
VICTORIA ST.
TRAFALGAR ST.
OTLEY ROAD
UNDERCLIFFE LANE
UNDERCLIFFE STREET
A658
BUTLER ST.
BARKEREND ROAD
A658
B6381
DREWTON ST.
SCHOOL ST.
Forster Square Sta.
Cath.
GPO
CHURCH BK.
NORTH WING
NORTH PARADE
EAST PARADE
HALL'S
A658
A647
LEEDS ROAD
WEST GATE
UNBRIDGE RD.
HORTON ROAD
GODWIN
IVEGATE
YORK GATE
MARKET ST.
BANK ST.
VICAR LA.
FILEY ST.
HAMMERTON ST.
Textile College
Bradford Univ.
City Hall
Courts
Exchange Sta.
RAC
Liby.
BRIDGE ST.
MORLEY ST.
GREAT HORTON ROAD
NEAL ST.
CROFT ST.
DRYDEN ST.
BUCK ST.
A145
A647
SBY RD.
TRINITY ROAD
PARK ROAD
MANCHESTER ROAD
CALEDONIA STREET
PROSPECT ST.
BOWLING BACK LANE
St. Lukes Hosp.
LITTLE HORTON LANE
A641
L.C.
A650
RIPLEYVILLE

BRIGHTON

PRESTON DROVE
HOLLINGBURY
ITCHING
A27
BEAR RD.
Museum
PRESTON PARK AVENUE
STANFORD
PRESTON PARK
Preston Park
HOLLING DEAN RD.
UPPER LEWES RD.
A23
RAC
ROAD
VIADUCT RD.
UNION RD.
ELM GROVE
LEWES ROAD
Park
Sports Field
DYKE RD.
OLD SHOREHAM RD.
A27
VIADUCT RD.
Play Gd.
DAVIGDOR RD.
BUCKINGHAM PLACE
Sta.
TRAFALGAR ST.
St. Peters Church
QUEENS PARK RD.
N
MONTPELIER RD.
Hosp.
QUEENS RD.
NORTH RD.
GRAND PARADE
Library & Museum
Police Station & Law Courts
EDWARD ST.
WESTERN ROAD
NORTH ST.
The Dome
The Royal Pavilion
ST. JAMES'S ST.
WEST ST.
AA
GPO
Town Hall
MARINE PDE.
KING'S ROAD
A259
MADEIRA DRIVE
West Pier
Palace Pier

Scale
0   ½ Mile

BRISTOL

Scale
0   ½ Mile

REDLAND
A4018
A38
Bristol Rovers F.C. Grd.
A432
FISHPONDS RD.
CLIFTON DOWN
B4468
WHITELADIES ROAD
RED LAND ROAD
CHELTENHAM RD.
ASHLEY HILL
ROBERTSONS RD.
BELGRAVE RD.
Sta.
Sta.
ST. ANDREWS ROAD
MINA RD.
M32
UPPER BELGRAVE RD.
HAMPTON RD.
ARLEY HILL
MONTPELIER
DEVON ROAD
CLIFTON DOWN
APSLEY RD.
REDLAND GROVE
COTHAM
LOWER ASHLEY ROAD
ASHLEY RD.
EASTON
Sta.
COTHAM HILL
ASHLEY ROAD
CLIFTON PARK
PEMBROKE ROAD
ALMA RD.
COTHAM
WOODLAND RD.
HORFIELD RD.
NEWFOUNDLAND ROAD
OUTER CIRCUIT ROAD
WHITEHALL RD.
COLLEGE RD.
Cathedral
ST. MICHAEL'S HILL
Hosp.
STOKES CROFT
JAMAICA ST.
ST. PAUL'S
STAPLETON ROAD
B4465
BRIDGE VALLEY RD.
RAC
Hosp.
Infmy.
BOND ST.
LAMB ST.
EASTON ROAD
A420
CLIFTON
LANSDOWN RD.
Univ.
PARK ROW
Bus Sta.
BROADMEAD
Sta.
LAWRENCE HILL
CHURCH RD.
DOWN
QUEENS RD.
BERKELEY PLACE
NELSON ST.
WINE ST.
NEWGATE
OLD MARKET ST.
BARROW ROAD
Clifton Suspension Bridge
REGENT STREET
JACOB'S WELLS
PARK ST.
AA
GPO
BALDWIN ST.
VICTORIA ST.
ST. PHILIP'S
AVONDALE ROAD
River HOTWELL ROAD
QUEENS RD.
Council Ho.
Cath.
ANCHOR RD.
REDCLIFF WAY
TEMPLE WAY
MIDLAND ROAD
The Feeder
River Avon
A4
ST. PAUL'S
Temple Meads Sta.
SILVERTHORNE LANE
A369
Floating Harbour
CUMBERLAND ROAD
Hosp.
Church
REDCLIFF HILL
YORK ROAD
BATH ROAD
FEEDER ROAD
BRUNEL WAY
CORONATION ROAD
A370
STACKPOOL RD.
CLARENCE RD.
ALBERT ROAD
A37
River Avon
A4
NORTH ST.
EAST STREET
BEDMINSTER
TOTTERDOWN

One-way Streets →   Car Parks P

© John Bartholomew & Son Ltd

CAMBRIDGE

CANTERBURY

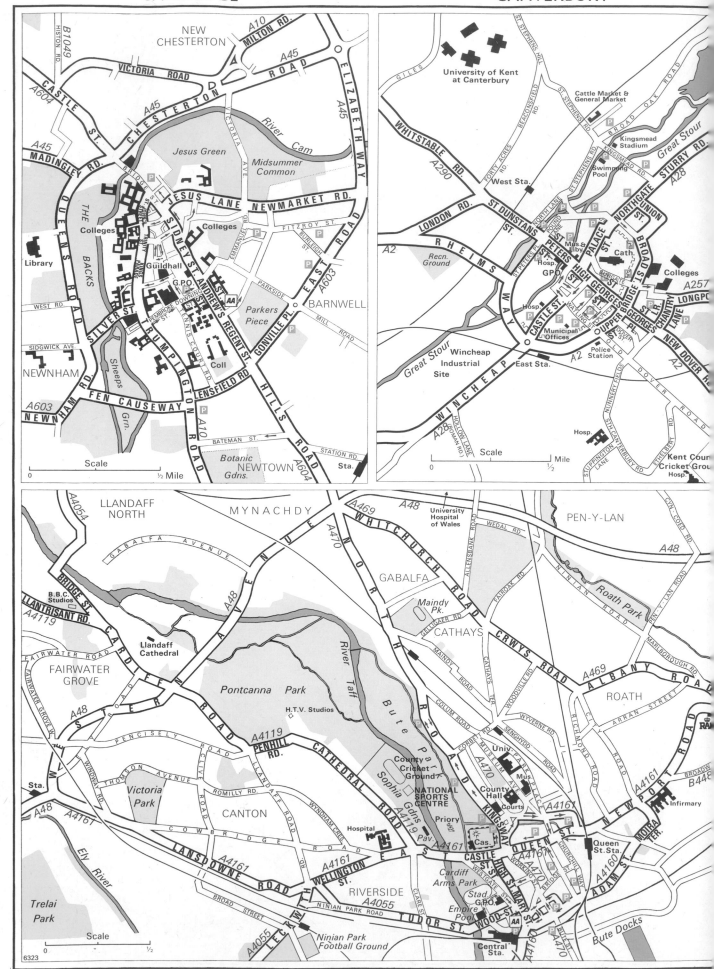

CAMBRIDGE

NEW CHESTERTON

MILTON RD.

A410

A45

B1049

HISTON RD.

VICTORIA ROAD

A45

CASTLE ST.

A604

CHESTERTON ROAD

A45

MADINGLEY RD.

A45

River Cam

Jesus Green

Midsummer Common

ELIZABETH WAY

A45

VICTORIA AVE.

JESUS LANE

NEWMARKET RD.

THE BACKS

Colleges

QUEENS ROAD

Library

Colleges

BRIDGE ST.

SIDNEY ST.

ST. ANDREW'S ST.

Guildhall

EMMANUEL RD.

FITZROY ST.

BURLEIGH ST.

EAST ROAD

A603

P

P

WEST RD.

G.P.O.

PARKSIDE

Parkers Piece

BARNWELL

AA

SILVER ST.

TRUMPINGTON ST.

REGENT ST.

GONVILLE PL.

MILL ROAD

SIDGWICK AVE.

PEMBROKE ST.

DOWNING ST.

TENNIS COURT RD.

Coll

NEWNHAM

Sheeps Grn.

LENSFIELD RD.

HILLS ROAD

A10

NEWNHAM RD.

FEN CAUSEWAY

A603

BATEMAN ST.

STATION RD.

Botanic Gdns.

NEWTOWN

A604

Sta.

Scale
0   ½ Mile

CANTERBURY

University of Kent at Canterbury

ST. STEPHENS HILL

GILES

WHITSTABLE RD.

A290

FORTY ACRES RD.

ST. STEPHENS RD.

BEACONSFIELD RD.

Cattle Market & General Market

BROAD OAK RD.

Kingsmead Stadium

Great Stour

STURRY RD.

A28

LONDON RD.

A2

RHEIMS WAY

ST. DUNSTANS ST.

West Sta.

NORTH LANE

KINGSMEAD RD.

Swimming Pool

NORTHGATE ST.

UNION ST.

BROAD ST.

Recn. Ground

ST. PETERS ST.

Hosp.

GPO

Mus & Liby.

Cath.

PALACE ST.

Colleges

A257

Great Stour

Wincheap Industrial Site

Hosp.

HIGH ST.

CASTLE ST.

GEORGES ST.

Municipal Offices

BURGATE

GEORGES PL.

UPPER BRIDGE ST.

CHANTRY LANE

LONGPORT

NEW DOVER RD.

A2

WINCHEAP

A28

HOLLOW LANE

ROMAN RD.

East Sta.

A2

Police Station

NUNNERY FIELDS

DOVER RD.

STH. CANTERBURY RD.

STUPPINGTON LANE

ETHELBERT RD.

Hosp.

Kent County Cricket Ground

Hosp.

Scale
0   ½ Mile

CARDIFF

LLANDAFF NORTH

A4054

MYNACHDY

A469

A48

A470

University Hospital of Wales

PEN-Y-LAN

A48

GABALFA AVENUE

WHITCHURCH ROAD

WEDAL RD.

CYN COED RD.

ALLENSBANK RD.

FAIROAK RD.

NINIAN ROAD

A48

B.B.C. Studios

CARDIFF ROAD

A48

Maindy Pk.

GABALFA

Roath Park

PEN-Y-LAN ROAD

BRIDGE ST.

LLANTRISANT RD.

A4119

Llandaff Cathedral

CATHAYS

GELLIGAER RD.

CRWYS ROAD

MARLBOROUGH RD.

FAIRWATER GROVE

FAIRWATER ROAD

STORE ROAD

River Taff

Pontcanna Park

H.T.V. Studios

Bute Park

MAINDY ROAD

CATHAYS TERRACE

WOODVILLE RD.

A469

ALBANY ROAD

ROATH

ARRAN STREET

RICHMOND ROAD

FAIRWATER GROVE W.

A48

PENCISELY ROAD

PENHILL RD.

A4119

CATHEDRAL ROAD

COLUM ROAD

CORBETT RD.

SENGHYDD RD.

WYVERNE RD.

A4161

PORT ROAD

WINDWAY RD.

Sta.

THOMSON AVENUE

CLIVE ROAD

LLANDAFF ROAD

ROMILLY RD.

Univ.

Mus.

County Hall

Courts

A470

MUSEUM AVE.

QUEEN ST.

NEW

B448

A48

A4161

Victoria Park

CANTON

WYNDHAM CRES.

COWBRIDGE ROAD

County Cricket Ground

Sophia Gdns.

NATIONAL SPORTS CENTRE

Priory

Pav.

KINGSWAY

Cas.

QUEEN ST.

CHURCHILL WAY

A4160

Queen St. Sta.

ADAM ST.

MOIRA TER.

Infirmary

ELY RIVER

A4161

A48

LANSDOWNE ROAD

A4161

WELLINGTON ST.

WYNDHAM CRES.

A4161

Hospital

A4161

High St.

ST. MARY'S

WESTGATE ST.

CASTLE ST.

WORKING ST.

Cardiff Arms Park

Stad.

G.P.O.

Empire Pool

AA

Trelai Park

Scale
0   ½

6323

BROAD STREET

RIVERSIDE

A4055

NINIAN PARK ROAD

TUDOR ST.

WOOD ST.

LECKWITH RD.

A4055

Ninian Park Football Ground

BUTE ST.

A470

Central Sta.

Bute Docks

CARDIFF

Car Parks P   One-way Streets →

© John Bartholomew & Son

CHESTER

PARKGATE RD. A540
LIVERPOOL RD. A5116
FLOOKERS BROOK
HOOLE RD. A56
HOOLE
BOUGHTON
HOOLE WAY
ST. OSWALD'S WAY
Sta.
GARDEN LANE
Canal
NEW CRANE ST.
Hosp.
Town Hall
Cath.
AA
FOREGATE ST.
BOUGHTON A51
A5115
Grosvenor Park
The Groves
GROSVENOR ST.
Cas.
RIVER DEE
THE MEADOWS
Race Course
ROODEE
QUEENS PARK
QUEENS PK. RD.
MEADOWS LANE
DEE BANKS
CURZON PARK
HAND BRIDGE
OVERLEIGH ROAD
EATON ROAD
HARTINGTON ROAD
PINFOLD LANE
B5130
WREXHAM RD. A483
Scale ½ Mile

COVENTRY

A423 RADFORD RD. A444
FOLESHILL RD.
B4109
Canal
B4110
Hosp.
HARNALL LANE WEST
HARNALL LANE EAST
STANTON
STONEY STANTON RD.
SWANSWELL ST.
PRIMROSE HILL ST.
KING WILLIAM ST.
PAYNES LA.
COX ST.
A4114 HOLYHD. RD.
COUNDON RD.
ABBOTS LA.
BISHOP ST.
BARRAS LA.
SPON ST.
CORPORATION ST.
HALES ST.
Bus Sta.
FAIRFAX
AA
Cath.
PRIORY ST.
COX ST.
GOSFORD ST.
A46
ST. VICTORIA RD.
BROAD GATE
BAYLEY
Council Bldgs.
HIGH ST.
EARL ST.
JORDAN WELL
GULSON ROAD
A4114
MARKET
PRECINCT
SMITHFORD
G.P.O.
Hosp.
PARK RD.
NEW UNION ST.
FRIARS RD.
ST. PATRICKS RD.
PARK SIDE
Sherbourne
LONDON ROAD
QUEENS RD.
PARADISE RD.
Sch.
Station
QUINTON ROAD
SPENCER RD.
WARWICK ROAD
LEAMINGTON RD.
KENILWORTH RD. A46
A4444
DAVENTRY ROAD
A423
Scale 0 ½ Mile

DERBY

Ring Road
BROADWAY A6
A5111
DUFFIELD ROAD
River Derwent
ALFRETON RD. A61
MANSFIELD RD. A608
PARK GROVE
WHITE ST.
BELPER RD.
HIGHFIELD
KINGSTON ST.
OLD CHESTER RD.
KEDLESTON ROAD
COWLEY ST.
OTTER ST.
NORTH ST.
CITY ROAD
MANSFIELD ROAD
STORES RD. A61 (A608)
Cricket Ground
Hosp.
ST. ALKMUNDS WAY
KING ST.
FOX ST.
NOTTINGHAM RD.
A52
WALKER LA.
Police Sta.
FRIAR GATE
FORD ST.
BRIDGE STREET
LODGE LA.
ST. MARYS GATE
Cath.
IRONGATE COURT
QUEEN ST.
Council Ho.
T.H.
Mus.
BECKET ST.
CURZON ST.
G.P.O.
ALBERT ST.
MORLEDGE
EAST ST.
ST. PETER'S ST.
GREEN LANE
Pedestrianised Area
ABBEY STREET
STAFFORD ST.
MACKLIN ST.
WILSON ST.
MONK ST.
NORMANTON RD.
BABINGTON LANE
OSMASTON RD.
TRAFFIC ST.
RAILWAY TER.
MIDLAND
Sta.
STOCKBROOK ST.
WOODS LA.
LACHE LANE
BURTON RD. A38
LEOPOLD ST.
CHARNWOOD ST.
LONDON ROAD A6
A5194
Infmy.
UTTOXETER NEW RD.
A516
Scale ½ Mile

DOVER

DEAL ROAD A258
Car Ferry Terminal
Eastern Docks
Hovercraft Port
Blériot Memorial
Castle
Connaught Park
CASTLE HILL ROAD
CONNAUGHT RD.
EAST CLIFF
Dover Harbour
FRITH RD.
B2059
MAISON DIEU RD.
Police Station
Town Hall
Bus Sta.
AA
Castle
Library
TOWNWALL ST.
MARINE PARADE
LONDON RD.
HIGH ST.
BIGGIN ST.
PENCESTER RD.
YORK ST.
RAC
A2
FOLKESTONE ROAD A20
Priory Sta.
SNARGATE ST.
Prince of Wales Pier
Western Docks
Train Ferry
Admiralty Pier
Marine Sta.
WESTERN HEIGHTS
Scale 0 ½ Mile

One-way Streets → Car Parks P

© John Bartholomew & Son Ltd

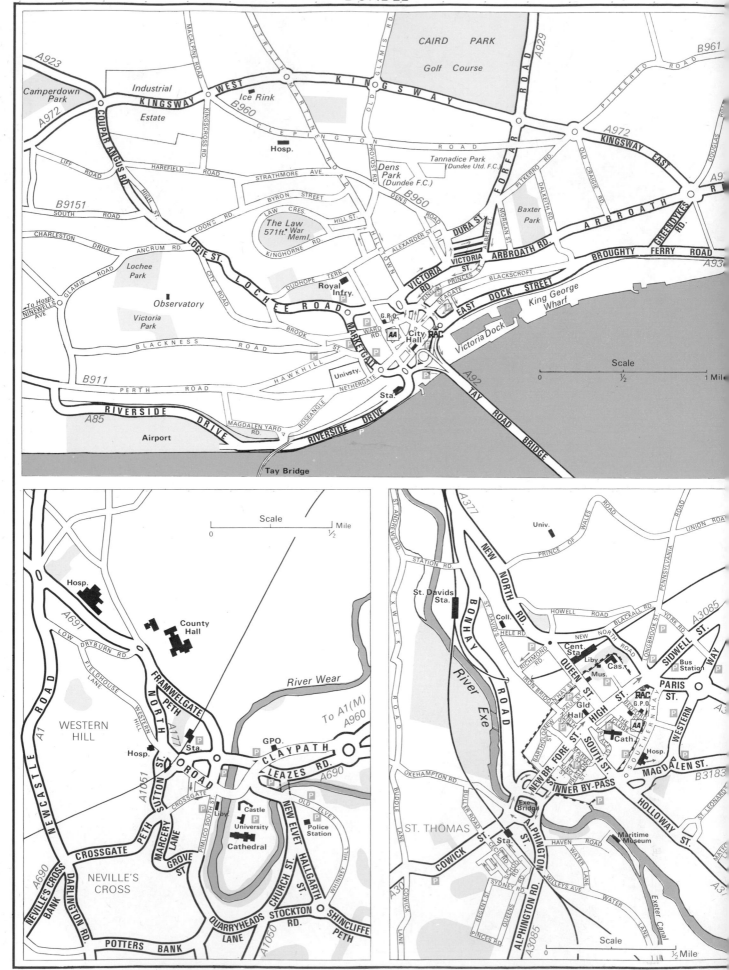

© John Bartholomew & Son

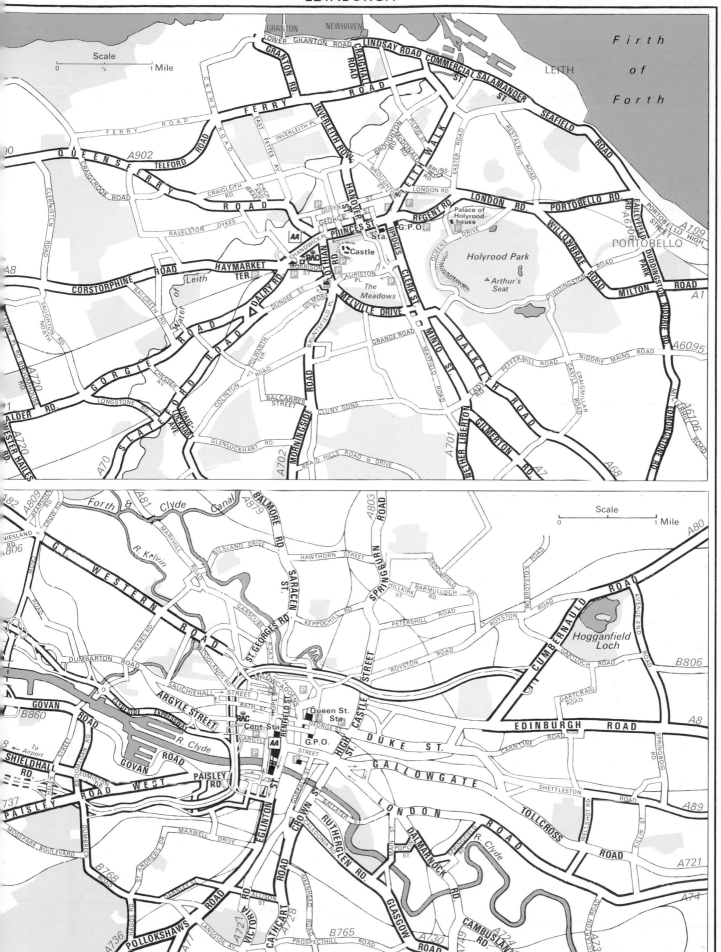

One-way Streets →

Car Parks P

© John Bartholomew & Son Ltd

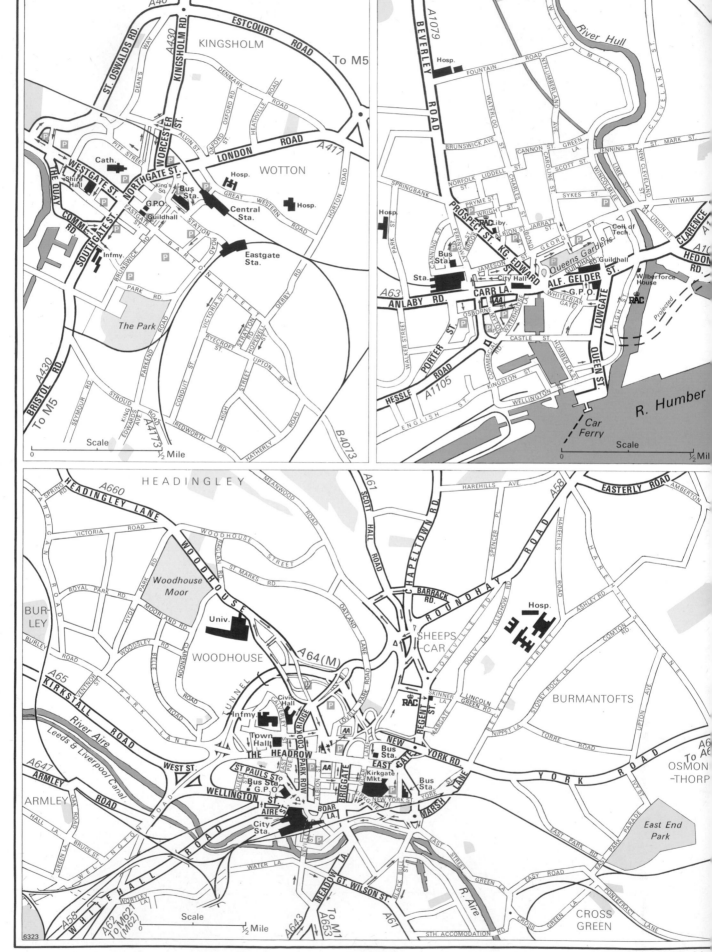

Car Parks **P**   One-way Streets

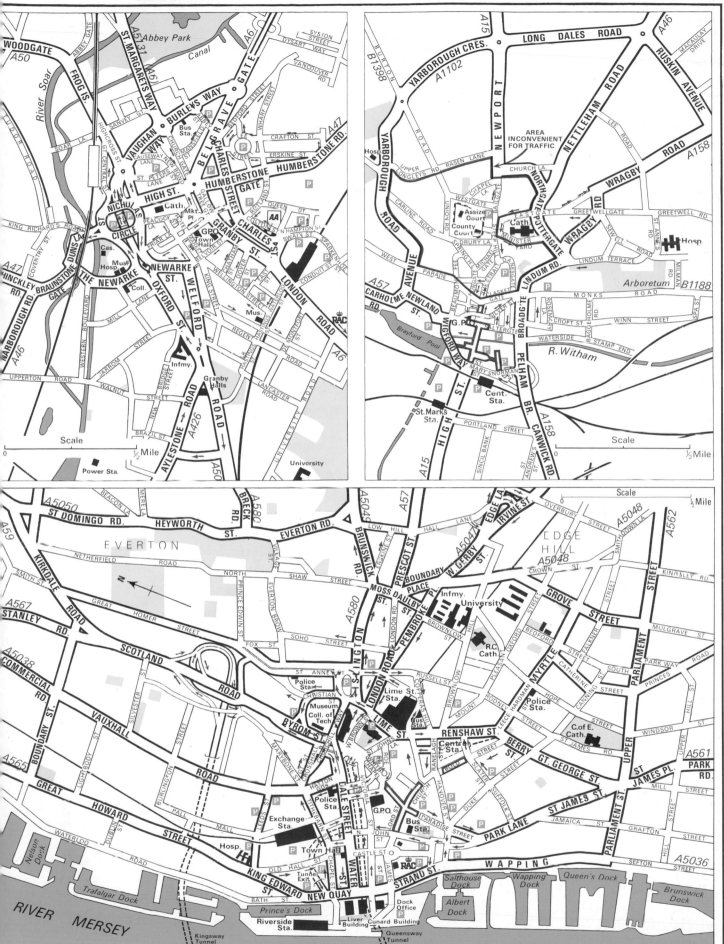

LEICESTER

WOODGATE
A50
Abbey Park
Canal
River Soar
FROG IS.
TUDOR ROAD
ST. MARGARETS WAY
ABBEY GATE
SARVEY G.
SOAR LA.
HIGHCROSS ST.
CENTRAL
A45/31 (A6)
BURLEY'S WAY
SYSTON STREET
DYSART WAY
VANCOUVER RD.
BEDFORD STREET
WHARF STREET
BELGRAVE GATE
Bus Sta.
CRAFTON ST.
ERSKINE ST.
VAUGHAN WAY
CAUSEWAY LANE
CHARLES ST.
LEE ST.
CHURCH GATE
ST. PETERS LANE
NEW RD.
ST. NICHOLAS ST.
CIRCLE
HIGH ST.
Cath.
Mkt. Pl.
HUMBERSTONE GATE
HUMBERSTONE RD.
A47
QUEEN ST.
Cas.
Mus. Hosp.
GRANBY ST.
CHARLES ST.
AA
Town Hall
GPO
CONDUIT ST.
SWAIN ST.
KING RICHARD'S RD.
NEWARKE ST.
COVENTRY ST.
BRAUNSTONE GATE
THE NEWARKE
OXFORD ST.
WELFORD ROAD
LONDON ROAD
A6
RAC
A47
HINCKLEY RD.
WELLINGTON STREET
KING STREET
NARBOROUGH RD.
A46
WESTERN BOULEVARD
BRIDGE ROAD
JARROM ST.
REGENT
Coll.
Mus.
Infmy.
Granby Halls
MILL LANE
BRAZIL ST.
WALNUT STREET
LANCASTER ROAD
UPPERTON ROAD
UPPERTON ROAD
BRAUNSTONE GATE
AYLESTONE ROAD
A426
A50
University
Scale
0   ½ Mile
■ Power Sta.

LINCOLN

A15
A46
LONG DALES ROAD
MACAULAY DRIVE
YARBOROUGH CRES.
A1102
RUSKIN AVENUE
BURTON B1398
YARBOROUGH ROAD
NEWPORT
NETTLEHAM ROAD
LEE ROAD
WRAGBY ROAD
A158
AREA INCONVENIENT FOR TRAFFIC
Hosp.
UPPER LONGLEYS
RASEN LANE
CHURCH LA.
NORTHGATE
POTTERGATE
EASTGATE
GREETWELLGATE
GREETWELL RD.
CHAPEL LA.
WESTGATE
BAILGATE
Cath.
MINSTER YARD
WRAGBY
ST. ANNE'S RD.
Hosp.
CARLINE ROAD
UNION RD.
Assize Court County Court
DRURY LA.
LINDUM RD.
SEW LL.
WEST PARADE
LINDUM TERRACE
MILMAN RD.
A57
CARHOLME RD.
NEWLAND
NEWLAND ST.
BEAUMONT
GATE
MONKS ROAD
Arboretum
B1188
Brayford Pool
G.P.O.
SALTERGATE
ROSEMARY
CROFT ST.
BAGGEHOLME RD.
WINN STREET
SPA RD.
WIGFORD WAY
BROADG'TE
PELHAM
WATERSIDE
STAMP END
R. Witham
ST. MARY'S
SNORMAN
Cent. Sta.
St. Marks Sta.
HIGH ST.
PONTLAND STREET
CANWICK RD.
BR.
A158
A15
SINCIL BANK
ST. ANDREW'S ST.
Scale
0   ½ Mile

LIVERPOOL

A5050
BEACON LA.
MERE LA.
BRECK RD.
A580
A57
A5049
A5047
EDGE LA.
IRVINE ST.
OVERBURY STREET
A5048
SMITH DOWN LA.
A562
ST. DOMINGO RD.
HEYWORTH ST.
EVERTON RD.
LOW HILL
HALL LA.
EDGE HILL A5048
A459
EVERTON
NETHERFIELD ROAD
VILLAGE
BRUNSWICK RD.
PRESCOT ST.
W. DERBY ST.
CROWN ST.
KINGSLEY RD.
KIRKDALE ROAD
SMITH ST.
NORTH
SHAW STREET
A580
MOSS ST.
DAULBY ST.
Infmy.
University
GROVE STREET
A567
STANLEY RD.
GREAT HOMER STREET
PRINCE EDWIN ST.
EVERTON BROW
FOX ST.
SOHO STREET
PEMBROKE PL.
LONDON RD.
BROWNLOW HILL
R.C. Cath.
MYRTLE
MULGRAVE ST.
SCOTLAND ROAD
ST. ANNE ST.
RUSSELL ST.
PLEASANT
OXFORD ST.
CATHERINE
PARK WAY
A5038
COMMERCIAL RD.
Police Sta.
CHRISTIAN ST.
Museum Coll. of Tech.
ISLINGTON
LIME ST.
Lime St. Sta.
BROWNLOW
MOUNT
RODNEY
HOPE ST.
Police Sta.
C. of E. Cath.
PRINCES
VAUXHALL ROAD
BYROM ST.
W. BROWN'S
LIME ST.
ST. JOHNS LA.
Bus Sta.
RENSHAW ST.
Central Sta.
BERRY ST.
GT. GEORGE ST.
WINDSOR ST.
A4565
BOUNDARY ST.
SILVESTER ST.
BIRLINGTON
MARYBONE
DALE STREET
Police Sta.
VICTORIA
CHURCH ST.
HANOVER ST.
DUKE ST.
SUFFOLK ST.
ST. JAMES ST.
JAMES PL.
A561
PARK RD.
GREAT HOWARD STREET
LIGHT BODY
PALL MALL
LEEDS ST.
G.P.O.
Bus Sta.
PARADISE
JAMAICA ST.
PARLIAMENT ST.
GRAFTON STREET
Exchange Sta.
Hosp.
Town Hall
WATER ST.
CASTLE ST.
RAC
PARK LANE
MILL
SEFTON ST.
A5036
WATERLOO ROAD
OLD HALL ST.
CHAPEL ST.
JAMES ST.
STRAND ST.
WAPPING
Nelson Dock
Trafalgar Dock
KING EDWARD ST.
Tunnel Exit
NEW QUAY
Dock Office
Salthouse Dock
Wapping Dock
Queen's Dock
Brunswick Dock
RIVER MERSEY
Kingsway Tunnel
Prince's Dock
Riverside Sta.
Liver Building
Cunard Building
Queensway Tunnel
Albert Dock

One-way Streets →   LIVERPOOL   Car Parks P

© John Bartholomew & Son Ltd

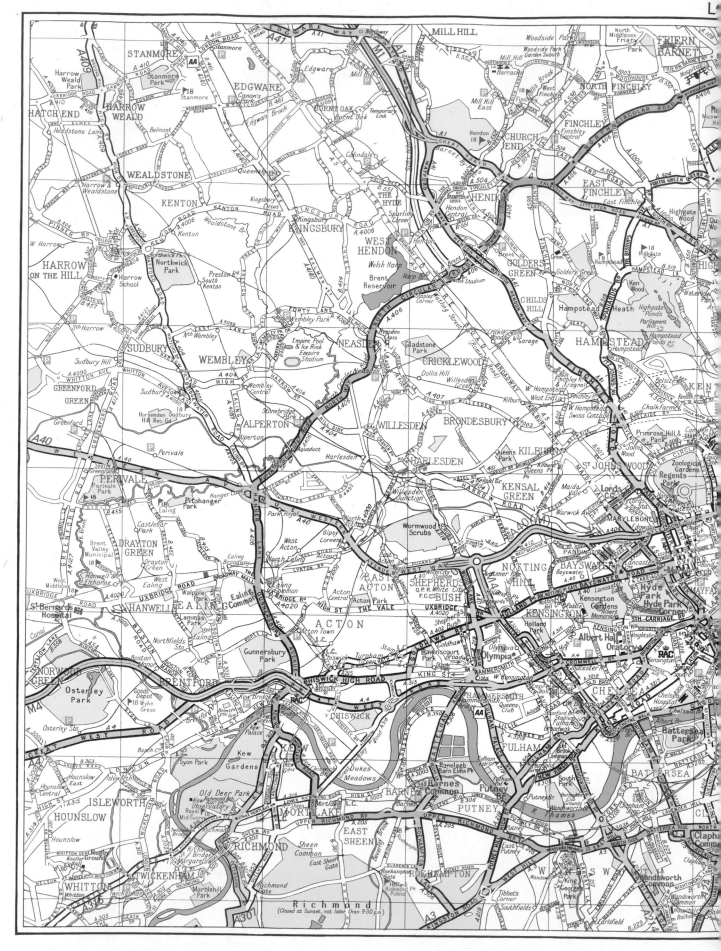

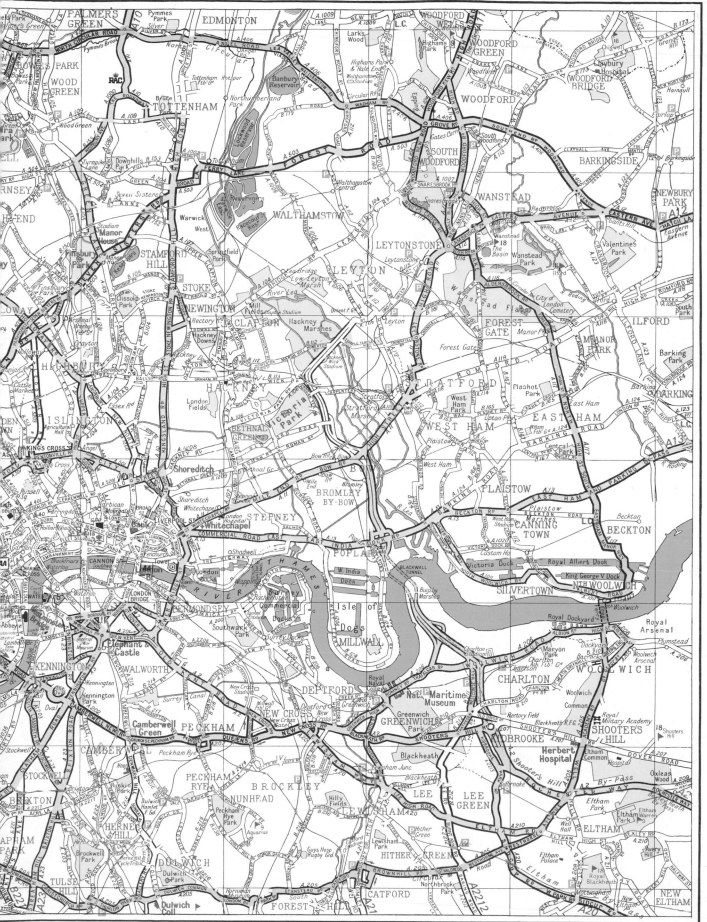

Recommended Through Routes ━━━━   One-way Streets →   Car Parks Ⓟ

MANCHESTER

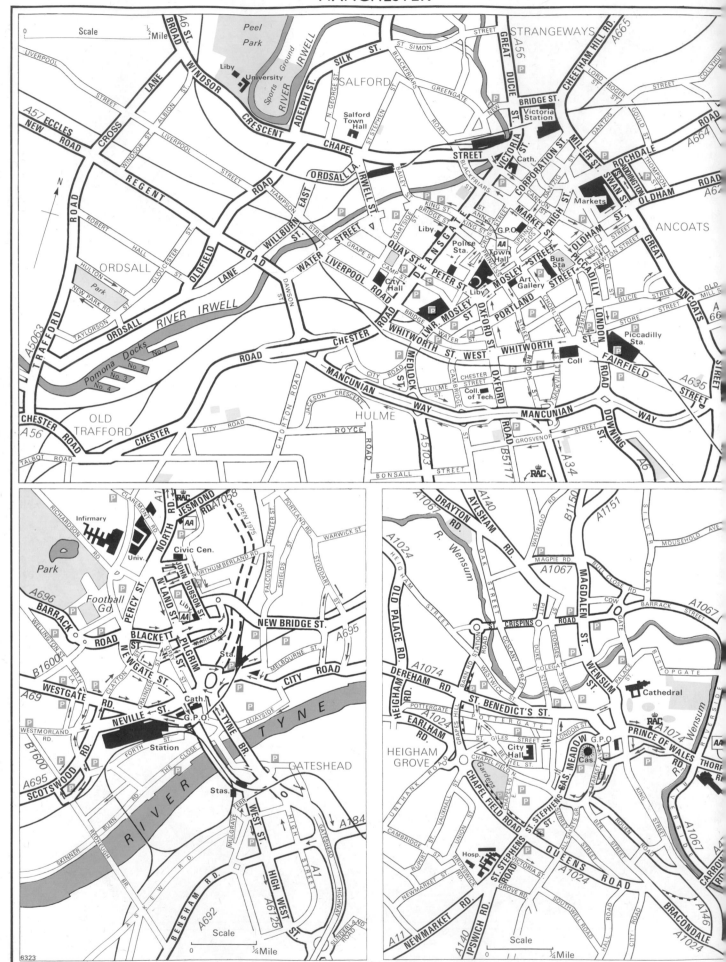

© John Bartholomew & Son Ltd.

NOTTINGHAM

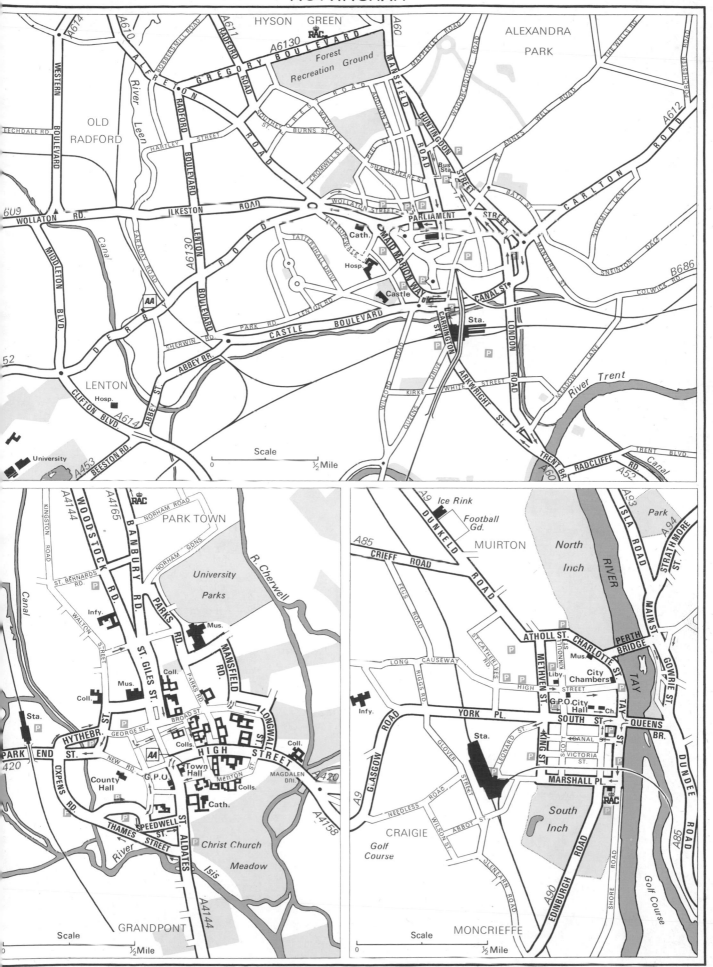

HYSON GREEN

ALEXANDRA PARK

A614
A610
A611
RADFORD ROAD
A6130
GREGORY BOULEVARD
A60
MAPPERLEY ROAD
WELLS RD.

WESTERN BOULEVARD
Forest Recreation Ground
MANSFIELD ROAD
WOODBOROUGH ROAD
WELL ROAD

OLD RADFORD
BOBBERS MILL ROAD
ALFRETON
ROAD

River Leen
HARTLEY STREET
RADFORD BOULEVARD
ROUTHEY HILL ST
BURNS ST
WAVERLEY ST
HUNTINGDON STREET
ADDISON ST
ANNE'S RD.
CARLTON
ROAD
A612

BEECHDALE RD.
ILKESTON ROAD
CROMWELL ST
SHAKESPEARE ST
BATH ST.

A609
WOLLATON RD.
A6130
ROAD
WOLLATON STREET
Cath.
PARLIAMENT STREET
Bus Sta.
MANNERS ST
VINCENT LANE
B686

52
CANAL
Hosp.
MAID MARIAN WAY
SNEINTON
COLWICK RD.

MIDDLETON BLVD.
FARADAY ROAD
LENTON BOULEVARD
TATTERSHALL DRIVE
THE ROPEWALK
Castle
CANAL ST.

AA
PARK RD.
LENTON RD.
Sta.
CARRINGTON
ARKWRIGHT ST
LONDON ROAD
MEADOW LANE

DERBY RD
SHERWIN
CASTLE BOULEVARD
ABBEY BR.
WILFORD DRIVE
KIRKE WHITE ST
River Trent

LENTON
Hosp.
CLIFTON BLVD.
A614
ABBEY ST.
QUEENS
TRENT BLVD.
TRENT BR.
RADCLIFFE RD.
Trent Canal

University
A453
BEESTON RD.

Scale
0 ——— ½ Mile

A9
Ice Rink
Football Gd.
A93
Park
A94

A4144
RAC
NORHAM ROAD
PARK TOWN
DUNKELD ROAD
MUIRTON
North Inch
ISLA ROAD
STRATHMORE ST.

KINGSTON RD.
WOODSTOCK RD.
A4165
BANBURY RD.
NORHAM GDNS.
University Parks
R. Cherwell
A85
CRIEFF ROAD
RIVER

St. BERNARD'S RD.
Infy.
PARKS RD.
Mus.
FEUS ROAD
ATHOLL ST.
CHARLOTTE ST.
MAIN ST.
PERTH BRIDGE

Canal
WALTON STREET
ST. GILES ST.
Coll.
MANSFIELD RD.
PARKS RD.
LONG CAUSEWAY
ST. CATHERINE'S RD.
Mus.
METHVEN ST.
Liby.
City Chambers
HIGH STREET
TAY
GOWRIE ST.

Mus.
Coll.
BROAD ST.
LONGWALL STREET
Coll.
RIGGS RD.
G.P.O.
City Hall
Ch.
QUEENS BR.

Sta.
GEORGE ST.
Colls.
HIGH STREET
A420
Infy.
YORK PL.
SOUTH ST.
TAY
DUNDEE ROAD

PARK END ST.
420
HYTHE BR.
AA
Town Hall
Colls.
Magdalen Bri.
GLASGOW ROAD
GLOVER STREET
Sta.
KING ST.
CANAL
VICTORIA ST.

OXPENS RD.
NEW RD.
G.P.O.
MERTON ST.
Colls.
A4158
A9
SCOTT ST.
MARSHALL PL.

County Hall
Cath.
ST. ALDATES
NEEDLESS ROAD
WILSON ST.
ABBOT ST.
RAC
RAC

THAMES STREET
SPEEDWELL ST.
River Isis
CRAIGIE
Golf Course
South Inch
SHORE ROAD
Golf Course

GRANDPONT
A4144
Christ Church Meadow
A4158
MONCRIEFFE
A90
EDINBURGH ROAD
GLENEARN ROAD
A85

Scale 0 ——— ½ Mile

Scale 0 ——— ½ Mile

OXFORD

One-way Streets →

Car Parks P

PERTH

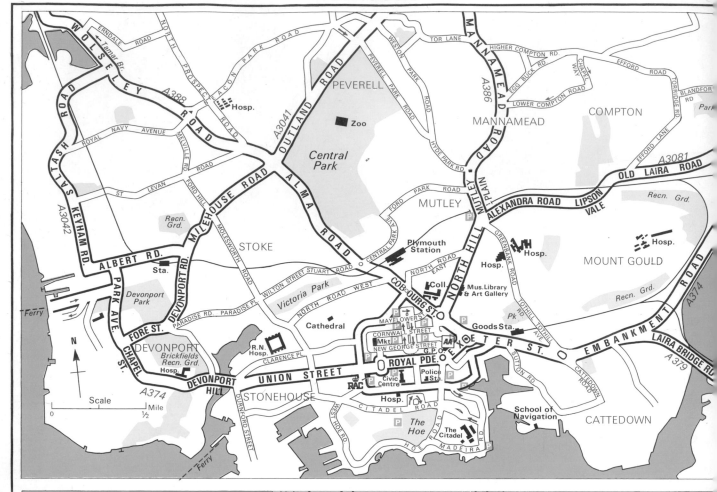

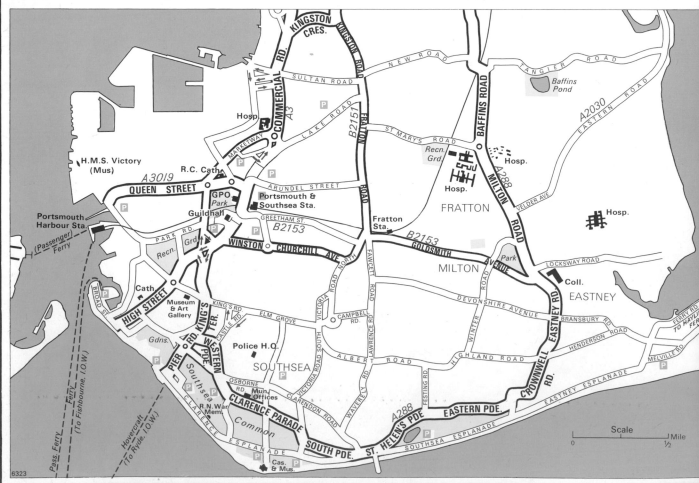

One-way Streets →

Car Parks P

© John Bartholomew & Son L

6323

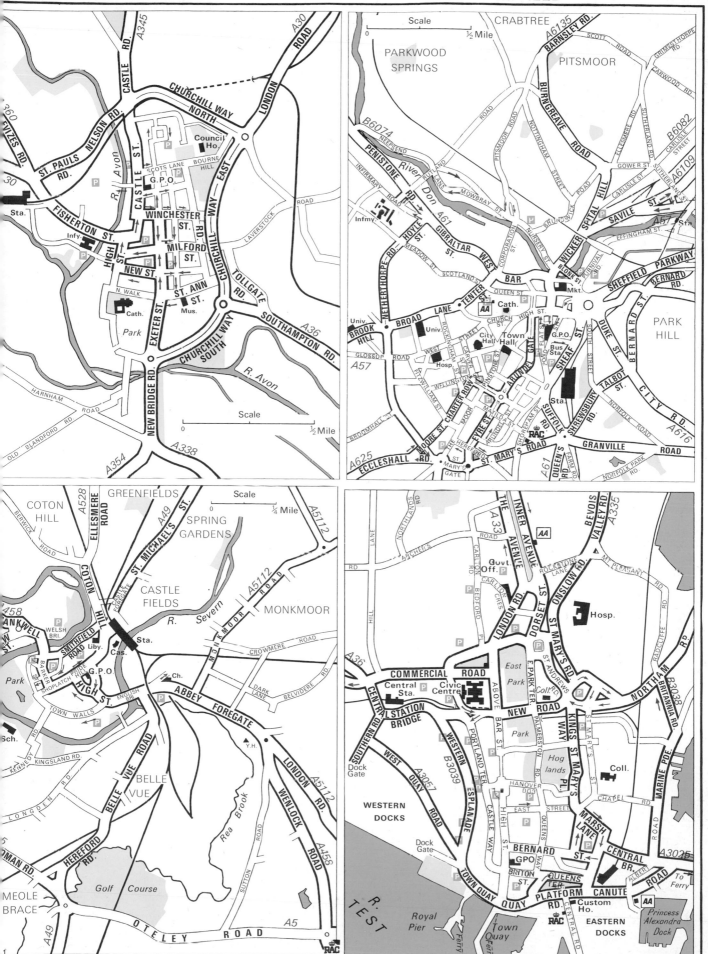

SALISBURY

CASTLE RD. A345
A360
FIZZES RD.
30
A430 LONDON ROAD
CHURCHILL WAY NORTH
Council Ho.
P
CASTLE ST.
NELSON RD.
ST. PAULS RD.
Scots Lane
BOURNE HILL
GPO
R. Avon
P
Sta.
FISHERTON ST.
WINCHESTER ST.
CHURCHILL WAY EAST
Infy.
H
MILFORD ST.
HIGH ST.
P
NEW ST.
P
N. WALK
ST. ANN ST.
EXETER ST.
Mus.
Cath.
Park
TOLLGATE RD.
CHURCHILL WAY SOUTH
SOUTHAMPTON RD. A36
LAVERSTOCK ROAD
R. Avon
NEW BRIDGE RD.
HARNHAM ROAD
OLD BLANDFORD RD.
A338
A354
Scale
0   1/2 Mile

SHEFFIELD

Scale
0   1/2 Mile
CRABTREE
PARKWOOD SPRINGS
PITSMOOR
BARNSLEY RD. A6135
SCOTT ROAD
GRIMESTHORPE RD.
B6074
NEEPSEND
BURNGREAVE ROAD
CARWOOD RD.
PENISTONE RD.
River Don 461
INFIRMARY ROAD
NOTTINGHAM STREET
PITSMOOR ROAD
ELLESMERE RD.
SUTHERLAND RD.
CARLISLE STREET
B6082
Infmy.
HOYLE ST.
MOWBRAY ST.
NURSERY STREET
GOWER ST.
SAVILE ST.
SUTHERLANDS A6109
GIBRALTAR ST.
CORPORATION ST.
MEADOW ST.
SCOTLAND ST.
WICKER
BRUNSWICK
SPITAL HILL
A57 Sta.
NETHERTHORPE RD.
BROAD LANE
BAR
BLONK ST.
ROCKINGHAM ST.
TENTER
QUEEN ST.
Mkt.
BRIDGE
EFFINGHAM ST.
BROOK HILL
AA
SHEFFIELD PARKWAY
Univ.
Univ
CHURCH ST.
HIGH ST.
GPO
BERNARD RD.
WEST ST.
City Hall
Town Hall
ARUNDEL GATE
SHEAF ST.
DUKE ST.
PARK HILL
GLOSSOP ROAD
A57
WELLINGTON ST.
Hosp.
CHARTER ROW
MOORE ST.
MOOR
PINSTONE ST.
MATILDA ST.
Bus Sta.
Sta.
BERNARD ST.
TALBOT ST.
CITY RD. A616
FITZWILLIAM ST.
BROOMHALL
CARVER
FURNIVAL ST.
SUFFOLK RD.
SHREWSBURY RD.
NORFOLK ROAD
RAC
B625
THE HEREFORD ST.
ST. MARY'S ROAD
GRANVILLE ROAD
ECCLESHALL RD.
A625
ST. MARY'S GATE
QUEEN'S RD.
FARM RD.
NORFOLK PARK RD.
A61

SHREWSBURY

COTON HILL
A528
GREENFIELDS
A49
ELLESMERE ROAD
ST. MICHAELS ST.
SPRING GARDENS
Scale
0   1/4 Mile
A5112
BERWICK RD.
COTON HILL
FORGATE
CASTLE FIELDS
A5112 ROAD
MONKMOOR
A458
BANKWELL ST.
WELSH BRI.
SMITHFIELD ROAD
Liby.
Cas.
Sta.
R. Severn
CROWMERE ROAD
MONKMOOR RD.
Park
BAKER
PRIDE HILL
ST.
GPO
SHOPLATCH
HIGH ST.
ENGLISH BRI.
ABBEY FOREGATE
DARK LANE
BELVIDERE RD.
TOWN WALLS
Sch.
P
Y.H.
KENNEDY RD.
KINGSLAND RD.
BELLE VUE ROAD
BELLE VUE
LONGDEN RD.
LONDON ROAD
WENLOCK ROAD A458
A5112
Rea Brook
MEOLE BRACE
HEREFORD RD.
ROMAN RD.
A49
Golf Course
OTELEY ROAD
A5
SUTTON ROAD
RAC

SOUTHAMPTON

LANE
ARCHERS RD.
THE AVENUE
INNER AVENUE
A33
BEVOIS VALLEY RD.
A335
NORTHLANDS ROAD
Govt. Off.
AA
ROCKSTONE LANE
MT. PLEASANT RD.
CARLTON RD.
CARLTON CRES.
LONDON RD.
DORSET ST.
ONSLOW RD.
ST. MARY'S RD.
Hosp.
BEDFORD
RADCLIFFE RD.
P
HILL
A36
COMMERCIAL ROAD
P
East Park
ST. ANDREWS RD.
NORTHAM RD. B3038
Central Sta.
Civic Centre
ABOVE BAR ST.
E. PARK TER.
Coll.
P
CENTRAL STATION BRIDGE
NEW ROAD
PALMERSTON RD.
KINGS WAY
ST. MARY'S RD.
BRITANNIA RD.
Park
ST. MARY'S PL.
SOUTHERN RD.
WESTERN
B3039
PORTLAND TER.
BAR ST.
Hog lands
Coll.
MARINE PDE.
Dock Gate
WEST QUAY
A3057
ESPLANADE
HANOVER BLDGS.
HIGH ST.
CHAPEL RD.
MARSH LANE
P
WESTERN DOCKS
CASTLE WAY
QUEENS
EAST STREET
BERNARD ST.
CENTRAL BR.
A3025
Dock Gate
GPO
BRITON ST.
QUEENS TER.
R. TEST
TOWN QUAY
PLATFORM RD.
CANUTE RD.
To Ferry
Royal Pier
Town Quay
Ferry
Custom Ho.
RAC
AA
EASTERN DOCKS
Princess Alexandra Dock

One-way Streets →   Car Parks P

© John Bartholomew & Son Ltd

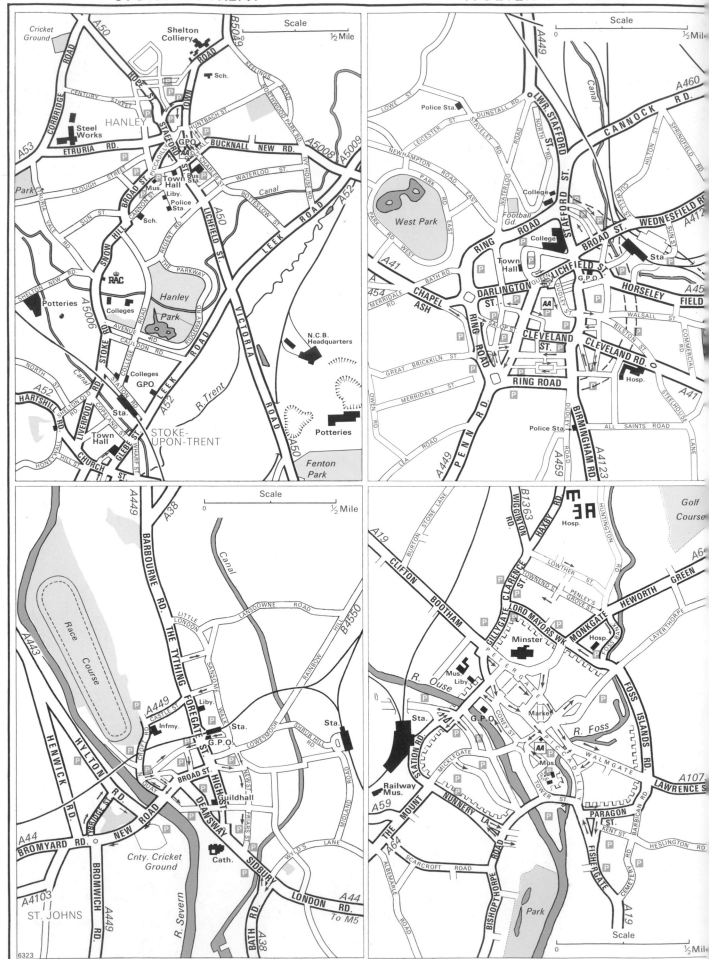

One-way Streets Car Parks P

© John Bartholomew & Son

—	Avon	—	Essex	Loth	Lothian	Tay	Tayside
Beds	Bedford	—	Fife	Mersey	Merseyside	Tyne/Wear	Tyne and Wear
Berks	Berkshire	Glos	Gloucester	Mid Glam	Mid Glamorgan	Warks	Warwick
—	Borders	Gramp	Grampian	Norf	Norfolk	W Glam	West Glamorgan
Bucks	Buckingham	Gtr Man	Greater Manchester	N Yorks	North Yorkshire	W Mid	West Midlands
Cambs	Cambridge	—	Gwent	N'thants	Northampton	W Sussex	West Sussex
Cent	Central	Gwyn	Gwynedd	N'land	Northumberland	W Yorks	West Yorkshire
Ches	Cheshire	Hants	Hampshire	Notts	Nottingham	W Isles	Western Isles
Clev	Cleveland	Heref/Worcs	Hereford and Worcester	—	Orkney	Wilts	Wiltshire
—	Clwyd	Herts	Hertford	Uxon	Oxford		
Corn	Cornwall	H'land	Highland	—	Powys		
Cumb	Cumbria	Humber	Humberside	—	Salop		
—	Derby	I of Man	Isle of Man	Shet	Shetland		
—	Devon	I of Wight	Isle of Wight	Som	Somerset		
—	Dorset	—	Kent	S Glam	South Glamorgan		
Dumf/Gal	Dumfries and Galloway	Lancs	Lancashire	S Yorks	South Yorkshire		
—	Durham	Leics	Leicester	Staffs	Stafford		
—	Dyfed	Lincs	Lincoln	S'clyde	Strathclyde		
E Sussex	East Sussex	—	London	Suff	Suffolk		
				—	Surrey		

B	Bay
Br	Bridge
C	Cape
co	county
div	division
E	East
Hd	Head
I	Island
L	Lake, Loch, Lough
mt	Mountain
N	North
pen	Peninsula
Pt	Point
R	River
reg	Region
Res	Reservoir
S	South
St	Saint
W	West
=	cross reference

Abbey St Bathans *Borders* 67 E3
Abbey Town *Cumb* 59 F6
Abbeystead *Lancs* 47 F3
Abbots Bromley *Staffs* 35 G2
Abbotsbury *Dorset* 8 D5
Abbotsford *Borders* 66 C5
Abbotsinch *S'clyde* 64 C2
Aber Falls *Gwyn* 40 D4
Aber Glaslyn, Pass of *Gwyn* 40 C6
Aberaeron *Dyfed* 24 A2
Aberavon *W Glam* 14 D3
Aberbeeg *Gwent* 15 G2
Abercarn *Gwent* 15 G2
Aberchirder *Gramp* 83 E2
Aberdare *Mid Glam* 15 E2
Aberdaron *Gwyn* 32 A2
Aberdeen *Gramp* 83 G6
Aberdour *Fife* 73 E5
Aberdyfi *Gwyn* 32 D5
Aberfeldy *Tay* 76 A6
Aberffraw *Gwyn* 40 A4
Aberford *W Yorks* 49 F4
Aberfoyle *Cent* 71 F4
Abergavenny *Gwent* 15 G1
Abergele *Clwyd* 41 F4
Abergiar *Dyfed* 24 B4
Abergwili *Dyfed* 24 A5
Aberlady *Loth* 66 C1
Aberlour *Gramp* 82 B3
Abernethy *Tay* 73 E3
Aberporth *Dyfed* 23 E1
Abersoch *Gwyn* 32 B2
Abersychan *Gwent* 15 G1
Aberthaw *S Glam* 15 F4
Abertillery *Gwent* 15 G1
Aberystwyth *Dyfed* 32 D6
Abingdon *Oxon* 17 H2
Abinger Common *Surrey* 11 G1
Abington *S'clyde* 65 F6
Aboyne *Gramp* 77 E2
Abram *Lancs* 42 B2
Accrington *Lancs* 47 H5
Acharacle *H'land* 68 C2
Achiltibuie *H'land* 85 A6
Achnasheen *H'land* 80 C2
Achray, Loch *Cent* 71 F4
Acherneed *H'land* 81 E2
Acle *Norf* 39 G4
Acocks Green *W Mid* 35 G5
Acton *London* 19 F3
Acton Turville *Glos* 16 C3
Adderbury *Oxon* 27 H4
Addlestone *Surrey* 19 E5
Adlington *Lancs* 42 B1
Adwick-le-Street *S Yorks* 44 A1
Ailort, Loch *H'land* 68 E2
Ailsa Craig, I *S'clyde* 56 A4
Aintree *Lancs* 42 A2
Aira Force, waterfall *Cumb* 52 D3
Aird of Sleat *Skye* 79 D7
Airdrie *S'clyde* 65 E2
Aireborough *W Yorks* 49 E4
Airth *Cent* 72 C5
Alcester *Warks* 27 E2
Alconbury *Cambs* 29 F1
Aldbourne *Wilts* 17 G4
Aldbrough *Humber* 51 F4
Aldeburgh *Suff* 31 H3
Alderley Edge *Ches* 42 D3
Aldermaston *Berks* 18 B5
Alderney, I *Channel Is* 3 G4
Aldershot *Hants* 18 C6
Alderton *Suff* 31 G4
Aldford *Ches* 42 A6
Aldridge-Brownhills *Staffs* 35 F4
Alexandra Park *London* 19 G3
Alexandria *S'clyde* 64 B1

Alfold *Surrey* 11 F2
Alford *Gramp* 83 E5
Alford *Lincs* 45 H4
Alfreton *Derby* 43 H5
Alfriston *E Sussex* 12 B6
All Stretton *Salop* 34 B4
Allendale Town *N'land* 60 D5
Allenheads *N'land* 53 G1
Allerston *N Yorks* 55 G6
Allerton *W Yorks* 48 D4
Alloa *Cent* 72 C5
Allonby *Cumb* 59 F6
Alloway *S'clyde* 56 D2
Allt na Caillich, waterfall *H'land* 84 E3
Alness *H'land* 81 F1
Alnmouth *N'land* 61 G1
Alnwick *N'land* 61 F1
Alrewas *Staffs* 35 G3
Alsager *Ches* 42 D5
Alston *Cumb* 53 F1
Altguish *H'land* 85 D8
Altnacealgach *H'land* 85 C6
Altnaharra *H'land* 84 F4
Alton *Hants* 10 D1
Altrincham *Gtr Man* 42 D3
Alva *Cent* 72 C5
Alvechurch *Heref/Worcs* 27 E1
Alwinton *N'land* 60 E1
Alyth *Tay* 76 C6
Amberley *W Sussex* 11 F4
Amble *N'land* 61 G2
Ambleside *Cumb* 52 D4
Amersham *Bucks* 18 D2
Amesbury *Wilts* 9 H1
Amlwch *Gwyn* 40 B2
Ammanford *Dyfed* 14 C1
Ampleforth *N Yorks* 50 B1
Ampthill *Beds* 29 E4
Amulree *Tay* 72 C1
Ancaster *Lincs* 44 D6
Ancrum *Borders* 66 D6
Andover *Hants* 10 B1
Angle *Dyfed* 22 B5
Angmering-on-Sea *W Sussex* 11 G5
Annan *Dumf/Gal* 59 G4
Annfield Plain *Durham* 61 F5
Anstruther *Fife* 73 H4
Apperley *Glos* 26 D4
Appersett *N Yorks* 53 G5
Appleby *Cumb* 53 F3
Applecross *H'land* 78 E4
Appledore *Devon* 6 C2
Appledore *Kent* 13 E4
Arborfield Cross *Berks* 18 C5
Arbroath *Tay* 73 H1
Archiestown *Gramp* 82 B3
Ardeonaig *Cent* 72 B2
Ardersier *H'land* 81 G2
Ardessie, waterfall *H'land* 85 A7
Ardgay *H'land* 85 B7
Ardgour *H'land* 74 B5
Ardleigh *Essex* 31 E3
Ardlui *S'clyde* 71 E3
Ardnamurchan *H'land* 68 B3
Ardrishaig *S'clyde* 70 A6
Ardrossan *S'clyde* 64 A4
Ardvasar *Skye* 79 E7
Arisaig *H'land* 68 E1
Arkaig, Loch *H'land* 74 B2
Arksey *S Yorks* 44 B1
Arlingham *Glos* 16 C1
Armadale *H'land* 86 A2
Armadale *Loth* 65 F2
Arnisdale *H'land* 79 F7
Arnold *Notts* 44 B5
Arnside *Cumb* 47 E1
Arran, I *S'clyde* 63 H5
Arrochar *S'clyde* 71 E4
Arthur's Seat, hill *Loth* 65 H2

Arundel *W Sussex* 11 F4
Ascog *Bute* 63 G2
Ascot *Berks* 18 D4
Ashbourne *Derby* 43 F6
Ashburton *Devon* 4 D5
Ashbury *Berks* 17 G3
Ashby-de-la-Zouch *Leics* 35 H3
Ashby Woulds *Leics* 35 H3
Ashdale Falls *Bute* 63 G5
Ashdown Forest *E Sussex* 12 B4
Ashford *Kent* 13 F3
Ashford *Surrey* 19 E4
Ashington *N'land* 61 G3
Ashkirk *Borders* 66 C6
Ashley *Staffs* 34 D1
Ashover *Derby* 43 H4
Ashstead *Surrey* 19 F5
Ashton-in-Makerfield *Gtr Man* 42 B2
Ashton-under-Lyne *Gtr Man* 43 E2
Askam *Lancs* 46 D1
Askrigg *N Yorks* 53 H5
Aspatria *Cumb* 52 B1
Aspull *Lancs* 42 B2
Assynt, Loch *H'land* 85 C6
Aston Cross *Glos* 26 D4
Atherstone *Warks* 35 H4
Atherton *Gtr Man* 42 C1
Attleborough *Norf* 39 E5
Attlebridge *Norf* 39 F3
Auchenblae *Gramp* 77 G3
Auchinleck *S'clyde* 64 C6
Auchmithie *Tay* 77 F6
Auchterarder *Tay* 72 C3
Auchterderran *Fife* 73 E5
Auchtermuchty *Fife* 73 E4
Audenshaw *Lancs* 42 D2
Audlem *Ches* 34 D1
Audley End *Essex* 30 A4
Auldearn *H'land* 81 H2
Aultbea *H'land* 78 F1
Aultguish, waterfall *H'land* 80 D6
Aust *Glos* 16 B3
Avebury *Wilts* 17 F4
Avening *Glos* 16 D2
Aveton Gifford *Devon* 4 D5
Aviemore *H'land* 81 H6
Avoch *H'land* 81 F2
Avonmouth *Avon* 16 A4
Avon, co 16 B4
Avonmouth *Avon* 16 A4
Awbridge *Hants* 10 A2
Awe, Loch *S'clyde* 70 B4
Axbridge *Som* 15 H5
Axe Edge *Derby-Staffs* 43 F5
Axminster *Devon* 5 H1
Aycliffe *Durham* 54 C3
Aylesbury *Bucks* 18 C1
Aylesford *Kent* 12 D1
Aylsham *Norf* 39 F2
Aymestrey *Heref/Worcs* 25 H1
Ayr *S'clyde* 56 D2
Aysgarth *N Yorks* 53 H5
Aysgarth Force, waterfall *N Yorks* 54 A5
Ayton *Borders* 67 F3
Babbacombe *Devon* 5 E4
Bacup *Lancs* 47 H5
Badachro *H'land* 78 E2
Badcall *H'land* 84 B3
Bagillt *Clwyd* 41 H5
Baginton *Warks* 35 H6
Bagshot *Surrey* 18 D5
Baildon *W Yorks* 48 D4
Baillieston *S'clyde* 64 D3
Bainbridge *N Yorks* 53 H5
Bakewell *Derby* 43 G4
Bala *Gwyn* 33 F1
Balallan *Lewis* 88 B2
Balby *S Yorks* 44 B1

Baldock *Herts* 29 F4
Baldwin *I of Man* 46 B5
Balerno *Loth* 65 H2
Balfron *Cent* 64 C1
Balintore *H'land* 81 G1
Ballachulish *H'land* 74 C5
Ballagan, Spout of, waterfall *Cent* 64 C1
Ballantrae *S'clyde* 57 B5
Ballasalla *I of Man* 46 B6
Ballater *Gramp* 76 D2
Ballaugh *I of Man* 46 B4
Ballindalloch Castle *Gramp* 82 B3
Ballinluig *Tay* 76 A5
Balloch *S'clyde* 64 B1
Balmacara *H'land* 79 F5
Balmaclellan *Dumf/Gal* 58 F3
Balmoral Castle *Gramp* 76 C2
Balquhidder *Cent* 71 F3
Balsham *Cambs* 30 B3
Bamber Bridge *Lancs* 47 F5
Bamburgh *N'land* 67 H5
Bampton *Devon* 7 G3
Bampton *Oxon* 17 G2
Banavie *H'land* 74 C4
Banbury *Oxon* 27 H3
Banchory *Gramp* 77 F2
Banff *Gramp* 83 E1
Bangor *Gwyn* 40 C4
Bankend *Dumf/Gal* 59 E4
Bankfoot *Tay* 72 D2
Bannockburn *Cent* 72 C5
Banstead *Surrey* 19 F5
Bardney *Lincs* 45 E4
Bardon Mill *N'land* 60 D5
Bardsea *Lancs* 46 D1
Bardsey, I *Gwyn* 32 A3
Barford *Warks* 27 G2
Barking *London* 19 H3
Barlborough *Derby* 44 A3
Barmouth *Gwyn* 32 D3
Barnard Castle *Durham* 54 A3
Barnby Moor *Notts* 44 B3
Barnet *London* 19 F2
Barnoldswick *Lancs* 47 H3
Barnsley *S Yorks* 43 G1
Barnstaple *Devon* 6 D2
Barr *S'clyde* 56 C4
Barra, I *W Isles* 88 D3
Barrhead *S'clyde* 64 C3
Barrhill *S'clyde* 57 C5
Barrow-in-Furness *Cumb* 46 D2
Barrowford *Lancs* 84 B4
Barry *Tay* 73 G1
Barry *S Glam* 15 F4
Barton-in-the-Clay *Beds* 29 E4
Barton-upon-Humber *Humber* 51 E5
Barton-under-Needwood *Staffs* 35 G3
Baschurch *Salop* 34 B2
Basildon *Essex* 20 D3
Basingstoke *Hants* 18 B6
Baslow *Derby* 43 G4
Bass Rock I. *I'nth* 73 H4
Bassenthwaite *Cumb* 52 C2
Bassingbourn *Cambs* 29 G3
Bath *Avon* 16 C5
Bathgate *Loth* 65 F2
Batley *W Yorks* 49 E5
Battle *E Sussex* 12 D5
Battlesbridge *Essex* 20 D2
Bawdeswell *Norf* 39 E3
Bawdsey *Suff* 31 G4
Bawtry *S Yorks* 44 B2
Baycliff *Lancs* 46 D1
Baythorn End *Essex* 30 C4
Beachley *Glos* 16 B3
Beachy Head *Sussex* 12 C6
Beaconsfield *Bucks* 18 D3
Beaminster *Dorset* 8 C4

Bearsden *S'clyde* 64 C2
Beattock *Dumf/Gal* 59 F2
Beaulieu *Hants* 10 B4
Beauly *H'land* 81 E3
Beaumaris *Gwyn* 40 C4
Bebington *Ches* 41 H3
Beccles *Suff* 39 H5
Beckenham *London* 19 G4
Beckingham *Notts* 44 C3
Beckington *Som* 16 C6
Bedale *N Yorks* 54 B5
Beddgelert *Gwyn* 40 C6
Bedford *Beds* 29 E3
Bedfordshire, co 29 E3
Bedgebury *Kent* 12 D3
Bedlington *N'land* 61 G3
Bedwas *Gwent* 15 G3
Bedwelty *Gwent* 15 G2
Bedworth *Warks* 36 A5
Beeley *Derby* 43 G4
Beer *Devon* 5 G2
Beeston *Notts* 36 B1
Beeston *W Yorks* 49 E5
Begelly *Dyfed* 22 D5
Beinn Dearg, mt *Tay* 75 H3
Beith *S'clyde* 64 B3
Belford *N'land* 67 G5
Bellingham *N'land* 60 D3
Belper *Derby* 43 H6
Belsay *N'land* 61 F4
Belvoir *Leics* 36 D1
Bembridge *I of Wight* 10 D5
Ben Alder, mt *H'land* 75 F4
Ben Cruachan, mt *S'clyde* 70 C2
Ben Hope, mt *H'land* 84 E3
Ben Lawers, mt *Tay* 71 G1
Ben Lomond, mt *Cent* 71 E4
Ben Macdui, mt *Gramp* 76 A2
Ben More, mt *Mull* 69 D5
Ben More, mt *Cent* 71 F3
Ben More Assynt, mt *H'land* 85 D5
Ben Nevis, mt *H'land* 74 C4
Ben Vorlich, mt *S'clyde* 71 E4
Ben Vorlich, mt *Tay* 72 A3
Ben Wyvis, mt *H'land* 85 E8
Benbecula, I *W Isles* 88 E2
Benfleet *Essex* 20 D3
Benington *Lincs* 37 H1
Benson *Oxon* 18 B2
Bentley *S Yorks* 44 B1
Bentworth *Hants* 10 D1
Berkeley *Glos* 16 B2
Berkhamsted *Herts* 19 E1
Berkshire, co 18 A4
Berneray, I *W Isles* 88 A4
Bernisdale *Skye* 78 B4
Berriedale *H'land* 87 D5
Berwick-upon-Tweed *N'land* 67 G3
Betchworth *Surrey* 19 F6
Bethersden *Kent* 13 E3
Bethesda *Gwyn* 40 C4
Bettws Bledrws *Dyfed* 24 B3
Bettws Gwerfil Goch *Clwyd* 41 F6
Bettyhill *H'land* 86 A2
Betws *Dyfed* 23 G4
Betws-y-Coed *Gwyn* 41 E5
Beverley *Humber* 51 E4
Bewdley *Heref/Worcs* 26 C1
Bexhill *E Sussex* 12 D6
Bexley *London* 19 H4
Bibury *Glos* 17 F1
Bicester *Oxon* 28 B5
Biddulph *Staffs* 42 D5
Bideford *Devon* 6 C3
Bidford *Warks* 27 F3
Bigbury-on-Sea *Devon* 4 C6
Biggar *S'clyde* 65 G5
Biggin Hill *Kent* 12 B1
Biggleswade *Beds* 29 F3

Bilbster H'land 86 F2
Billericay Essex 20 C2
Billesdon Leics 36 C4
Billing Northants 28 C2
Billingborough Lincs 37 F1
Billinge Lancs 42 B2
Billingham Clev 54 D3
Billinghay Lincs 45 F5
Billingshurst W Sussex 11 G3
Bilston W Mid 35 F4
Binbrook Lincs 45 F2
Bingham Notts 36 C1
Bingley W Yorks 48 D4
Bircham Newton Norf 38 C2
Birchgrove W Glam 14 C2
Birchington Kent 13 H1
Birdham E Sussex 11 E5
Birkenhead Mersey 41 H3
Birmingham W Mid 35 G5
Birnam Tay 72 D1
Birstall W Yorks 49 E5
Birtley Tyne/Wear 61 G5
Bishop Auckland Durham 54 B2
Bishopbriggs S'clyde 64 D2
Bishop's Castle Salop 34 A5
Bishop's Stortford Herts 29 H5
Bishop's Waltham Hants 10 C3
Bishopsteignton Devon 5 E3
Bishopston W Glam 14 B3
Bishopton S'clyde 64 B2
Black Isle, pen H'land 81 F2
Black Mt Dyfed 24 C6
Black Mts Powys 25 G5
Blackboys E Sussex 12 B4
Blackburn Lancs 47 G5
Blackburn Loth 65 F2
Blackbushe Hants 18 C5
Blackdown Hills Devon 8 A3
Blackford Tay 72 C4
Blackhill Durham 61 F6
Blackness Loth 65 G1
Blackpool Lancs 46 D4
Blackrod Lancs 42 B1
Blackshiels Loth 66 C3
Blackwater Hants 18 C5
Blackwater I of Wight 10 C6
Blackwaterfoot Arran 63 F5
Blackwood Gwent 15 G2
Blaenau Ffestiniog Gwyn 32 E1
Blaenavon Gwent 15 G1
Blaenffos Dyfed 22 D2
Blaina Gwent 15 G1
Blair Atholl Tay 75 H4
Blairgowrie Tay 73 E1
Blakeney Glos 16 B1
Blakeney Norf 39 E1
Blanchland N'land 61 E6
Blandford Forum Dorset 9 F4
Blaxton S Yorks 44 B1
Blaydon Tyne/Wear 61 F5
Blencathra, mt Cumb 52 C2
Blenheim Palace Oxon 27 H6
Bletchley Bucks 28 D4
Bletsoe Beds 29 E2
Bloxham Oxon 27 H4
Bloxwich W Mid 35 F4
Bluntisham Cambs 29 G1
Blyth N'land 61 G3
Blyth Notts 44 B3
Blythburgh Suff 31 H1
Boat of Garten H'land 81 H5
Bocking Essex 30 C5
Boddam Gramp 83 H3
Bodiam Castle E Sussex 12 D4
Bodinnick Corn 3 F3
Bodmin Corn 3 F2
Bodmin Moor Corn 3 F1
Bognor Regis W Sussex 11 F5
Boldon Durham 61 H5
Bollington Ches 43 E3
Bolsover Derby 43 H4
Bolton Gtr Man 42 C1
Bolton Bridge N Yorks 48 D3
Bolton-le-Sands Lancs 47 E2
Bonar Bridge H'land 85 F7
Bo'ness Cent 72 D6
Bonhill S'clyde 64 B1
Bonnyrigg Loth 66 B2
Bonvilston S Glam 15 F4
Booker Bucks 18 C2
Boosbeck Clev 55 E3
Bootle Cumb 52 B6
Bootle Mersey 41 H2
Borders, reg 66 A5
Boreham Street E Sussex 12 C5
Boroughbridge N Yorks 49 F2
Borrowdale Fells Cumb 52 C4
Borthwick Borders 66 B3
Boscastle Corn 6 A6
Boston Lincs 37 H1
Botesdale Suff 31 E1
Bothal N'land 61 G3
Bothwell S'clyde 64 D3
Botley Hants 10 C3
Bottesford Leics 36 D1
Bottisham Cambs 30 A2
Bourne Lincs 37 F3
Bourne End Bucks 18 D3
Bournemouth Dorset 9 G5
Bournville W Mid 35 F6
Bourton-on-the-Water Glos 27 F5
Bovey Tracy Devon 5 E3
Bovingdon Herts 19 E2
Bowdon Ches 42 C3
Bowes Durham 53 H3
Bowmore Islay 62 B2
Bowness Cumb 52 D5
Bracadale Skye 79 B5
Brackenthwaite Cumb 52 B3
Brackley Northants 28 B4
Bracknell Berks 18 D4
Braco Tay 72 C4
Bradford W Yorks 48 D4
Bradford-on-Avon Wilts 16 C5
Brading I of Wight 10 C6
Bradninch Devon 5 F1
Bradwell-on-Sea Essex 21 F1
Braemar Gramp 76 C2
Braintree Essex 30 C5
Braithwaite Cumb 52 C3
Bramber W Sussex 11 G4
Bramdean Hants 10 C2
Bramford Suff 31 E3
Bramhall Ches 42 D3
Bramham W Yorks 49 F4
Bramley W Yorks 49 E4
Brampton Cumb 60 B5
Brampton Cambs 29 F1
Bramshaw Hants 10 A3
Bramshott Hants 11 E2
Brancaster Norf 38 C1
Brancepeth Durham 54 B1
Branderburgh Gramp 82 B1
Brandesburton Humber 51 F3
Brandon Durham 54 B1
Brandon Suff 38 C5
Brandon Warks 36 A6
Brands Hatch Kent 20 C5
Bransons Cross Heref/Worcs 27 E1
Branston Staffs 35 H2
Brassington Derby 43 G5
Braunston Northants 28 B1
Braunton Devon 6 D2
Brechin Tay 77 F5
Breckland Norf 38 C5
Brecon Powys 25 F5
Brecon Beacons, mts Powys 25 E5
Bredbury Ches 42 E2
Breedon-on-the-Hill Leics 36 A2
Brendon Hills Som 7 G2
Brent London 19 F3
Brentford London 19 F4
Brentwood Essex 20 C2
Bride I of Man 46 C3
Bridge of Allan Cent 72 B5
Bridge of Cally Tay 76 C5
Bridge of Earn Tay 73 E3
Bridge of Lochay Tay 71 F2
Bridge of Orchy S'clyde 71 E1
Bridge of Weir S'clyde 64 B3
Bridgend Mid Glam 15 E3
Bridgend Islay 62 B2
Bridgend Tay 73 E2
Bridgnorth Salop 34 D5
Bridgtown Staffs 35 F3
Bridgwater Som 8 B1
Bridlington Humber 51 F2
Bridport Dorset 8 C5
Brierfield Lancs 47 H4
Brierley Hill W Mid 35 E5
Brigg Humber 45 E1
Brigham Cumb 52 B2
Brighouse W Yorks 48 D5
Brightlingsea Essex 31 E6
Brighton E Sussex 11 H4
Brig o' Turk Cent 71 F4
Brigstock Northants 37 E5
Brill Bucks 18 B1
Bristol Avon 16 B4
Briton Ferry W Glam 14 C2
Brixham Devon 5 E5
Brixworth Northants 28 C1
Broad Chalke Wilts 9 G2
Broad Clyst Devon 5 F1
Broad Haven Dyfed 22 B4
Broadford Skye 79 E6
Broads, The Norf 39 G3
Broadstairs Kent 13 H1
Broadstone Dorset 9 G4
Broadway Heref/Worcs 27 E4
Brockdish Suff 31 F1
Brockenhurst Hants 10 A4
Brockley Som 16 A5
Brodick Arran 63 G4
Bromborough Mersey 42 A3
Bromley London 19 G4
Bromsgrove Heref/Worcs 26 D1
Bromyard Heref/Worcs 26 B2
Brookman's Park Herts 19 F2
Broom, Loch H'land 85 B7
Broomfield Essex 20 D1
Brora H'land 87 C6
Brotton Clev 55 E3
Brough Cumb 53 G3
Brough Humber 50 D5
Broughton Hants 10 A2
Broughton-in-Furness Cumb 52 C6
Broughton Borders 65 G5
Broughton Poggs Oxon 17 F1
Broughty Ferry Tay 73 G2
Brownhills W Mid 35 F4
Brownsea I Dorset 9 G5
Broxbourne Herts 19 G1
Broxburn Loth 65 G2
Bruar, Falls of Tay 75 H4
Bruton Som 8 D1
Brynamman Dyfed 14 C1
Bryncir Gwyn 32 C1
Brynmawr Gwent 15 G1
Bubwith Humber 50 C4
Buchlyvie Cent 72 A5
Buckden Cambs 29 F1
Buckfastleigh Devon 4 D4
Buckhaven Fife 73 F4
Buckie Gramp 82 C1
Buckingham Bucks 28 C4
Buckinghamshire co 28 B5
Buckley Clwyd 41 H5
Bucknell Salop 25 H1
Buckspool Dyfed 22 G6
Buddon Ness Tay 73 H2
Bude Corn 6 B4
Budleigh Salterton Devon 5 F3
Bugle Corn 3 E3
Builth Wells Powys 25 E3
Bulford Wilts 17 F6
Bulwell Notts 44 A6
Bunessan Mull 69 C6
Bungay Suff 39 G5
Buntingford Herts 29 G5
Burbage Wilts 17 F5
Bures Essex/Suff 30 D4
Burford Oxon 17 F1
Burgess Hill W Sussex 12 A4
Burgh-by-Sands Cumb 59 G5
Burgh-le-Marsh Lincs 45 H4
Burghead Gramp 82 A1
Burghley House Cambs 37 F4
Burley Hants 9 H4
Burley in Wharfedale W Yorks 48 D3
Burlton Salop 34 B2
Burnaston Derby 35 H1
Burnham Bucks 18 D3
Burnham Market Norf 38 C1
Burnham-on-Crouch Essex 21 E2
Burnham-on-Sea Som 15 G6
Burnley Lancs 47 H4
Burnt Stub Surrey 19 F5
Burntisland Fife 73 F5
Burry Port Dyfed 14 A2
Burscough Bridge Lancs 42 A1
Bursledon Hants 10 B4
Burslem Staffs 42 D6
Burton Bradstock Dorset 8 C5
Burton-in-Kendal Cumb 47 F1
Burton-in-Lonsdale N Yorks 47 G1
Burton Latimer Northants 28 D1
Burton upon Trent Staffs 35 H2
Burwash Common E Sussex 12 C4
Bury Gtr Man 42 D1
Bury St Edmunds Suff 30 D2
Busby S'clyde 64 C3
Bushey Herts 19 F2
Bute, Isle of S'clyde 63 G1
Bute, Kyles of 63 G1
Buttermere Cumb 52 B3
Buxton Derby 43 F4
Byfield Northants 28 A2
Byfleet Surrey 19 E5
Bylchau Clwyd 41 F5
Byshottles Durham 54 B1
Cader Idris, mt Gwyn 33 E3
Cadishead Lancs 42 C2
Cadnam Hants 10 A3
Cadwell Park Lincs 45 G3
Caenby Corner Lincs 44 D2
Caergwrle Clwyd 41 H5
Caerleon Gwent 15 H2
Caernarfon Gwyn 40 B5
Caerphilly Mid Glam 15 F3
Caersws Powys 33 G5
Caerwys Clwyd 41 G4
Cairngorm Mts 82 A6
Cairntoul, mt Gramp 76 A2
Caister-on-Sea Norf 39 H4
Caistor Lincs 45 E1
Caldbeck Cumb 52 C1
Caldicot Gwent 16 A3
Caldron Snout, waterfall Cumb/Durham 53 G2
Calgary Mull 68 B4
Callander Cent 72 A4
Callanish Lewis 88 B2
Callington Corn 3 H2
Calne Wilts 17 E4
Calstock Corn 3 H2
Calverton Notts 44 B6
Camberley Surrey 18 D5
Camborne Corn 2 C4
Cambridge Cambs 29 H2
Cambridge, co 29 F2
Cambuslang S'clyde 64 D3
Camden London 19 G3
Campbeltown S'clyde 63 E5
Campsie Fells Cent 64 C1
Candlesby Lincs 45 H4
Canna, I H'land 79 A7
Cannich H'land 80 D4
Cannock Staffs 35 F3
Cannock Chase Staffs 35 F3
Canonbie Dumf/Gal 60 A4
Canterbury Kent 13 G2
Canvey I Essex 20 D3
Caol H'land 74 C4
Capel Surrey 11 G1
Capel-Bangor Dyfed 24 C1
Capel Curig Gwyn 40 D5
Capel Gwynfe Dyfed 23 H3
Capesthorne Ches 42 D4
Cardiff S Glam 15 G4
Cardigan Dyfed 22 D2
Cardington Beds 29 E3
Cardross S'clyde 64 B2
Carfraemill Borders 66 C3
Carisbrooke I of Wight 10 B5
Carlisle Cumb 60 A5
Carlops Borders 65 G3
Carloway Lewis 88 B2
Carlton Notts 36 C1
Carluke S'clyde 65 E4
Carmarthen Dyfed 23 F4
Carnaby Humber 51 F2
Carnforth Lancs 47 F1
Carnoustie Tay 73 H2
Carnwath S'clyde 65 F4
Carrbridge H'land 81 H5
Carrington Mersey 42 C2
Carrs, The N Yorks 51 D1
Carsphairn Dumf/Gal 58 B2
Carstairs S'clyde 65 F4
Carter Bar Borders/N'land 60 C1
Cartmel Cumb 47 E1
Castle Acre Norf 38 C3
Castle Bromwich W Mid 35 G5
Castle Carrock Cumb 60 B5
Castle Cary Som 8 D2
Castle Combe Wilts 16 D4
Castle Donington Leics 36 A2
Castle Douglas Dumf/Gal 58 D5
Castle Hedingham Essex 30 C4
Castle Howard N Yorks 50 C2
Castlebay Barra 88 D4
Castleford W Yorks 49 F5
Castlemartin Pemb 22 B5
Castleton Derby 43 F3
Castleton Lancs 42 D1
Castletown H'land 86 E1
Castletown I of Man 46 A6
Caterham Surrey 12 A2
Catrine S'clyde 64 C6
Catterick N Yorks 54 B5
Catterick Force, waterfall N Yorks 47 H2
Caversham Berks 18 C4
Cawdor H'land 81 G3
Cawood N Yorks 49 G4
Cellardyke Fife 73 H4
Cemaes Bay Gwyn 40 B2
Cemmaes Road Powys 33 E4
Cenarth Falls Dyfed 23 E2
Central, reg 72 A4
Ceres Fife 73 G3
Cerne Abbas Dorset 8 D4
Cerrigydrudion Clwyd 41 F6
Chacewater Corn 2 C4
Chadderton Gtr Man 42 D1
Chagford Devon 4 D2
Chalfont St Giles Bucks 18 D2
Chalfont St Peter Bucks 19 E3
Chalford Glos 16 D2
Chalk Kent 20 C4
Channel Is 3 G5
Chapel-en-le-Frith Derby 43 F3
Chapel Hill Gwent 16 A2
Chapel St. Leonards Lincs 45 H4
Chard Som 8 B3
Charing Kent 13 E2
Charlbury Oxon 27 G5
Charlestown Corn 3 E3
Charlton Kings Glos 26 D5
Charnwood Forest Leics 36 B3
Charterhouse Som 16 A5
Chartwell Kent 12 B2
Chatburn Lancs 48 A4
Chatham Kent 20 D5
Chatsworth House Derby 43 G4
Chatteris Cambs 37 H5
Chatton N'land 67 G5
Cheadle Ches 42 D3
Cheadle Staffs 43 E6
Cheddar Som 16 A6
Cheddar Gorge Som 16 A5
Cheddleton Staffs 43 E5
Chedgrave Norf 39 G5
Chedworth Glos 27 E6
Chelford Ches 42 D4
Chelmsford Essex 20 D1
Cheltenham Glos 26 D5
Chepstow Gwent 16 A2
Cheriton Kent 13 G3
Chertsey Surrey 19 E5
Chesham Bucks 18 D2
Cheshire, co 42 B4
Cheshunt Herts 19 G2
Chesil Bank Dorset 8 D6
Chessington London 19 F4
Chester Ches 42 A5
Chesterfield Derby 43 H4
Chester-le-Street Durham 61 G6
Chesters Fort N'land 60 D4
Chetwynd Salop 34 D3
Cheviot Hills 67 E6
Chew Stoke Avon 16 B5
Chichester W Sussex 11 E4
Chiddingfold Surrey 11 F2
Chigwell Essex 19 H2
Chilbolton Hants 10 B1
Childwall Lancs 42 A3
Chilham Kent 13 F2
Chiltern Hills 18 B3
Chiltern Hundreds Bucks 18 D2
Chingford London 20 A2
Chinnor Oxon 18 C2
Chippenham Wilts 16 D4
Chipping Campden Glos 27 F4
Chipping Norton Oxon 27 G5
Chipping Ongar Essex 20 C2
Chipping Sodbury Avon 16 C3
Chirnside Borders 67 F3
Chisledon Wilts 17 F3
Chislehurst London 20 B4
Chiswick London 19 F4
Chobham Surrey 18 D5
Chollerton N'land 61 E4
Cholstrey Heref/Worcs 25 H2
Chorley Lancs 47 F6
Chorleywood Herts 19 E2
Christchurch Dorset 9 H4
Christchurch Gwent 15 H3
Christian Malford Wilts 16 D3
Chudleigh Devon 5 E3
Chulmleigh Devon 7 E4
Church Lancs 47 G5
Church Cobham Surrey 19 E5
Church Fenton N Yorks 49 G4
Church Stretton Salop 34 B5
Churchdown Glos 26 D5
Churston Ferrers Devon 5 E5
Cinderford Glos 16 B1
Cirencester Glos 17 E2
Clackmannan Cent 72 C5
Clacton-on-Sea Essex 31 F6
Claerwen Res Powys 24 D2
Clanfield Oxon 17 G2
Clare Suff 30 C3
Clashmore H'land 87 A7
Clashnessie H'land 84 B4
Claughton Lancs 47 F2
Claverley Staffs 35 E5
Clay Cross Derby 43 H4
Claydon Suff 31 F3
Clayton W Yorks 48 D5
Clayton-le-Moors Lancs 47 G5
Cleator Cumb 52 A4
Cleckheaton W Yorks 48 D5
Cleethorpes Humber 45 G1
Cleobury Mortimer Salop 26 B1
Clevedon Avon 15 H4
Cleveland, co 54 D3
Cleveleys Lancs 46 D4
Cley Norf 39 E1
Clifford Heref/Worcs 25 G3
Clifton Avon 16 B4
Clifton Lancs 42 D1
Clifton upon Dunsmore Warks 36 B6
Clitheroe Lancs 47 G4
Clophill Beds 29 E4
Closeburn Dumf/Gal 58 D2
Cloughton N Yorks 55 H5
Clova Tay 76 D4
Clovelly Devon 6 C3
Clovenfords Borders 66 C5
Clowne Derby 44 A3
Cluanie Bridge H'land 80 B6
Cluanie, Loch H'land 80 B6
Clun Salop 34 A6
Clun Forest Salop 34 A5
Clwyd, co 41 F5
Clydach W Glam 14 C2
Clyde, R S'clyde 64 B2
Clyde, Falls of S'clyde 65 F4
Clydebank S'clyde 64 C2
Coalville Leics 36 A3
Coatbridge S'clyde 64 D2
Cock Bridge Gramp 82 B6
Cockburnspath Borders 67 E2
Cockenzie Loth 66 B1
Cockerham Lancs 47 E3
Cockermouth Cumb 52 B2
Coggeshall Essex 30 C5
Colchester Essex 31 E5
Cold Ashton Glos 16 C4
Cold Norton Essex 21 E2
Coldingham Borders 67 F2
Coldstream Borders 67 E4
Coleford Glos 16 B1
Coleshill Warks 35 G5
Colinsburgh Fife 73 G4
Colintraive S'clyde 63 G1
Coll, I S'clyde 68 A3
Collingham Notts 44 C5
Colmonell S'clyde 57 B5
Colne Lancs 47 H4
Colne Valley W Yorks 48 D6
Colonsay, I S'clyde 69 C7
Coltishall Norf 39 G3
Colwinston S Glam 15 E4
Colwyn Bay Clwyd 41 E3
Colyton Devon 5 G2
Combe Martin Devon 6 D1
Comrie Tay 72 B3

Congleton Ches 42 D5
Congresbury Avon 16 A5
Coningsby Lincs 45 F5
Conisbrough S Yorks 44 A2
Coniston Cumb 52 C5
Connah's Quay Clwyd 41 H4
Connel S'clyde 70 B2
Conon Bridge H'land 81 E2
Consett Durham 61 F6
Constantine Corn 2 C5
Contin H'land 81 E2
Conwy Gwyn 40 D4
Conwil Elvet Dyfed 23 E3
Cookham Berks 18 D3
Coombe Bissett Wilts 9 H2
Corbridge N'land 61 E5
Corby Northants 36 D5
Corby Glen Lincs 37 E2
Corfe Castle Dorset 9 G6
Cornhill-on-Tweed N'land 67 F4
Cornwall, co 3 E2
Cornwood Devon 4 C4
Corpach H'land 74 C4
Corran H'land 74 B5
Corrie Arran 63 G3
Corsham Wilts 16 D4
Corstopitum N'land 61 E5
Corwen Clwyd 33 G1
Coryton Essex 20 D3
Coseley W Mid 35 F5
Cosham Hants 10 D4
Cotswold Hills Glos 16 D1
Cottenham Cambs 29 H1
Cottesmore Leics 37 E3
Cottingham Humber 51 E5
Coulter S'clyde 65 G5
Coupar-Angus Tay 73 E1
Cove S'clyde 70 D6
Coventry W Mid 35 H6
Coverack Corn 2 D6
Cowbridge S Glam 15 E4
Cowdenbeath Fife 73 E5
Cowes I of Wight 10 B5
Cowfold W Sussex 11 H3
Cowley Oxon 18 A1
Cradley Heref/Worc 35 F5
Craggie H'land 81 G3
Craigellachie Gramp 82 C3
Craighouse Jura 62 C2
Craignure Mull 68 E4
Crail Fife 73 H4
Cramlington N'land 61 G4
Cranborne Dorset 9 G3
Cranbrook Kent 12 D3
Cranfield Beds 28 D3
Cranleigh Surrey 11 F1
Cranwell Lincs 45 E6
Crarae S'clyde 70 C5
Crathie Church Gramp 76 C2
Craven Arms Salop 34 B6
Crawford S'clyde 65 F6
Crawley W Sussex 11 H2
Credenhill Herf/Worc 26 A3
Crediton Devon 4 D1
Creetown Dumf/Gal 57 E6
Cressage Salop 34 C4
Crewe Ches 42 C5
Crewkerne Som 8 C3
Crianlarich Cent 71 E3
Criccieth Gwyn 32 C1
Crickhowell Powys 25 G6
Cricklade Wilts 17 E2
Crieff Tay 72 C3
Crimond Gramp 83 H2
Croft N Yorks 54 C4
Cromarty H'land 81 G1
Cromdale H'land 82 A4
Cromer Norf 39 F1
Cromford Derby 43 G5
Crompton Lancs 43 E1
Crook Durham 54 B2
Crook of Alves Gramp 82 A1
Crook of Devon Tay 72 D4
Crooklands Cumb 53 E6
Crosby I of Man 46 B5
Crosby Mersey 41 H2
Cross Hands Dyfed 24 B6
Cross Inn Dyfed 24 A3
Crossford S'clyde 65 E4
Crossgates Fife 73 E5
Crossgates Powys 25 F2
Crosshill S'clyde 56 D3
Crosshills N Yorks 48 C4
Cross-in-Hand E Sussex 12 B4
Crossway Green Heref/Worcs 26 D1
Croston Lancs 47 F6
Crowborough E Sussex 12 B4
Crowland Lincs 37 G3
Crowle Humber 44 C1
Crown Hill Devon 4 B5
Crowthorne Berks 18 C5
Croxley Green Herts 19 E2
Croyde Devon 6 C2
Croydon London 19 G5
Cruachan, Falls of S'clyde 70 B4
Cruden Bay Gramp 83 H3
Crudgington Salop 34 C4
Crummock Water Cumb 52 B3
Cuckfield W Sussex 11 H3
Cuckney Notts 44 A4
Cudworth S Yorks 43 H1
Cuillin Hills Skye 79 C6
Culbin Sandhills Gramp 81 H1
Cullen Gramp 82 D1
Cullingworth W Yorks 48 D4
Culloden Moor H'land 81 G3
Cullompton Devon 7 G4
Culmstock Devon 7 H4
Culross Fife 72 D5
Cults Gramp 77 H1
Culworth Northants 28 B3
Culzean Castle S'clyde 63 H6
Cumbernauld S'clyde 65 E2
Cumbria, co 52 C4
Cumnock S'clyde 56 F2
Cupar Fife 73 F3
Curragh, The I of Man 46 B4
Cwmamman Dyfed 15 E2
Cwmbran Gwent 15 G2
Dagenham London 19 H3
Dalbeattie Dumf/Gal 58 D5
Dalcross H'land 81 G3
Dalegarth Force = Stanley Force
Dalkeith Loth 66 B2
Dallas Gramp 82 A2
Dalmally S'clyde 70 D2
Dalmellington S'clyde 56 E3
Dalmeny Loth 65 G1
Dalnaspidal Tay 75 G4
Dalry S'clyde 64 A4
Dalry Dumf/Gal 58 C3
Dalrymple S'clyde 56 D3
Dalston Cumb 59 H6
Dalton Dumf/Gal 59 F4
Dalton in Furness Cumb 46 D1
Dalwhinnie H'land 75 F3
Darfield S Yorks 43 H1
Darlaston W Mid 35 F4
Darlington Durham 54 C3
Dartford Kent 19 H4
Dartmoor Devon 4 C3
Dartmouth Devon 5 E5
Darton S Yorks 43 G1
Darvel S'clyde 64 C5
Darwen Lancs 47 G5
Datchet Berks 19 E4
Daventry Northants 28 B2
Dawley Salop 34 D4
Dawlish Devon 5 F3
Deal Kent 13 H2
Dean, Forest of Glos 16 B1
Dearham Cumb 52 B2
Dearne S Yorks 43 H1
Debden Essex 30 A4
Debenham Suff 31 F2
Deddington Oxon 27 H4
Dee, R Gramp 77 G2
Dee, Linn of, waterfall Gramp 76 B2
Deepcar S Yorks 43 G2
Deeping St James Lincs 37 F3
Delamere Forest Ches 42 B4
Denbigh Clwyd 41 F4
Denby Dale W Yorks 43 G1
Denham Bucks 19 E3
Denholme W Yorks 48 D4
Dennington Suff 31 G2
Denny Cent 65 E1
Denton Gtr Man 43 E2
Deptford Wilts 9 G1
Derby Derby 36 A1
Derbyshire, co 43 G4
Dervaig Mull 68 C4
Derwen Clwyd 41 G6
Desborough Northants 36 D5
Devauden Gwent 16 A2
Devil's Beef Tub Dumf/Gal 59 F1
Devil's Bridge Dyfed 33 E6
Devil's Dyke E Sussex 11 H4
Devil's Elbow Derby 43 E2
Devil's Elbow Tay 76 C3
Devizes Wilts 17 E5
Devon, co 4 C1
Devon, Falls of Tay 72 D4
Devonport Devon 3 H3
Dewsbury W Yorks 49 E5
Didcot Oxon 18 A3
Didmarton Glos 16 C3
Digby Lincs 45 E5
Dinas Mawddwy Gwyn 33 F3
Dingwall H'land 81 E2
Dirleton Loth 66 C1
Dishforth N Yorks 49 F1
Diss Norf 31 F1
Dittisham Devon 5 E5
Ditton Priors Salop 34 C5
Doddington Cambs 37 H5
Doddington N'land 67 G5
Dodworth S Yorks 43 G1
Dolgarrog Gwyn 41 E4
Dolgarrog Cascade Gwyn 40 D4
Dolgellau Gwyn 33 E3
Dollar Cent 72 D4
Dolphinton S'clyde 65 G4
Dolwyddaelan Gwyn 40 D6
Doncaster S Yorks 44 B1
Donington Lincs 37 G1
Dorchester Dorset 8 D5
Dores H'land 81 F4
Dorking Surrey 19 F6
Dornie H'land 80 A5
Dornoch H'land 87 B7
Dorset, co 8 D4
Douglas I of Man 46 B5
Douglas S'clyde 65 E5
Doune Cent 72 B4
Dounreay H'land 86 C2
Dove Dale Derby/Staffs 43 F5
Dover Kent 13 H3
Dovercourt Essex 31 F5
Dowally Tay 76 B6
Dowlais Mid Glam 15 F1
Downham Market Norf 38 B4
Downton Hants 10 A5
Downton Wilts 9 H2
Downton Devon 4 B2
Dreghorn S'clyde 64 B5
Drigg Cumb 52 B5
Droitwich Heref/Worcs 26 D2
Dronfield Derby 43 H3
Droylsden Gtr Man 42 D2
Drumbeg H'land 84 B4
Drumelzier Borders 65 G5
Drumlithie Gramp 77 G3
Drummore Dumf/Gal 57 B8
Drumnadrochit H'land 81 E4
Drumochter, Pass of H'land 75 G3
Dryburgh Abbey Borders 66 D5
Drymen Cent 64 C1
Drynoch Skye 79 C5
Ducklington Oxon 17 G1
Duddington Northants 37 E4
Dudley W Mid 35 F5
Duffield Derby 36 A1
Dufftown Gramp 82 C3
Duich, Loch H'land 80 A5
Dukeries, The Notts 44 A3
Dukestown Gwent 15 F1
Dukinfield Gtr Man 43 E2
Dulnain Bridge Gramp 81 H4
Dumbarton S'clyde 64 B2
Dumfries Dumf/Gal 59 E4
Dumfries and Galloway, reg 58 C4
Dunbar Loth 66 D1
Dunbeath H'land 86 E4
Dunblane Cent 72 B4
Duncansby H'land 86 F1
Dunchurch Warks 27 H1
Dundee Tay 73 F2
Dundonald S'clyde 64 B5
Dundonnell H'land 85 B7
Dundrennan Dumf/Gal 58 D6
Dunfermline Fife 73 E5
Dungeness Kent 13 F5
Dunipace Cent 65 E1
Dunkeld Tay 72 D1
Dunlop S'clyde 64 B4
Dunnet H'land 86 E1
Dunning Tay 72 D3
Dunottar Castle Gramp 77 H3
Dunoon S'clyde 63 H1
Duns Borders 67 E3
Dunscore Dumf/Gal 58 D3
Dunsfold Surrey 11 F2
Dunsop Bridge Lancs 47 G3
Dunstable Beds 29 E5
Dunstaffnage Castle S'clyde 70 B2
Dunster Som 7 G1
Dunsyre S'clyde 65 G4
Duntulm Skye 78 C2
Dunvegan Skye 78 A4
Durham Durham 54 C1
Durham, co 54 A1
Durness H'land 84 D2
Durnford Wilts 9 H1
Dursley Glos 16 C2
Durston Som 8 B2
Duthil H'land 81 H5
Duxford Cambs 29 H3
Dyce Gramp 83 G5
Dyfed, co 24 B3
Dyffryn Gwyn 32 D2
Dymchurch Kent 13 F4
Dymock Heref/Worcs 26 C4
Dysart Fife 73 F5
Eaglesfield Dumf/Gal 59 G4
Eaglesham S'clyde 64 C4
Ealing London 19 F3
Earby Lancs 48 B3
Eardisley Heref/Worcs 25 G3
Earith Cambs 29 G1
Earl Shilton Leics 36 A4
Earls Colne Essex 30 C5
Earlsferry Fife 73 G4
Earlston Borders 66 D4
Earn, Loch Tay 72 A3
Earsdon Tyne/Wear 61 G4
Eas-Coul-Aulin, waterfall H'land 84 C4
Easebourne W Sussex 11 E3
Easington Durham 54 C1
Easingwold N Yorks 49 G2
East Cowes I of Wight 10 C5
East Dereham Norf 38 D3
East Grinstead W Sussex 12 A3
East Ham London 20 B3
East Harling Norf 39 E6
East Kilbride S'clyde 64 D3
East Linton Loth 66 D1
East Markham Notts 44 C4
East Retford Notts 44 B3
East Sussex, co 12 B4
East Wemyss Fife 73 F5
Eastbourne E Sussex 12 C6
Eastington Glos 16 C1
Eastleigh Hants 10 B3
Eastry Kent 13 H2
Eastwood Notts 44 A6
Eaton Norf 39 F4
Eaton Socon Cambs 29 F2
Ebbw Vale Gwent 15 F1
Ebchester Durham 61 F5
Ecclefechan Dumf/Gal 59 G4
Eccles Border 67 E4
Eccles Gtr Man 42 C2
Ecclesfield S Yorks 43 H2
Eccleshall Staffs 35 E2
Echt Gramp 77 G1
Eckford Borders 66 D5
Eckington Derby 43 H3
Eddleston Borders 66 A4
Edenbridge Kent 12 B2
Edgbaston W Mid 35 F5
Edgware London 19 F2
Edinburgh Loth 65 H2
Edingham N'land 61 F1
Edmondbyers Durham 61 E6
Edmonton London 19 G2
Edzell Tay 77 F4
Egham Surrey 19 E4
Eglingham N'land 67 G6
Egmanton Notts 44 C4
Egremont Cumb 52 A4
Egton N Yorks 55 F4
Eil, Loch H'land 74 B4
Eilean, Loch an H'land 81 H6
Elderslie S'clyde 64 C3
Elgin Gramp 82 B1
Elgol Skye 79 D7
Elie Fife 73 G4
Elland W Yorks 48 D6
Ellesmere Salop 34 B1
Ellesmere Port Ches 42 A4
Ellington N'land 61 G3
Ellon Gramp 83 G4
Ellsley Berks 17 H3
Elmdon W Mid 35 G5
Elphin H'land 85 C6
Elrick Gramp 83 F6
Elsdon N'land 61 E2
Elstree Herts 19 F2
Eltham London 19 H4
Elvington N Yorks 50 C3
Ely Cambs 38 A6
Embleton N'land 67 H6
Empingham Leics 37 E4
Emsworth Hants 10 D4
Enard B H'land 85 A5
Enfield London 20 A2
Ennerdale Water Cumb 52 B3
Epping Essex 20 B2
Epping Forest Essex 20 B2
Epsom Surrey 19 F5
Epworth Humber 44 C1
Erdington W Mid 35 G5
Eriboll, Loch H'land 84 D2
Ericht, Loch H'land 75 F4
Eriskay, I W Isles 88 E3
Erith London 19 H4
Ermine Street Lincs 44 D3
Errol Tay 73 F2
Erskine S'clyde 64 C2
Esher Surrey 19 F5
Eskdale Cumb 52 C4
Essex, co 20 C1
Eston Clev 53 D3
Etive, Loch S'clyde 70 C2
Eton Berks 18 D4
Ettington Warks 27 G3
Ettrick Church Borders 66 A6
Euston Suff 38 D6
Evanton H'land 81 F1
Evesham Heref/Worcs 27 E3
Evesham, Vale of Heref/Worcs 27 E3
Ewe, Loch H'land 78 F1
Ewell Surrey 19 F5
Exeter Devon 5 E2
Exmoor 7 E1
Exmouth Devon 5 F3
Eyam Derby 43 G3
Eye Suff 31 F1
Eye, pen H'land 88 C2
Eyemouth Borders 67 F2
Eynort, Loch S Uist 88 E3
Eynsford Kent 20 B5
Failsworth Lancs 42 D1
Fair Oak Hants 10 C3
Faitford Glos 17 F2
Fairlie S'clyde 63 H2
Fairwood Common W Glam 14 B3
Fakenham Norf 38 D2
Falkirk Cent 72 C6
Falkland Fife 73 F4
Falmouth Corn 2 D5
Falstone N'land 60 C3
Fannich, Loch H'land 80 C2
Fareham Hants 10 C4
Faringdon Oxon 17 G2
Farnborough Hants 18 D6
Farne Is N'land 67 H4
Farnham Surrey 18 C6
Farningham Kent 20 C5
Farnsfield Notts 44 B5
Farnworth Gtr Man 42 C1
Farrington Gurney Som 16 B5
Farsley W Yorks 49 E4
Faversham Kent 13 F1
Fearn H'land 87 B8
Featherstone W Yorks 49 F5
Felixstowe Suff 31 G4
Felling Tyne/Wear 61 G5
Feltham London 19 E4
Felton N'land 61 F2
Feltwell Norf 38 B5
Fender, Falls of Tay 75 H4
Fenny Stratford Bucks 28 D4
Fenwick S'clyde 64 C4
Fern Down Dorset 9 G4
Fernhurst W Sussex 11 E2
Ferrybridge W Yorks 50 A5
Ferryden Tay 77 G5
Ferryfield Kent 13 F5
Fettercairn Gramp 77 F4
Ffestiniog Gwyn 33 E1
Ffor, y Gwyn 32 B1
Fforestfach W Glam 14 C2
Fife, reg 73 F4
Filey N Yorks 51 F1
Filton Glos 16 B3
Finchingfield Essex 30 B4
Finchley London 19 F3
Findhorn Gramp 82 A1
Findochty Gramp 82 D1
Findon Gramp 77 H2
Findon E Sussex 11 G4
Finella Fall Gramp 77 G4
Fingal's Cave S'clyde 69 B5
Finningham Suff 31 E2
Finningley Notts 44 B2
Fintry, Loup of, waterfall Cent 64 D1
Fishbourne E Sussex 11 E4
Fishguard Dyfed 22 B2
Fittleworth W Sussex 11 F3
Flamborough Hd Humber 51 G2
Fleet Hants 18 C6
Fleetwood Lancs 46 D3
Fletching E Sussex 12 B4
Flimby Cumb 52 A2
Flint Clwyd 41 H4
Flockton W Yorks 49 E6
Flodden Field N'land 67 F5
Flookburgh Lancs 47 E1
Fobbing Essex 20 D3
Fochabers Gramp 82 C2
Folkestone Kent 13 G3
Folkingham Lincs 37 F2
Fontwell E Sussex 11 F4
Fordingbridge Hants 9 H3
Fordwich Kent 13 G2
Forfar Tay 77 E5
Formby Mersey 41 H1
Forres Gramp 82 A2
Fort Augustus H'land 74 D1
Fort George H'land 81 G2
Fort William H'land 74 C4
Forth Br 65 G1
Forth, R 72 C5
Fortingall Tay 75 G6
Fortrose H'land 81 F2
Fortuneswell Dorset 9 E6
Foss Way Notts 36 C3
Foulness I Essex 21 F3
Fountains Abbey N Yorks 49 E2
Fowey Corn 3 F3
Foyers H'land 81 E5
Framlingham Suff 31 G2
Frampton Cotterell Glos 16 B3
Frant E Sussex 12 C3
Fraserburgh Gramp 83 H1
Freckleton Lancs 47 E5
Freshwater I of Wight 10 B5
Fressingfield Suff 31 F1
Freswick H'land 86 F1
Frimley Surrey 18 D5
Frinton-on-Sea Essex 31 F6
Friockheim Tay 77 F6
Fritham Hants 10 A3
Frizington Cumb 52 A3
Frodsham Ches 42 B3
Frome Som 16 C6
Fulford N Yorks 50 B3
Fulwood Lancs 47 F5
Fyne, Loch S'clyde 70 B5
Fyvie Gramp 83 F3
Gailey Staffs 35 E3
Gainsborough Lincs 44 C2
Gairloch H'land 78 F2
Galashiels Borders 66 C5
Galgate Lancs 47 F3
Galloway Dumf/Gal 57 C6
Galston S'clyde 64 C5
Gamlingay Cambs 29 F3
Gamston Notts 44 B3
Garboldisham Norf 39 E6
Garelochhead S'clyde 70 D5
Garforth W Yorks 49 F4
Gargunnock Cent 72 B5
Garlieston Dumf/Gal 57 E7
Garmouth Gramp 82 C1
Garry, Loch H'land 74 D2
Garstang Lancs 47 F4
Garston Mersey 42 A3
Garth Powys 25 E3
Garthmyl Powys 33 H4
Garton-on-the-Wolds Humber 51 E2
Garvald Loth 66 D2
Garve H'land 80 D2

Garw Mid Glam 14 D4
Garynahine Lewis 88 B2
Gateacre Lancs 42 A3
Gatehouse-of-Fleet Dumf/Gal 58 C5
Gateshead Tyne/Wear 61 G5
Gatley Ches 42 D3
Gelligaer Mid Glam 15 F2
Gerrards Cross Bucks 19 E3
Gifford Loth 66 C2
Gilfach Mid Glam 15 F2
Gillingham Dorset 9 E2
Gillingham Kent 20 D4
Gilsland Cumb/N'land 60 C4
Girvan S'clyde 56 B4
Gisburn Lancs 47 H3
Glamis Tay 73 F1
Glas Maol, mt Tay 76 C3
Glascarnoch Res H'land 80 C1
Glasgow S'clyde 64 C2
Glass Houghton W Yorks 49 F5
Glastonbury Som 8 C1
Glen Affric H'land 80 B5
Glen Almond Tay 72 B2
Glen Coe H'land 74 C5
Glen Garry Tay 74 C2
Glen Lyon Tay 71 G1
Glen Moriston H'land 80 C6
Glen Shee Tay 76 B4
Glen Shiel H'land 80 A6
Glen Trool Dumf/Gal 57 D5
Glenboig S'clyde 64 D2
Glenbuck S'clyde 65 E5
Glendevon Tay 72 D4
Gleneagles Tay 72 C3
Glenelg H'land 79 F6
Glenfarg Tay 73 E3
Glenfinnan H'land 74 A3
Glengarry H'land 74 D2
Glenisla Tay 76 C5
Glenluce Dumf/Gal 57 C7
Glenridding Cumb 52 D3
Glenrothes Fife 73 F4
Glomach, Falls of H'land 80 B5
Glossop Derby 43 E2
Gloucester Glos 26 C5
Gloucestershire, co 26 C6
Glyn Neath W Glam 14 D1
Glyncorrwg W Glam 14 D2
Glyndebourne E Sussex 12 B5
Goat Fell, mt Arran 63 F3
Goathland N Yorks 55 F4
Godalming Surrey 18 D6
Godmanchester Cambs 29 F1
Godshill I of Wight 10 C6
Golborne Lancs 42 B2
Golcar W Yorks 48 D6
Golden Valley Heref/Worcs 25 H4
Golspie H'land 87 B6
Gomersal W Yorks 49 E5
Goodwick Dyfed 22 B2
Goodwood E Sussex 11 E4
Goole Humber 49 H5
Gordonstown Gramp 82 F3
Gordonstown Gramp 82 D2
Gorebridge Loth 66 B3
Goring Oxon 18 B3
Goring W Sussex 11 G5
Gorleston Norf 39 H4
Gorseinon W Glam 14 B2
Gosforth Cumb 52 B4
Gosforth Tyne/Wear 61 G4
Gosport Hants 10 C4
Gourock S'clyde 63 H1
Govan S'clyde 64 C2
Gower Pen W Glam 14 B3
Gowerton W Glam 14 B2
Grampian, reg 82 B4
Grampound Corn 3 E3
Grange Cumb 47 E1
Grangemill Derby 43 G5
Grangemouth Cent 64 F1
Grantchester Cambs 29 H2
Grantham Lincs 37 E1
Granton Loth 65 H1
Grantown-on-Spey H'land 82 A4
Grantshouse Borders 67 E2
Grasmere Cumb 52 D4
Gravesend Kent 20 C4
Grays Essex 20 C4
Grayshott Hants 11 F2
Great Ayton N Yorks 55 E4
Great Casterton Leics 37 E3
Great Chesterford Essex 30 A3
Great Cumbrae, I S'clyde 63 H2
Great Driffield Humber 51 E3
Great Dunmow Essex 30 B5
Great Gidding Cambs 37 F6
Great Grimsby = Grimsby, Great
Great Harwood Lancs 47 G5
Great Limber Lincs 45 E1
Great Malvern Herf/Worcs 26 C3
Great Missenden Bucks 18 D2
Great Orme's Head Gwyn 40 D3
Great Orton Cumb 59 H5
Great Salkeld Cumb 53 E2
Great Shefford Berks 17 G4
Great Shelford Cambs 30 A3
Great Staughton Cambs 29 F2
Great Torrington Devon 6 D3
Great Wakering Essex 21 E3
Great Waltham Essex 20 D1
Great Witchingham Norf 39 E3
Great Witley Heref/Worcs 26 C1
Great Yarmouth Norf 39 H4
Greater Manchester, co 42 C1
Greatham Clev 54 D2
Greatham Hants 11 E2
Greenfield Clwyd 41 G4
Greenhead N'land 60 C5
Greenhithe Kent 20 C4
Greenlaw Borders 66 D4
Greenock S'clyde 63 H1
Greenwich London 19 G4
Gretna Dumf/Gal 59 G4
Gretna Green Dumf/Gal 59 G4
Grey Mare's Tail, waterfall Dumf/Gal 59 F1
Greysouthen Cumb 52 B2
Greystoke Cumb 52 D2
Griffithstown Gwent 15 G2
Grimsby, Great Humber 45 G1
Grimsetter Orkney 89 B6
Gringley-on-the-Hill Notts 44 C2
Gronant Clwyd 40 G3
Groombridge E Sussex 12 B3
Grosmont N Yorks 55 F4
Gruinard B H'land B5 A7
Guernsey, I Channel Is 3 F5
Guildford Surrey 19 E6
Guisborough Clev 55 E3
Guiseley W Yorks 48 D4
Gullane Loth 66 C1
Gunnislake Corn 3 H1
Gunwalloe Corn 2 C6
Guyhirn Cambs 37 H4
Gwalchmai Gwyn 40 B4
Gwbert-on-Sea Dyfed 22 D1
Gweek Corn 2 C5
Gwent, co 15 G1
Gwithian Corn 2 B4
Gwyddgrug Dyfed 23 F2
Gwynedd, co 40 C6
Gyffylliog Clwyd 41 F5
Hackney London 19 G3
Hackthorpe Cumb 53 E3
Haddenham Bucks 18 C1
Haddenham Cambs 29 H1
Haddington Loth 66 D2
Haddiscoe Norf 29 H5
Hadleigh Essex 20 D3
Hadleigh Suff 31 E4
Hailsham E Sussex 12 C5
Hale Ches 42 A3
Hale Gtr Man 42 D3
Halesowen W Mid 35 F5
Halesworth Suff 31 G1
Halfway Powys 24 D4
Halifax W Yorks 48 D5
Halkirk H'land 86 D2
Hallsands Devon 5 E6
Halstead Essex 30 C5
Haltemprice Humber 51 E5
Haltwhistle N'land 60 C5
Halwell Devon 4 D5
Ham Street Kent 13 F4
Hamble Hants 10 B4
Hambleden Bucks 18 C3
Hambledon Hants 10 D3
Hambledon Surrey 11 F2
Hambleton Hills N Yorks 54 D5
Hamilton S'clyde 64 D3
Hammersmith London 19 F4
Hampshire, co 10 B2
Hampstead London 19 F3
Hampton London 19 F4
Hampton Court London 19 F4
Hampton-in-Arden W Mid 35 G6
Hanbury Heref/Worcs 26 D2
Handcross E Sussex 11 H2
Handsworth S Yorks 43 H3
Hanley Staffs 42 D6
Hanworth London 19 E4
Happisburgh Norf 39 G2
Harbury Warks 27 G2
Harby Leics 36 C2
Harewood W Yorks 49 E4
Haringey London 19 G3
Harlech Gwyn 32 D2
Harleston Norf 39 F6
Harlow Essex 20 B1
Harpenden Herts 18 E1
Harrington Cumb 52 A3
Harris W Isles 88 A3
Harrogate N Yorks 49 E3
Harrow London 19 F3
Harrow-on-the-Hill London 19 F3
Harston Cambs 29 H3
Hartburn N'land 61 F3
Hartfield E Sussex 12 B3
Harthill Ches 42 B5
Harthill S'clyde 65 F2
Hartington Derby 43 F5
Hartland Devon 6 B3
Hartlepool Clev 54 D2
Harwell Oxon 18 A3
Harwich Essex 31 F5
Haslemere Surrey 11 E2
Haslingden Lancs 47 H5
Hastings E Sussex 12 D5
Haswell Durham 54 F1
Hatfield Herts 19 F1
Hatfield S Yorks 44 B1
Hatfield Broad Oak Essex 30 A6
Hatfield Peverel Essex 30 C6
Hatherleigh Devon 6 D4
Hathern Leics 36 B2
Hathersage Derby 43 G3
Hatton Gramp 83 H3
Havant Hants 10 D4
Haverfordwest Dyfed 22 C4
Haverhill Suff 30 B3
Havering London 20 B3
Haverton Hill Durham 54 D3
Hawarden Clwyd 41 H4
Haweswater Cumb 53 E3
Hawick Borders 60 B1
Hawkshead Cumb 52 D5
Hawkstone Park Salop 34 C2
Haworth W Yorks 48 C4
Haxey Lincs 44 C2
Hay-on-Wye Powys 25 G4
Haydock Lancs 42 B2
Haydon Bridge N'land 60 D5
Hayes London 19 E3
Hayfield Derby 43 E3
Hayle Corn 2 B4
Hayling I Hants 10 D4
Hayton Humber 50 C4
Haywards Heath W Sussex 12 A4
Hazel Grove Gtr Man 43 E3
Headington Oxon 28 A6
Headless Cross Heref/Worcs 27 E2
Heanor Derby 43 H6
Heathfield E Sussex 12 C4
Heaton Park Lancs 42 D1
Hebburn Tyne/Wear 61 G5
Hebden Bridge W Yorks 48 C5
Heckington Lincs 37 F1
Heckmondwike W Yorks 48 D5
Heddon-on-the-Wall N'land 61 F5
Hednesford Staffs 35 F3
Hedon Humber 51 F5
Helensburgh S'clyde 64 A1
Helmdon Northants 28 B3
Helmsdale H'land 87 D5
Helmsley N Yorks 55 E6
Helston Corn 2 C5
Helvellyn, mt Cumb 52 D3
Hemel Hempstead Herts 18 E1
Hemswell Lincs 44 D2
Hemsworth W Yorks 49 F6
Hendon London 19 F3
Hendy Dyfed 23 G5
Henfield W Sussex 11 H3
Henley-in-Arden Warks 27 F1
Henley-on-Thames Oxon 18 C3
Henstridge Som 9 E3
Hereford Heref/Worcs 26 A3
Hereford and Worcester, co 25 H3
Heriot Loth 66 B3
Herne Bay Kent 13 G1
Herriard Hants 18 B6
Herstmonceux E Sussex 12 C5
Hertford Herts 19 G1
Hertfordshire, co 29 E6
Hesketh Bank Lancs 47 E5
Hethersett Norf 39 F4
Hetton-le-Hole Tyne/Wear 61 H6
Hever Castle Kent 12 B2
Hexham N'land 61 E5
Heyford, Upr & Lr Oxon 28 A5
Heysham Lancs 47 E2
Heytesbury Wilts 16 D6
Heywood Gtr Man 42 D1
High Bentham N Yorks 47 G2
High Force, waterfall Durham 53 G2
High Halden Kent 13 E3
High Ongar Essex 20 C2
High Wycombe Bucks 18 D2
Higham Derby 43 H5
Higham Ferrers Northants 29 E1
Highbridge Som 15 G6
Highgate London 19 F3
Highland, reg 80 B4
Highworth Wilts 17 F2
Hilderstone Staffs 35 F1
Hill of Fearn H'land 87 B8
Hillingdon London 19 E3
Hillington S'clyde 64 C3
Hillington Norf 38 C2
Hillside Gramp 77 F5
Hinckley Leics 36 A5
Hinderwell N Yorks 55 F3
Hindhead Surrey 10 E2
Hindley Gtr Man 42 B1
Hindon Wilts 9 F1
Hingham Norf 39 E4
Hirwaun Mid Glam 15 E1
Hitchin Herts 29 F5
Hobbs Pt Dyfed 22 C5
Hobkirk Borders 60 B1
Hockering Norf 39 E3
Hockley Heath Warks 27 F1
Hoddesdon Herts 20 A1
Hodnet Salop 34 C2
Hogs Back Surrey 11 F1
Holbeach Lincs 37 H2
Hollington Derby 43 G6
Holmbury St Mary Surrey 11 G1
Holme upon Spalding Moor Humber 50 C4
Holmes Chapel Ches 42 D4
Holmesfield Derby 43 G3
Holmfirth W Yorks 43 F1
Holmwood Surrey 19 F6
Holsworthy Devon 6 C4
Holt Clwyd 42 A5
Holt Norf 39 E1
Holy I N'land 67 G4
Holyhead Gwyn 40 A3
Holywell Clwyd 41 G4
Honington Suff 38 D6
Honiton Devon 5 G1
Hope under Dinmore Heref/Worcs 26 A2
Horbury W Yorks 49 E6
Horeb Card 24 A4
Horley W Sussex 11 H1
Horncastle Lincs 45 F4
Hornchurch London 20 B3
Horndean Hants 10 D3
Hornsea Humber 51 F3
Hornsey London 19 G3
Horsebridge E Sussex 12 C5
Horsebridge Hants 10 B2
Horsforth W Yorks 49 E4
Horsham W Sussex 11 G2
Horsham St Faith Norf 39 F3
Horwich Gtr Man 42 C1
Houghton Cambs 29 G1
Houghton-le-Spring Tyne/Wear 61 H6
Hounslow London 19 E4
Housesteads N'land 60 D4
Hove E Sussex 11 H4
Howden Humber 49 H5
Howwood S'clyde 64 B3
Hoy, I Orkney 89 A7
Hoylake Mersey 41 G3
Hoyland Nether S Yorks 43 H1
Hucknall Notts 44 A6
Huddersfield W Yorks 48 D6
Huggate Humber 50 D3
Hugh Town Scilly Is. 2 A1
Hull, Kingston upon Humber 51 E5
Hullavington Wilts 16 D3
Humberside, co 50 D4
Hungerford Berks 17 G4
Hunmanby Humber 51 E1
Hunstanton Norf 38 B1
Huntingdon Cambs 29 F1
Huntly Gramp 82 D3
Hurlford S'clyde 64 C5
Hurn Hants 9 H4
Hursley Hants 10 B2
Hurst Green E Sussex 12 D4
Hurstpierpoint W Sussex 11 H3
Husbands Bosworth Leics 36 C5
Hutton-le-Hole N Yorks 55 E5
Huyton Mersey 42 A3
Hyde Gtr Man 43 E2
Hythe Hants 10 B4
Hythe Kent 13 G3
Ibsley Hants 9 H3
Ickenham London 19 E3
Idle W Yorks 48 D4
Ilchester Som 8 C2
Ilford London 19 H3
Ilfracombe Devon 6 D1
Ilkeston Derby 36 B1
Ilkley W Yorks 48 D3
Ilminster Som 8 B3
Immingham Humber 51 F6
Immingham Dock Lincs 51 F6
Ince-in-Makerfield Lancs 42 B1
Inchcolm Fife 73 E6
Inchkeith Fife 73 F6
Inchnadamph H'land 85 C5
Ingatestone Essex 20 C2
Ingleby Cross N Yorks 54 D5
Ingliston Loth 65 G2
Ingleton N Yorks 47 G1
Ingoldmells Lincs 45 H4
Innellan S'clyde 63 G1
Innerleithen Borders 66 B5
Insch Gramp 83 E4
Inverallochy Gramp 83 H1
Inveran H'land 85 F6
Inveraray S'clyde 70 C4
Inverbervie Gramp 77 G4
Inveresk Loth 66 B2
Inverewe H'land 78 F2
Inverfarigaig H'land 81 E5
Invergarry H'land 74 D2
Invergordon H'land 81 F1
Inverinate H'land 80 A5
Inverkeilor Tay 77 G5
Inverkeithing Fife 73 E6
Inverkirkaig H'land 85 B5
Invermay, Birks of, waterfall Tay 72 D3
Invermoriston H'land 80 D5
Inverness H'land 81 F3
Invershiel H'land 80 A5
Invershin H'land 83 F6
Inverurie Gramp 83 F4
Iona I S'clyde 69 B6
Ipstones Staffs 43 E6
Ipswich Suff 31 F4
Irlam Lancs 42 C2
Ironbridge Salop 34 D4
Irthington Cumb 60 B5
Irthlingborough Northants 28 D1
Irvine S'clyde 64 B5
Islay, I S'clyde 62 A2
Isle of Man 46 A4
Isle of Wight, co 10 B6
Isle Oronsay Skye 79 E7
Islington London 19 G3
Itchen Hants 10 B4
Iver Bucks 19 E3
Ivybridge Devon 4 C5
Ixworth Suff 30 D1
Jameston Dyfed 22 C5
Jamestown S'clyde 64 B1
Janetstown H'land 86 D2
Janetstown H'land 86 E4
Jarrow Tyne/Wear 61 G5
Jedburgh Borders 66 D6
Jersey, I Channel Is 3 G6
Jodrell Bank Ches 42 D4
John o' Groat's H'land 86 F1
Johnshaven Gramp 77 G4
Johnstone S'clyde 64 B3
Jura, I S'clyde 62 C1
Jurby I of Man 46 B4
Katrine, Loch Cent 71 E4
Kearsley Lancs 42 C1
Keighley W Yorks 48 C4
Keiss H'land 86 F2
Keith Gramp 82 D2
Kelling Pines Norf 39 E1
Kelsall Ches 42 B4
Kelso Borders 67 E5
Kelty Fife 73 E5
Kelvedon Essex 30 D6
Kemble Glos 17 E2
Kempsey Heref/Worcs 26 D3
Kempston Beds 29 E3
Kempton Park Surrey 19 E4
Kendall Cumb 53 E5
Kenilworth Warks 27 G1
Kenley Surrey 12 A1
Kenmore Tay 75 H6
Kenninghall Norf 39 E6
Kennoway Fife 73 F4
Kensington and Chelsea London 19 F3
Kent, co 12 D2
Kentford Suff 30 C2
Kenton Devon 5 E2
Kerrera, I S'clyde 70 A2
Kessingland Suff 39 H6
Kessock, N H'land 81 F3
Kessock, S H'land 81 F3
Keswick Cumb 52 C3
Kettering Northants 36 D6
Kettlewell N Yorks 48 C1
Kew Gardens London 19 F4
Keynsham Avon 16 B5
Kidderminster Heref/Worcs 35 E6
Kidlington Oxon 18 A1
Kidsgrove Staffs 42 D5
Kidwelly Dyfed 14 A1
Kilbarchan S'clyde 64 B3
Kilbirnie S'clyde 64 B3
Kilchoan H'land 68 C3
Kilconquhar Fife 73 G4
Kilcreggan S'clyde 70 D6
Kildrummy Gramp 82 D5
Kilfinan S'clyde 70 B6
Kilkhampton Corn 6 B4
Killearn Cent 64 C1
Killicrankie, Pass of Tay 76 A4
Killin Cent 72 A2
Killinaig Mull 69 D5
Killinghall N Yorks 49 E2
Killingworth Tyne/Wear 61 G4
Kilmacolm S'clyde 64 B2
Kilmaluag Skye 78 C2
Kilmarnock S'clyde 64 B5
Kilmartin S'clyde 70 A5
Kilmaurs S'clyde 64 B4
Kilmelford S'clyde 69 F6
Kilmichael Glassary S'clyde 70 B5
Kilmory S'clyde 69 D2
Kilmory Arran 63 F5
Kilmuir H'land 87 A8
Kilninver S'clyde 70 A3
Kilpatrick Hills S'clyde 64 B2
Kilrenny Fife 73 H4
Kilsyth S'clyde 64 D1
Kilt Rock, waterfall Skye 78 C3
Kilwinning S'clyde 64 B4
Kimbolton Cambs 29 E1
Kinbrace H'land 86 B4
Kincardine-on-Forth Fife 72 C5
Kincardine O'Neil Gramp 77 F1
Kincraig H'land 75 H1
Kineton W Mid 27 G3
King Harry Corn 2 D4
Kinghorn Fife 73 E5
King's Cliffe Northants 37 E4
King's Langley Herts 18 E2

King's Lynn *Norf* 38 B3
King's Somborne *Hants* 10 B2
Kings Worthy *Hants* 10 B2
Kingsand *Corn* 3 H3
Kingsbarns *Fife* 73 H3
Kingsbridge *Devon* 4 D6
Kingsburgh *Skye* 78 B4
Kingsbury *Warks* 35 H4
Kingsclere *Hants* 18 A5
Kingshouse *S'clyde* 74 D5
Kingskettle *Fife* 73 F4
Kingsteignton *Devon* 5 E3
Kingsthorpe *Northants* 28 C2
Kingston upon Thames *London* 19 F4
Kingston Bagpuize *Berks* 17 H2
Kingston upon Hull= Hull, Kingston upon
Kingswear *Devon* 5 E5
Kingswood *Avon* 16 B4
Kingston *Heref/Worcs* 25 G2
Kingussie *H'land* 75 G2
Kinloch Hourn *H'land* 74 B1
Kinloch Rannoch *Tay* 75 G5
Kinlochbervie *H'land* 84 C2
Kinlochewe *H'land* 80 B2
Kinlochleven *H'land* 74 C5
Kinlochmoidart *H'land* 68 E2
Kinloss *Gramp* 82 A1
Kinneff *Gramp* 77 H3
Kinross *Tay* 73 E4
Kintore *Gramp* 83 F5
Kintyre, Mull of *S'clyde* 62 D6
Kippford *Dumf/Gal* 58 D6
Kirby Hill *N Yorks* 49 F2
Kirby Misperton *N Yorks* 50 C1
Kirk Michael *I of Man* 46 B4
Kirk of Mochrum *Dumf/Gal* 57 D7
Kirk Yetholm *Borders* 67 E5
Kirkbride *Cumb* 59 G5
Kirkburton *W Yorks* 48 D6
Kirkby *Mersey* 42 A2
Kirkby-in-Ashfield *Notts* 44 A5
Kirkby Lonsdale *Cumb* 47 F1
Kirkbymoorside *N Yorks* 55 E6
Kirkby Stephen *Cumb* 53 G4
Kirkcaldy *Fife* 73 F5
Kirkcolm *Dumf/Gal* 57 A6
Kirkconnel *Dumf/Gal* 58 C1
Kirkcowan *Dumf/Gal* 58 A5
Kirkcudbright *Dumf/Gal* 58 C6
Kirkfieldbank *S'clyde* 65 E4
Kirkham *Lancs* 47 E5
Kirkheaton *W Yorks* 48 D6
Kirkintilloch *S'clyde* 64 D2
Kirkmaiden *Dumf/Gall* 67 B8
Kirkmichael *S'clyde* 56 D3
Kirkmichael *Tay* 76 B5
Kirknewton *Loth* 65 G2
Kirknewton *N'land* 67 F5
Kirkoswald *S'clyde* 56 C3
Kirkoswald *Cumb* 53 E1
Kirkpatrick-Fleming *Dumf/Gal* 59 G4
Kirksanton *Cumb* 41 C1
Kirktown of Rayne *Gramp* 83 E4
Kirkwall *Orkney* 89 B6
Kirn *S'clyde* 64 A2
Kirriemuir *Tay* 76 D5
Kirton *Lincs* 37 G1
Kirton-in-Lindsey *Humber* 44 D2
Knaresborough *N Yorks* 49 F3
Knarsdale *N'land* 60 C6
Knighton *Powys* 25 G1
Knockandhu *Gramp* 82 B4
Knottingley *W Yorks* 50 A5
Knutsford *Ches* 42 D3
Kyleakin *Skye* 79 E6
Kylerhea *Skye* 79 F6
Kylesku *H'land* 84 C3
Kylestrome *H'land* 84 C4
Lacock *Wilts* 16 D4
Ladybank *Fife* 73 F3
Laggan *H'land* 75 F2
Laggan, Loch *H'land* 75 E3
Lairg *H'land* 85 F6
Lakenheath *Suff* 38 C5
Lambeth *London* 19 G4
Lambourn *Berks* 17 G3
Lamington *S'clyde* 65 F5
Lamlash *Arran* 63 G4
Lammermuir Hills 66 C3
Lampeter *Dyfed* 24 B3
Lanark *S'clyde* 65 F4
Lancashire, co 47 F6
Lancaster *Lancs* 47 F2
Lanchester *Durham* 61 F6
Land's End *Corn* 2 A5
Langdale *Cumb* 52 C4
Langford *Beds* 29 F4
Langholm *Dumf/Gal* 60 A3
Langport *Som* 8 C2
Langwathby *Cumb* 53 E2
Lapford *Devon* 7 E4
Larbert *Cent* 64 E1
Largo *Fife* 73 G4
Largo Ward *Fife* 73 G4
Largs *S'clyde* 63 H2
Larkhall *S'clyde* 65 E4
Lasswade *Loth* 66 B2
Lastingham *N Yorks* 55 F5
Latchingdon *Essex* 21 E2
Latherton *H'land* 86 E4
Lauder *Borders* 66 C4
Laugharne *Dyfed* 23 E4
Launceston *Corn* 4 A2
Laurencekirk *Gramp* 77 G4
Lavenham *Suff* 30 D3
Laxey *I of Man* 46 C5
Laxfield *Suff* 31 G1
Laxford Bridge *H'land* 84 C3
Laxton *Notts* 44 C4
Lazonby *Cumb* 53 F1
Leaden Roding *Essex* 30 B6
Leadenham *Lincs* 44 D5
Leadhills *Dumf/Gal* 58 D1
Leamington Spa, Royal *Warks* 27 G1
Leatherhead *Surrey* 19 F5
Lechlade *Glos* 17 F2
Leconfield *Humber* 51 E4
Ledbury *Heref/Worcs* 26 C4
Leeds *W Yorks* 49 E5
Leek *Staffs* 43 E5
Lees *Lancs* 43 E1
Leeming Bar *N Yorks* 54 C5
Leicester *Leics* 36 B4
Leicestershire, co 36 A3
Leigh *Gtr Man* 42 C2
Leigh *Surrey* 19 F6
Leigh-on-Sea *Essex* 20 D3
Leighterton *Glos* 16 C3
Leighton Buzzard *Beds* 28 D5
Leintwardine *Heref/Worcs* 25 H1
Leiston *Suff* 31 H2
Leith *Loth* 65 H1
Lelant *Corn* 2 B4
Lendalfoot *S'clyde* 56 B4
Lennoxtown *S'clyde* 64 D1
Leny, Falls of *Tay* 72 A4
Leny, Pass of *Tay* 71 G4
Lenzie *S'clyde* 64 D2
Leominster *Heref/Worcs* 26 A2
Lerwick *Shet* 89 E7
Lesbury *N'land* 61 G1
Leslie *Fife* 73 F4
Lesmahagow *S'clyde* 65 E4
Letchworth *Herts* 29 F4
Letham *Tay* 77 E6
Leuchars *Fife* 73 G3
Leven *Fife* 73 G4
Leven, Loch *H'land* 74 C5
Leven, Loch *Tay* 73 E4
Levenshulme *Lancs* 42 D2
Lewes *E Sussex* 12 B5
Lewis *W Isles* 88 A2
Lewisham *London* 19 G4
Leyburn *N Yorks* 54 A5
Leyland *Lancs* 47 F5
Leyton *London* 19 G3
Lhanbryde *Gramp* 82 B1
Lichfield *Staffs* 35 G3
Lifton *Devon* 4 A2
Lilliesleaf *Borders* 66 C6
Lincoln *Lincs* 44 D4
Lincoln Wolds *Lincs* 45 F2
Lincolnshire, co 44 D5
Lindisfarne I *N'land* 67 G4
Lingen *Heref/Worcs* 25 H2
Lingfield *Surrey* 12 A2
Linlithgow *Loth* 65 F1
Linnhe, L. *H'land/S'clyde* 74 B5
Linslade *Beds* 28 D5
Linthwaite *W Yorks* 48 D6
Linton *Cambs* 30 A3
Linton-on-Ouse *N Yorks* 49 G2
Liphook *Hants* 11 E2
Liskeard *Corn* 3 G2
Lismore, I *S'clyde* 70 A2
Liss *Hants* 10 D2
Litherland *Mersey* 41 H2
Little Cheverell *Wilts* 17 E6
Little Lever *Lancs* 42 C1
Little Rissington *Glos* 27 F5
Little Snoring *Norf* 38 D2
Littleborough *Gtr Man* 48 C6
Littlebury *Essex* 30 A4
Littledean *Glos* 16 B1
Littlehampton *W Sussex* 11 F5
Littleport *Cambs* 38 A5
Littlestone-on-Sea *Kent* 13 F4
Liverpool *Mersey* 42 A2
Liversedge *W Yorks* 48 D5
Livingston *Loth* 65 G2
Lizard Pt *Corn* 2 C6
Llanaelhaern *Gwyn* 32 B1
Llanallgo *Gwyn* 40 C3
Llanarth *Dyfed* 24 A3
Llanbedrog *Gwyn* 32 B2
Llanberis *Gwyn* 40 C5
Llanbister *Powys* 25 F1
Llandaff *S Glam* 15 F4
Llanddarog *Dyfed* 24 B6
Llanddeiniolen *Gwyn* 40 C5
Llandderfel *Gwyn* 33 F1
Llandeilo *Dyfed* 23 G3
Llandinam *Powys* 33 G5
Llandissilio *Dyfed* 22 D4
Llandovery *Dyfed* 23 H2
Llandow *S Glam* 15 E4
Llandrillo *Gwyn* 33 G1
Llandrindod Wells *Powys* 25 F2
Llandudno *Gwyn* 41 E3
Llandybie *Dyfed* 23 G4
Llandyssul *Dyfed* 23 F2
Llanelltyd *Gwyn* 33 E3
Llanelli *Dyfed* 14 B2
Llanerchymedd *Gwyn* 40 B3
Llanerfyl *Powys* 33 G3
Llanfaethlu *Gwyn* 40 A3
Llanfair Caereinion *Powys* 33 G4
Llanfair Talhaiarn *Clwyd* 41 F4
Llanfairfechan *Gwyn* 40 D4
Llanfairpwllgwyngyll *Gwyn* 40 C4
Llanfarian *Dyfed* 24 B1
Llanfihangel-ar-arth *Dyfed* 23 F2
Llanfihangel Glyn Myfyr *Clwyd* 41 F6
Llanfyllin *Powys* 33 H3
Llanfynydd *Dyfed* 23 G3
Llangadog *Dyfed* 24 C5
Llangarron *Heref/Worcs* 26 A5
Llangefni *Gwyn* 40 B4
Llangelynin *Gwyn* 32 D4
Llangernyw *Clwyd* 41 E4
Llangoed *Gwyn* 40 C3
Llangollen *Clwyd* 33 H1
Llangranog *Dyfed* 22 E1
Llangrove *Heref/Worcs* 26 A5
Llangurig *Powys* 33 F6
Llangynllo *Powys* 25 G1
Llangynog *Powys* 33 G2
Llangynog *Dyfed* 23 B4
Llanidloes *Powys* 33 F5
Llanilar *Dyfed* 24 B1
Llanllwni *Dyfed* 23 F2
Llanpumsaint *Dyfed* 23 F3
Llanrhystyd *Dyfed* 24 B2
Llansanffraid *Dyfed* 24 B2
Llanrwst *Gwyn* 41 E5
Llansannan *Clwyd* 41 F5
Llansawel *Dyfed* 24 C4
Llanstephan *Dyfed* 23 E4
Llantrisant *Mid Glam* 15 F3
Llantwit Major *S Glam* 15 E4
Llanuwchllyn *Gwyn* 33 F3
Llanwrda *Dyfed* 23 H3
Llanwrtyd Wells *Powys* 24 D3
Llanybydder *Dyfed* 24 B4
Llanyre *Powys* 25 E2
Llechryd *Dyfed* 22 D2
Lleyn, pen *Gwyn* 32 A2
Llyswen *Powys* 25 F4
Loanhead *Loth* 66 A2
Lochaline *H'land* 68 E4
Lochalsh, Kyle of *H'land* 79 F6
Lochboisdale *S Uist* 88 E3
Lochbuie *Mull* 69 E5
Lochcarron *H'land* 80 A4
Lochdonhead *Mull* 69 E5
Lochearnhead *Cent* 72 A3
Lochgelly *Fife* 73 E5
Lochgilphead *S'clyde* 70 B6
Lochgoilhead *S'clyde* 70 D4
Lochinver *H'land* 85 B5
Lochmaben *Dumf/Gal* 59 F3
Lochmaddy *N Uist* 88 E1
Lochnagar, mt *Gramp* 76 C3
Lochranza *Arran* 63 F3
Lochwinnoch *S'clyde* 64 B3
Lochy, Loch & R *H'land* 74 C3
Lockerbie *Dumf/Gal* 59 F3
Loddon *Norf* 39 G5
Loftus *Clev* 55 F3
Logierait *Tay* 76 A5
Lomond Hills *Fife* 73 E4
Lomond, Loch *Cent/S'clyde* 71 E5
London 19 F4
London Airport (Gatwick) *W Sussex* 11 H1
London Airport (Heathrow) *London* 19 E4
London Colney *Herts* 19 F2
Long, Loch *S'clyde* 70 D5
Long Bennington *Lincs* 44 C6
Long Buckby *Northants* 28 B1
Long Compton *Warks* 27 G4
Long Crendon *Bucks* 18 B1
Long Eaton *Derby* 36 B1
Long Houghton *N'land* 61 G1
Long Itchington *Warks* 27 H1
Long Melford *Suff* 30 D3
Long Mynd, The *Salop* 34 B5
Long Preston *N Yorks* 48 B2
Long Riston *Humber* 51 F4
Long Sutton *Lincs* 37 H2
Longbenton *Tyne/Wear* 61 G4
Longdendale *Ches* 43 E2
Longforgan *Tay* 73 F2
Longformacus *Borders* 66 D3
Longframlington *N'land* 61 F2
Longhorsley *N'land* 61 F2
Longleat House *Wilts* 16 C6
Longniddry *Loth* 66 C1
Longnor *Staffs* 43 F4
Longridge *Lancs* 47 F4
Longriggend *S'clyde* 65 E2
Longton *Lancs* 47 F5
Longton *Staffs* 35 E1
Longtown *Cumb* 60 A4
Looe, E and W *Corn* 3 G3
Lopcombe Corner *Wilts* 10 A2
Loppington *Salop* 34 B2
Lorn, Firth of *S'clyde* 69 E6
Lossiemouth *Gramp* 82 B1
Lostwithiel *Corn* 3 F2
Lothian, reg 66 A2
Loudwater *Bucks* 18 D3
Loughborough *Leics* 36 B3
Loughor *W Glam* 14 B2
Loughton *Essex* 19 H2
Louth *Lincs* 45 G3
Lowdham *Notts* 44 B6
Lowestoft *Suff* 39 H5
Loweswater *Cumb* 52 B3
Lowick *N'land* 67 G4
Lowther Hills *S'clyde* 59 E1
Loyal, Loch *H'land* 84 F3
Lubnaig, Loch *Tay* 72 A3
Ludford Magna *Lincs* 45 F3
Ludgershall *Wilts* 17 G6
Ludlow *Salop* 26 A1
Luichart, Loch *H'land* 80 D2
Lullingstone *Kent* 12 B1
Lulsgate *Glos* 16 A5
Lulworth Cove *Dorset* 9 F6
Lumphanan *Gramp* 77 F1
Lunan B *Tay* 77 F5
Lundin Links *Fife* 73 G4
Luss *S'clyde* 71 E5
Lustleigh *Devon* 4 D3
Luton *Beds* 29 E5
Lutterworth *Leics* 36 B5
Lybster *H'land* 86 E4
Lydd *Kent* 13 F5
Lydden *Kent* 13 G3
Lydford *Devon* 4 B2
Lydney *Glos* 16 B2
Lye *Herf/Worcs* 35 F5
Lyme Regis *Dorset* 5 H2
Lymington *Hants* 10 A5
Lymm *Ches* 42 C3
Lympne *Kent* 13 F3
Lyndhurst *Hants* 10 A4
Lyneham *Wilts* 17 E3
Lyneholme Ford *Cumb* 60 B4
Lynmouth *Devon* 7 E1
Lynton *Devon* 7 E1
Lytham St Anne's *Lancs* 46 D5
Mablethorpe *Lincs* 45 H3
Macclesfield *Ches* 43 E4
Macduff *Gramp* 83 E1
Machen *Gwent* 15 G3
Machrihanish *S'clyde* 62 D5
Machynlleth *Powys* 33 E4
Madley *Heref/Worcs* 25 H4
Maenclochog *Dyfed* 22 C3
Maesteg *Mid Glam* 14 D3
Maghull *Lancs* 42 A2
Magor *Gwent* 15 H3
Maiden Bradley *Wilts* 9 E1
Maiden Newton *Dorset* 8 D4
Maidenhead *Berks* 18 D3
Maidstone *Kent* 12 D2
Malden *London* 19 F5
Maldon *Essex* 20 D1
Mallaig *H'land* 79 E8
Mallardoch, Loch *H'land* 80 C4
Mallory Park *Leics* 36 A4
Malmesbury *Wilts* 16 D3
Malpas *Ches* 42 B6
Maltby *S Yorks* 44 A2
Malton *N Yorks* 50 C1
Malvern Hills *Heref/Worcs* 26 C4
Malvern Link *Heref/Worcs* 26 C3
Mam Soul, mt *H'land* 80 B5
Man, Isle of 46 A4
Manaccan *Corn* 2 C5
Manby *Lincs* 45 G3
Manchester *Gtr Man* 42 D1
Mangotsfield *Glos* 16 C4
Manningtree *Essex* 31 E5
Mansfield *Notts* 44 A5
Mansfield Woodhouse *Notts* 44 A4
Manston *Kent* 13 H1
Marazion *Corn* 2 B5
March *Cambs* 37 H5
Marden, N and E *E Sussex* 11 E3
Maree, Loch *H'land* 80 A1
Margate *Kent* 13 H1
Marham *Norf* 38 C4
Market Bosworth *Leics* 36 A4
Market Deeping *Lincs* 37 F3
Market Drayton *Salop* 34 D1
Market Harborough *Leics* 36 C5
Market Lavington *Wilts* 17 E5
Market Rasen *Lincs* 45 E2
Market Weighton *Humber* 50 D4
Markinch *Fife* 73 F4
Marks Tey *Essex* 30 D5
Marlborough *Wilts* 17 F4
Marloes *Dyfed* 22 A5
Marlow *Bucks* 18 C3
Marple *Ches* 43 E3
Marsden *W Yorks* 43 E1
Marshfield *Avon* 16 C4
Marske *Clev* 55 E3
Marston Green *Warks* 35 G5
Marston Montgomery *Derby* 35 G1
Marstow *Heref/Worcs* 26 B5
Martinhoe *Devon* 7 E1
Martlesham *Suff* 31 F3
Martley *Heref/Worcs* 26 C2
Martock *Som* 8 C3
Maryculter *Gramp* 77 H1
Marykirk *Gramp* 77 F4
Maryport *Cumb* 52 A2
Masham *N Yorks* 49 E1
Massingham *Norf* 38 C2
Matlock *Derby* 43 G5
Mauchline *S'clyde* 64 C5
Maud *Gramp* 83 G2
Maxton *Borders* 66 D5
Maxwelltown *Dumf/Gal* 59 E4
May, Isle of *Fife* 73 H4
Maybole *S'clyde* 56 C3
Mayfield *E Sussex* 12 C4
Measach, Falls of *H'land* 85 C8
Meigle *Tay* 73 F1
Meikleour *Tay* 73 E1
Melbourn *Cambs* 29 G3
Melbourne *Derby* 36 A2
Melcombe Regis *Dorset* 9 E6
Melksham *Wilts* 16 D5
Melmerby *Cumb* 53 E2
Melness *H'land* 84 F2
Melrose *Borders* 66 C5
Meltham *W Yorks* 43 F1
Melton Constable *Norf* 39 E2
Melton Mowbray *Leics* 36 C3
Melton Ross *Lincs* 45 E1
Melvaig *H'land* 78 E1
Melvich *H'land* 86 B2
Menai Bridge *Gwyn* 40 C4
Mendip Hills *Som* 16 A5
Menteith, L of *Cent* 71 G4
Mere *Ches* 42 C3
Mere *Wilts* 9 E1
Mere Brow *Lancs* 47 E6
Mersea I *Essex* 31 E6
Mersey, R *Ches, etc* 42 A3
Merseyside, co 41 42
Merstham *Surrey* 19 G6
Merthyr Tydfil *Mid Glam* 15 F1
Merton *London* 19 F4
Metheringham *Lincs* 45 E5
Methil *Fife* 73 F4
Methlick *Gramp* 83 G3
Methven *Tay* 72 D2
Methwold *Norf* 38 C5
Mevagissey *Corn* 3 E4
Mexborough *S Yorks* 43 H1
Mey, Castle of *H'land* 86 F1
Micklefield, New & Old *W Yorks* 49 F5
Mickleton *Glos* 27 F3
Mid Calder *Loth* 65 G2
Mid Glamorgan, co 15 E2
Middle Wallop *Hants* 10 A1
Middlebie *Dumf/Gal* 59 G4
Middleham *N Yorks* 54 A6
Middlesbrough *Clev* 54 D3
Middleton *Gtr Man* 42 D1
Middleton-in-Teesdale *Durham* 53 H2
Middleton-One Row *Durham* 54 C4
Middleton Stoney *Oxon* 28 A5
Middlewich *Ches* 42 C4
Midhurst *W Sussex* 11 E3
Midtown Brae *H'land* 78 F2
Milborne *Dorset* 9 E4
Milborne Port *Som* 9 E3
Mildenhall *Suff* 30 C1
Milford *Surrey* 11 F1
Milford Haven *Dyfed* 22 B5
Milford-on-Sea *Hants* 10 A5
Millom *Cumb* 46 C1
Millport *Bute* 63 H2
Milnathort *Tay* 73 E4
Milngavie *S'clyde* 64 C2
Milnrow *Lancs* 43 E1
Milnthorpe *Cumb* 47 F1
Milton *Kent* 13 E1
Milton Keynes *Bucks* 28 D4
Milverton *Som* 8 A2
Minchinhampton *Glos* 16 D2
Minehead *Som* 7 G1
Mingulay, I *W Isles* 88 D4
Mintlaw *Gramp* 83 H2
Mirfield *W Yorks* 48 D6
Misterton *Notts* 44 C2
Mitcheldean *Glos* 26 B5
Modbury *Devon* 4 C5
Moffat *Dumf/Gal* 59 F1
Mold *Clwyd* 41 H5
Moness Falls *Tay* 75 H6
Moniaive *Dumf/Gal* 58 D3
Monifieth *Tay* 73 G2
Monkhopton *Salop* 34 C5
Monkton *S'clyde* 64 B5
Monmouth *Gwent* 16 A1
Montgomery *Powys* 33 H4
Montrose *Tay* 77 G5
Monymusk *Gramp* 83 E5
Moorfoot Hills 66 B3
Morar *H'land* 68 E1
Morden *London* 19 F4
More, Loch *H'land* 84 D4
Morebattle *Borders* 67 E6
Morecambe *Lancs* 47 E2
Moretonhampstead *Devon* 4 D2
Moreton-in-Marsh *Glos* 27 F4
Morley *W Yorks* 49 E5
Morlich, Loch *H'land* 81 H6
Morpeth *N'land* 61 F3
Morriston *W Glam* 14 C2
Mortehoe *Devon* 6 D1
Mortimer's Cross *Heref/Worcs* 25 H2

Morvah *Corn* **2 A5**
Morven, mt *Gramp* **76 D1**
Morven, mt *H'land* **86 C4**
Morvern *S'clyde* **68 E3**
Morville *Salop* **34 D5**
Mossley *Gtr Man* **43 E1**
Mostyn *Clwyd* **41 G3**
Motherwell *S'clyde* **65 E3**
Mottram *Ches* **43 E2**
Mountain Ash *Mid Glam* **15 F2**
Mountsorrel *Leics* **36 B3**
Mousehole *Corn* **2 A5**
Mouswald *Dumf/Gal* **59 F4**
Moy *H'land* **75 E3**
Moy *H'land* **81 G4**
Much Birch *Heref/Worcs* **26 A4**
Much Hadham *Herts* **29 H5**
Much Wenlock *Salop* **34 C4**
Muchalls *Gramp* **77 H2**
Mucklestone *Staffs* **34 D1**
Muir-of-Ord *H'land* **81 E3**
Muirdrum *Tay* **71 H1**
Muirkirk *S'clyde* **56 F2**
Mull, I *S'clyde* **69 D5**
Mull of Galloway *Dumf/Gal* **57 B8**
Mullion *Corn* **2 C6**
Mumbles *W Glam* **14 C3**
Mundesley *Norf* **39 G2**
Mundford *Norf* **38 C5**
Munlochy *H'land* **81 F2**
Murthly *Tay* **72 D1**
Musselburgh *Loth* **66 B2**
Muthill *Tay* **72 C3**
Mybster *H'land* **86 E2**
Mynyddislwyn *Gwent* **15 G3**
Mytholmroyd *W Yorks* **48 C5**
Nailsworth *Glos* **16 D2**
Nairn *H'land* **81 H2**
Nant-y-glo *Gwent* **15 G1**
Nantgaredig *Dyfed* **23 F3**
Nantwich *Ches* **42 C6**
Narberth *Dyfed* **22 D4**
Naunton *Glos* **27 F5**
Naver, Loch *H'land* **84 F4**
Nayland *Suff* **30 D4**
Neath *W Glam* **14 D2**
Needham Market *Suff* **31 E3**
Needles, The *I of Wight* **10 A6**
Nefyn *Gwyn* **32 B1**
Nelson *Lancs* **47 H4**
Ness, Loch *H'land* **81 E5**
Neston *Ches* **41 H4**
Nether Stowey *Som* **8 A1**
Netherton *Devon* **5 E3**
Nethybridge *H'land* **82 A5**
Netley *Hants* **10 B4**
Nettlebed *Oxon* **18 B3**
New Abbey *Dumf/Gal* **59 E5**
New Aberdour *Gramp* **83 G1**
New Alresford *Hants* **10 C2**
New Barnet *London* **19 F2**
New Brighton *Mersey* **41 H2**
New Buckenham *Norf* **39 E5**
New Coylton *S'clyde* **64 B6**
New Cumnock *S'clyde* **56 F3**
New Dailly *S'clyde* **56 C4**
New Deer *Gramp* **83 G2**
New Forest *Hants* **10 A4**
New Galloway *Dumf/Gal* **58 C4**
New Holland *Lincs* **51 E5**
New Hunstanton *Norf* **38 B1**
New Mills *Derby* **43 E3**
New Pitsligo *Gramp* **83 G2**
New Quay *Dyfed* **24 A2**
New Radnor *Powys* **25 G2**
New Romney *Kent* **13 F4**
New Scone *Tay* **73 E2**
Newark-on-Trent *Notts* **44 C5**
Newbiggin-by-the-Sea *N'land* **61 G3**
Newborough *Gwyn* **40 B5**
Newbridge *Corn* **3 H2**
Newbridge *Gwent* **15 G2**
Newbridge-on-Wye *Powys* **25 E2**
Newbrough *N'land* **60 D4**
Newburgh *Gramp* **83 H4**
Newburgh *Fife* **73 F3**
Newburn *Tyne/Wear* **61 F5**
Newbury *Berks* **17 H5**
Newby Bridge *Cumb* **52 D6**
Newcastle Emlyn *Dyfed* **23 E2**
Newcastleton *Borders* **60 B3**
Newcastle-under-Lyme *Staffs* **42 D6**
Newcastle upon Tyne *Tyne/Wear* **61 G5**
Newent *Glos* **26 C5**
Newham *London* **19 G3**
Newhaven *E Sussex* **12 B6**
Newhouse *S'clyde* **65 E3**
Newlands Corner *Surrey* **19 E6**
Newlyn *Corn* **2 A5**
Newlyn East *Corn* **2 D3**
Newmachar *Gramp* **83 G5**
Newmarket *Suff* **30 B2**
Newmilns *S'clyde* **64 C5**
Newnham *Glos* **26 C6**
Newport *Essex* **30 A4**
Newport *I of Wight* **10 C5**
Newport *Gwent* **15 G3**
Newport *Dyfed* **22 C2**
Newport *Salop* **34 D3**
Newport-on-Tay *Fife* **73 G2**
Newport Pagnell *Bucks* **28 D3**
Newquay *Corn* **2 D2**
Newton *Dumf/Gal* **59 F2**
Newton *Notts* **44 B6**
Newton Abbot *Devon* **5 E3**
Newton Aycliffe *Durham* **54 C3**
Newton Ferrers *Devon* **4 C5**
Newton Heath *Gtr Man* **42 D2**
Newton-le-Willows *Mersey* **42 B2**
Newton-on-the-Moor *N'land* **61 F1**
Newton Poppleford *Devon* **5 F2**
Newton Stewart *Dumf/Gal* **57 D6**
Newtongrange *Loth* **66 B2**
Newtonmore *H'land* **75 G2**
Newtown *Powys* **33 H5**
Newtown St Boswells *Borders* **66 D5**
Newtyle *Tay* **73 F1**
Neyland *Dyfed* **22 C5**
Nigg *H'land* **87 B8**
Norfolk, co **38 C3**
Norham *N'land* **67 F4**
Normanton *W Yorks* **49 F5**
Normanton-on-Trent *Notts* **44 C4**
North Berwick *Loth* **66 C1**
North Chapel *W Sussex* **11 F2**
North Downs *Kent/Surrey* **12 D1**
North Foreland *Kent* **13 H1**
North Luffenham *Leics* **37 E4**
North Molton *Devon* **7 E2**
North Shields *Tyne/Wear* **61 H4**
North Tawton *Devon* **7 E5**
North Uist, I *W. Isles* **88 D1**
North Walsham *Norf* **39 G2**
North Weald Bassett *Essex* **20 B2**
North Yorkshire, co **48 B1**
Northallerton *N Yorks* **54 C5**
Northam *Devon* **6 C3**
Northampton *Northants* **28 C2**
Northamptonshire, co **28 B1**
Northfield *W Mid* **35 F6**
Northfleet *Kent* **20 C4**
Northleach *Glos* **17 F1**
Northolt *London* **19 E3**
Northop *Clwyd* **41 H4**
Northumberland, co **60 D3**
Northwich *Ches* **42 C4**
Northwood *London* **19 E3**
Norton *Durham* **54 D3**
Norton *N Yorks* **50 C1**
Norton Radstock *Som* **16 C5**
Norwich *Norf* **39 F4**
Nottingham *Notts* **36 B1**
Nottinghamshire, co **44 A5**
Nuneaton *Warks* **36 A5**
Oadby *Leics* **36 C4**
Oakengates *Salop* **34 D3**
Oakham *Leics* **36 D3**
Oakhill *Som* **16 B6**
Oakington *Cambs* **29 H2**
Oakley *Bucks* **18 B1**
Oakworth *W Yorks* **48 C4**
Oban *S'clyde* **70 B2**
Ochil Hills **72 C4**
Ochiltree *S'clyde* **64 C6**
Ockley *Surrey* **11 G1**
Odiham *Hants* **18 C6**
Ogmore *W Glam* **14 D4**
Oich, Loch *H'land* **74 D2**
Okehampton *Devon* **4 C2**
Old Brampton *Derby* **43 H4**
Old Deer *Gramp* **83 G2**
Old Fletton *Cambs* **37 G4**
Old Kilpatrick *S'clyde* **64 C2**
Old Meldrum *Gramp* **83 F4**
Old Sarum *Wilts* **9 H1**
Old Shoreham *W Sussex* **11 H4**
Old Warden *Beds* **29 F3**
Oldbury *W Mid* **35 F5**
Oldham *Gtr Man* **43 E1**
Ollerton *Notts* **44 B4**
Olney *Bucks* **28 D3**
Ombersley *Heref/Worcs* **26 D2**
Onchan *I of Man* **46 B5**
Onich *H'land* **74 B5**
Orford *Suff* **31 G3**
Orkney, Is & reg **89**
Ormiston *Loth* **66 B2**
Ormskirk *Lancs* **42 A1**
Oronsay, I *S'clyde* **69 C8**
Orpington *London* **19 H5**
Orrell *Lancs* **42 B1**
Orrell Post *Lancs* **42 B1**
Orsett *Essex* **20 C3**
Orton *Cumb* **53 F4**
Osbaldeston *Lancs* **47 G5**
Osborne House *I of Wight* **10 C5**
Osbournby *Lincs* **37 F1**
Ossett *W Yorks* **49 E5**
Oswaldtwistle *Lancs* **47 G5**
Oswestry *Salop* **34 A2**
Otford *Kent* **12 B1**
Othery *Som* **8 B2**
Otley *W Yorks* **49 E4**
Otter Ferry *S'clyde* **70 B6**
Otterburn *N'land* **60 D2**
Ottershaw *Surrey* **19 E5**
Otterton *Devon* **5 F2**
Ottery St Mary *Devon* **5 F2**
Ottringham *Humber* **51 G5**
Oulton Park *Ches* **42 B4**
Oundle *Northants* **37 E5**
Outwell *Cambs/Norf* **38 A4**
Over *Ches* **42 C4**
Over Whitacre *Warks* **35 H5**
Overscaig *H'land* **85 D5**
Overton *Clwyd* **34 B1**
Ower *Hants* **10 A3**
Oxford *Oxon* **18 A1**
Oxfordshire, co **27 G5**
Oxshott *Surrey* **19 F5**
Oykel Bridge *H'land* **85 D6**
Padiham *Lancs* **47 H4**
Padstow *Corn* **2 D1**
Paignton *Devon* **5 E4**
Painswick *Glos* **16 D1**
Paisley *S'clyde* **64 C3**
Pakefield *Suff* **39 H5**
Pangbourne *Berks* **18 B4**
Pannal *N Yorks* **49 E3**
Paps of Jura, mt *Jura* **62 C1**
Par *Corn* **3 F3**
Parkeston *Essex* **31 F5**
Parkgate *Dumf/Gal* **59 E3**
Pateley Bridge *N Yorks* **48 D2**
Pathhead *Fife* **73 F5**
Pathhead *Loth* **66 B2**
Patna *S'clyde* **56 D3**
Patrington *Humber* **51 G5**
Patterdale *Cumb* **52 D3**
Paul *Corn* **2 A5**
Peacehaven *E Sussex* **12 A6**
Peak, The, mt *Derby* **43 F3**
Peaslake *Surrey* **11 G1**
Peebles *Borders* **66 A4**
Peel *I of Man* **46 A5**
Pembrey *Dyfed* **14 A2**
Pembridge *Heref/Worcs* **25 H2**
Pembroke *Dyfed* **22 C5**
Pembroke Dock *Dyfed* **22 C5**
Pen-y-groes *Gwyn* **40 B6**
Penarth *S Glam* **15 G4**
Pendennis Pt *Corn* **2 D5**
Pendlebury *Gtr Man* **42 D1**
Penicuik *Loth* **65 H3**
Penistone *S Yorks* **43 G1**
Penkridge *Staffs* **35 F3**
Penmaen-mawr *Gwyn* **40 D4**
Penn *Bucks* **18 D2**
Pennan *Gramp* **83 F1**
Penrhyndeudraeth *Gwyn* **32 D1**
Penrith *Cumb* **53 E2**
Penruddock *Cumb* **52 D2**
Penryn *Corn* **2 D5**
Pensarn *Clwyd* **41 F3**
Penshurst *Kent* **12 B3**
Pentland Firth **89 A7**
Pentland Hills **65 G3**
Pentraeth *Gwyn* **40 C4**
Pentrefoelas *Gwyn* **41 E6**
Penzance *Corn* **2 A5**
Perranporth *Corn* **2 C3**
Pershore *Heref/Worcs* **26 D3**
Perth *Tay* **72 D2**
Peterborough *Cambs* **37 G4**
Peterculter *Gramp* **77 G1**
Peterhead *Gramp* **83 H2**
Peterlee *Durham* **54 D1**
Petersfield *Hants* **10 D3**
Petworth *W Sussex* **11 F3**
Pewsey *Wilts* **17 F5**
Philleigh *Corn* **2 D4**
Pickering *N Yorks* **55 F6**
Pickering, Vale of *N Yorks* **50 C2**
Piercebridge *Durham* **54 B3**
Pill *Som* **16 A4**
Pinner *London* **19 E3**
Pinwherry *S'clyde* **56 C4**
Pistyll Rhaiadr, waterfall *Denb, Powys* **33 G2**
Pitchcombe *Glos* **16 D1**
Pitlochry *Tay* **76 A5**
Pittenweem *Fife* **73 H4**
Plockton *H'land* **79 F5**
Pluckley *Kent* **13 E3**
Plumpton *E Sussex* **12 A5**
Plymouth *Devon* **4 B5**
Plympton *Devon* **4 C5**
Plynlimon Fawr, mts *Dyfed* **33 E5**
Pocklington *Humber* **50 C3**
Polegate *E Sussex* **12 C6**
Polesden Lacey *Surrey* **19 E6**
Pollokshaws *S'clyde* **64 C3**
Polmont *Cent* **65 F1**
Polperro *Corn* **3 G3**
Polruan *Corn* **3 F3**
Ponders End *London* **19 G2**
Pont-erwyd *Dyfed* **33 E6**
Pont-y-Berem *Dyfed* **23 F4**
Pontardawe *W Glam* **23 H5**
Pontardulais *W Glam* **23 G5**
Pontefract *W Yorks* **49 F5**
Ponteland *N'land* **61 F4**
Pontrhydfendigaid *Dyfed* **24 C2**
Pontrilas *Heref/Worcs* **25 H5**
Pontypool *Gwent* **15 G2**
Pontypridd *Mid Glam* **15 F3**
Poole *Dorset* **9 G5**
Poolewe *H'land* **78 F2**
Porlock *Som* **7 F1**
Port Appin *S'clyde* **74 B6**
Port Askaig *Islay* **62 B1**
Port Carlisle *Cumb* **59 G5**
Port Charlotte *Islay* **62 A2**
Port Ellen *Islay* **62 B3**
Port Erin *I of Man* **46 A6**
Port Erroll *Gramp* **83 H3**
Port Eynon *W Glam* **14 B3**
Port Glasgow *S'clyde* **64 B2**
Port of Menteith *Cent* **72 A4**
Port of Ness *Lewis* **88 C1**
Port St Mary *I of Man* **46 A6**
Port Seton *Loth* **66 B1**
Port Talbot *W Glam* **14 D3**
Port William *Dumf/Gal* **57 D7**
Portencross *S'clyde* **64 A4**
Portessie *Gramp* **82 D1**
Portgordon *Gramp* **82 C1**
Porthcawl *Mid Glam* **14 D4**
Porthleven *Corn* **2 C5**
Portinscale *Cumb* **52 C3**
Portishead *Avon* **16 A4**
Portknockie *Gramp* **82 D1**
Portland *Dorset* **9 E6**
Portlethen *Gramp* **77 H2**
Porthmadoc *Gwyn* **32 D1**
Portmahomack *H'land* **87 C7**
Portnacroish *S'clyde* **74 B6**
Portnahaven *Islay* **62 A3**
Portpatrick *Dumf/Gal* **57 A7**
Portreath *Corn* **2 C4**
Portree *Skye* **79 C5**
Portsea *Hants* **10 D4**
Portskewett *Gwent* **16 A3**
Portslade-by-sea *E Sussex* **11 H4**
Portsmouth *Hants* **10 D4**
Portsonachan *S'clyde* **70 C3**
Portsoy *Gramp* **83 E1**
Postbridge *Devon* **4 C3**
Potters Bar *Herts* **19 F2**
Potton *Beds* **29 F3**
Poulton-le-Fylde *Lancs* **47 E4**
Powys, co **25 E3**
Praze-an-Beeble *Corn* **2 C5**
Preesall *Lancs* **47 E3**
Predergast *Dyfed* **22 C4**
Prescot *Mersey* **42 A2**
Prestatyn *Clwyd* **41 G3**
Presteigne *Powys* **25 G2**
Preston *Lancs* **47 F5**
Preston Candover *Hants* **10 C1**
Prestonpans *Loth* **66 B2**
Prestwich *Lancs* **42 D1**
Prestwick *S'clyde* **64 B6**
Princes Risborough *Bucks* **18 C2**
Princetown *Devon* **4 C3**
Probus *Corn* **2 D3**
Prudhoe *N'land* **61 F5**
Puckeridge *Herts* **29 G5**
Puddletown *Dorset* **9 E5**
Pudsey *W Yorks* **49 E5**
Pulborough *E Sussex* **11 F3**
Pumpsaint *Dyfed* **24 C4**
Purbeck, I of *Dorset* **9 F6**
Purfleet *Essex* **20 B4**
Purley *London* **19 G5**
Purston Jaglin *W Yorks* **49 F6**
Putford E and W *Devon* **6 C4**
Putsham *Som* **15 F6**
Pwllheli *Gwyn* **32 B2**
Quantock Hills *Som* **8 A1**
Queenborough *Kent* **21 E4**
Queensbury *W Yorks* **48 D5**
Queensferry, N *Fife* **73 E6**
Queensferry, S *Loth* **73 E6**
Quiraing, mt *Skye* **78 C3**
Quoich, Loch *H'land* **74 B2**
Quoich Bridge *H'land* **74 B2**
Raasay, I *H'land* **79 D5**
Radcliffe *Gtr Man* **42 D1**
Radcliffe-on-Trent *Notts* **36 C1**
Radlett *Herts* **19 F2**
Radnor Forest *Powys* **25 F2**
Radstock *Avon* **16 C5**
Raglan *Gwent* **15 H1**
Rainford *Lancs* **42 B2**
Rainham *London* **20 B3**
Ram *Dyfed* **24 B3**
Ramasaig *Skye* **79 A5**
Rampside *Lancs* **46 D2**
Ramsbottom *Gtr Man* **47 H6**
Ramsey *Cambs* **37 G5**
Ramsey *I of Man* **46 C4**
Ramsey I *Dyfed* **22 A3**
Ramsgate *Kent* **13 H1**
Rannoch, Loch *Tay* **75 F5**
Rannoch, Moor of *S'clyde/Tay* **75 E6**
Ratho *Loth* **65 G2**
Ratinghope *Salop* **34 B4**
Rattlesden *Suff* **30 D2**
Rattray *Tay* **73 E1**
Raunds *Northants* **29 E1**
Ravenglass *Cumb* **52 B5**
Ravenscar *N Yorks* **55 G4**
Ravensthorpe *W Yorks* **49 E6**
Rawdon *W Yorks* **49 E4**
Rawmarsh *S Yorks* **43 H2**
Rawtenstall *Lancs* **47 H5**
Rayleigh *Essex* **20 D3**
Raynham *Norf* **38 D2**
Reading *Berks* **18 C4**
Reay *H'land* **86 C2**
Redbourn *Herts* **19 E1**
Redbridge *London* **19 G3**
Redcar *Clev* **55 E3**
Redditch *Heref/Worcs* **27 E1**
Redhill *Surrey* **19 G6**
Redruth *Corn* **2 C4**
Redwick *Glos* **16 B3**
Reedham *Norf* **39 H4**
Reekie Linn, waterfall *Tay* **76 C5**
Reepham *Norf* **39 E3**
Reeth *N Yorks* **54 A5**
Regent's Park *London* **19 F3**
Reigate *Surrey* **19 F6**
Reighton *N Yorks* **51 F1**
Rempstone *Notts* **36 B2**
Renfrew *S'clyde* **64 C2**
Renton *S'clyde* **64 B1**
Rest and be Thankful *S'clyde* **70 D4**
Reston *Borders* **67 F3**
Rhayader *Powys* **25 E2**
Rhayadr Mawr = Aber Falls
Rhayadr-y-Wennol = Swallow Falls
Rhiconich *H'land* **84 C3**
Rhondda *Mid Glam* **15 E2**
Rhoose *S Glam* **15 F4**
Rhos *Dyfed* **23 E2**
Rhosili *W Glam* **14 A3**
Rhosllanerchrugog *Clwyd* **41 H6**
Rhosneigr *Gwyn* **40 A4**
Rhu *S'clyde* **64 A1**
Rhuddlan *Clwyd* **41 F4**
Rhyd Owen *Dyfed* **24 A4**
Rhydtalog *Clwyd* **41 H5**
Rhyl *Clwyd* **41 F3**
Rhymney *Mid Glam* **15 F1**
Riccall *N Yorks* **50 B4**
Riccarton *S'clyde* **64 B5**
Richards Castle *Salop* **26 A1**
Richmond *N Yorks* **54 B4**
Richmond upon Thames *London* **19 F4**
Rickinghall *Suff* **31 E1**
Rickmansworth *Herts* **19 E2**
Riding Mill *N'land* **61 E5**
Ridsdale *N'land* **61 E3**
Rievaulx *N Yorks* **55 E6**
Ringford *Dumf/Gal* **58 C5**
Ringway *Gtr Man* **42 D3**
Ringwood *Hants* **9 H4**
Rinns of Galloway **57 A6**
Rinns of Islay **62 A3**
Rinns of Kells *Dumf/Gal* **58 B3**
Ripley *Derby* **43 H5**
Ripley *N Yorks* **49 E2**
Ripley *Surrey* **19 E5**
Ripon *N Yorks* **49 E1**
Ripponden *W Yorks* **48 C6**
Risca *Gwent* **15 G3**
Rishton *Lancs* **47 G5**
Rivington *Lancs* **47 G6**
Robertsbridge *E Sussex* **12 D4**
Robin Hood's Bay *N Yorks* **55 G4**
Roborough *Devon* **4 B4**
Rochdale *Gtr Man* **42 D1**
Roche *Corn* **3 E2**
Rochester *Kent* **20 D5**
Rochford *Essex* **20 E3**
Rockcliffe *Cumb* **59 H5**
Rode *Som* **16 C5**
Rodel *Harris* **88 A4**
Romford *London* **19 H3**
Romiley *Ches* **42 E2**
Romney Marsh *Kent* **13 F4**
Romsey *Hants* **10 A3**
Rona, S, I *H'land* **78 D3**
Ronaldsway *I of Man* **46 B6**
Rosehearty *Gramp* **83 G1**
Rosemarkie *H'land* **81 G2**
Roslin *Loth* **66 A2**
Ross-on-Wye *Heref/Worcs* **26 B5**
Rosyth *Fife* **73 E6**
Rothbury *N'land* **61 F2**
Rotherfield *E Sussex* **12 B4**
Rotherham *S Yorks* **43 H2**
Rothes *Gramp* **82 B2**
Rothesay *S'clyde* **63 G2**
Rothwell *Northants* **36 D6**
Rothwell *W Yorks* **49 E5**
Rouken Glen *S'clyde* **64 C3**
Rousay, I *Orkney* **89 B6**
Rowardennan *Cent* **71 E5**
Rowley Regis *W Mid* **35 F5**
Roxburgh *Borders* **66 D5**
Roy Bridge *H'land* **74 D3**
Royal Leamington Spa = Leamington Spa, Royal
Royal Tunbridge Wells = Tunbridge Wells, Royal
Roydon *Essex* **20 B1**
Royston *Herts* **29 G4**
Royston *S Yorks* **43 H1**
Royton *Gtr Man* **42 D1**
Ruabon *Clwyd* **34 A1**
Ruddington *Notts* **36 B2**
Rufforth *N Yorks* **50 A3**
Rufus's Stone *Hants* **10 A3**
Rugby *Warks* **27 H1**
Rugeley *Staffs* **35 F3**

Ruislip *London* **19 E3**
Rum, I *H'land* **68 B1**
Rumbling Bridge *Tay* **72 D4**
Runcorn *Ches* **42 B3**
Rushden *Northants* **28 D1**
Rushyford *Durham* **54 C2**
Rutherglen *S'clyde* **64 D3**
Ruthin *Clwyd* **41 G5**
Ryde *I of Wight* **10 C5**
Rye *E Sussex* **13 E5**
Ryhope *Tyne/Wear* **61 H6**
Ryton *Tyne/Wear* **61 F6**
Saddleback (Blencathra), mt *Cumb* **52 C2**
Saddleworth *Gtr Man* **43 E1**
Saffron Walden *Essex* **30 A4**
St Abb's Hd *Borders* **67 F2**
St Agnes *Corn* **2 C3**
St Albans *Herts* **19 F1**
St Andrews *Fife* **73 G3**
St Arvans *Gwent* **16 A2**
St Asaph *Clwyd* **41 F4**
St Austell *Corn* **3 E3**
St Bees *Cumb* **52 A4**
St Blazey *Corn* **3 F3**
St Boswells *Borders* **66 D5**
St Briavels *Glos* **16 B1**
St Bride's B *Dyfed* **22 A4**
St Buryan *Corn* **2 A5**
St Catherines Pt *I of Wight* **10 B6**
St Clears *Dyfed* **23 E4**
St Columb Major *Corn* **3 E2**
St Cyrus *Gramp* **77 G4**
St David's *Dyfed* **22 A3**
St Day *Corn* **2 C4**
St Dennis *Corn* **3 E3**
St Dogmaels *Dyfed* **22 D2**
St Eval *Corn* **2 D2**
St Fillans *Tay* **72 B2**
St Helens *I of Wight* **10 C5**
St Helens *Mersey* **42 B2**
St Ives *Corn* **2 B4**
St Ives *Cambs* **29 G1**
St Johns *I of Man* **46 B5**
St John's Chapel *Durham* **53 G1**
St Just *Corn* **2 A5**
St Keverne *Corn* **2 D6**
St Leonard's *E Sussex* **12 D5**
St Margaret's-at-Cliffe *Kent* **13 H3**
St Mary's *Scilly Is* **2 A1**
St Mary's Loch *Borders* **66 A6**
St Mawes *Corn* **2 D5**
St Mawgan *Corn* **2 D2**
St Merryn *Corn* **2 D1**
St Michaels-on-Wye *Lancs* **47 F4**
St Monance *Fife* **73 H4**
St Neots *Cambs* **29 F2**
St Osyth *Essex* **31 F6**
St Peter Port *Channel Is* **3 G5**
St Peter's *Kent* **13 H1**
Salcombe *Devon* **4 D6**
Sale *Gtr Man* **42 D2**
Salen *H'land* **68 E3**
Salen *Mull* **68 D4**
Salford *Gtr Man* **42 D2**
Salisbury *Wilts* **9 H2**
Salisbury Plain *Wilts* **17 E6**
Salop, co **34 B4**
Saltaire *W Yorks* **48 D4**
Saltash *Corn* **3 H2**
Saltburn-by-the-Sea *Clev* **55 E3**
Saltcoats *S'clyde* **64 A5**
Saltoun, E & W *Loth* **66 C2**
Sampford Peverell *Devon* **7 G4**
Sandal Magna *W Yorks* **49 E6**
Sandbach *Ches* **42 D5**
Sandbank *S'clyde* **70 D6**
Sandbanks *Dorset* **9 G5**
Sandford on Thames *Oxon* **18 A2**
Sandgate *Kent* **13 G3**
Sandhaven *Gramp* **83 G1**
Sandhurst *Berks* **18 C5**
Sandown *I of Wight* **10 C6**
Sandown *Surrey* **19 E5**
Sandringham *Norf* **38 B2**
Sandwich *Kent* **13 H2**
Sandy *Beds* **29 F3**
Sanquhar *Dumf/Gal* **58 D1**
Sarn Meillteyrn *Gwyn* **32 A2**
Satterthwaite *Cumb* **52 C5**
Saundersfoot *Dyfed* **22 D5**
Sawbridgeworth *Herts* **30 A6**
Sawtry *Cambs* **37 F6**
Saxilby *Lincs* **44 D4**
Saxmundham *Suff* **31 G2**
Saxthorpe *Norf* **39 E2**
Scafell Pikes, mt *Cumb* **52 C4**
Scalby *N Yorks* **55 H5**
Scale Force, waterfall *Cumb* **52 B3**
Scaleber Force, waterfall *N Yorks* **47 H2**
Scalloway *Shet* **89 E7**
Scalpay, I *Skye* **79 D5**
Scampton *Lincs* **44 D3**
Scapa Flow *Orkney* **89 B7**
Scarba, I *S'clyde* **69 E7**
Scarborough *N Yorks* **55 H6**
Scarinish *S'clyde* **69 A7**
Schiehallion, mt *Tay* **75 G5**
Scilly, Isles of, co **2 A1**
Scole *Norf* **39 F6**
Scotch Corner *N Yorks* **54 B4**
Scotforth *Lancs* **47 F2**
Scourie *H'land* **84 B3**
Scrabster *H'land* **86 D1**
Sculthorpe *Norf* **38 D2**
Scunthorpe *Humber* **44 D1**
Scwd Henrhyd *Powys* **14 D1**
Sea Houses *N'land* **67 H5**
Seaford *E Sussex* **12 B6**
Seaforth, Loch *Lewis* **88 B3**
Seaham *Durham* **61 H6**
Seamer *N Yorks* **55 H6**
Seascale *Cumb* **52 A5**
Seaton *Devon* **5 G2**
Seaton Delaval *N'land* **61 G4**
Seaton Sluice *N'land* **61 H4**
Seaton Valley *N'land* **61 G4**
Sedbergh *Cumb* **53 F5**
Sedgfield *Durham* **54 C2**
Sedgley *Staffs* **35 E5**
Seil, I *S'clyde* **70 A3**
Selbourne *Hants* **10 D2**
Selby *N Yorks* **49 G5**
Selkirk *Borders* **66 C5**
Selsey *E Sussex* **11 E5**
Sennybridge *Powys* **25 E5**
Settle *N Yorks* **47 H2**
Sevenoaks *Kent* **12 B2**
Severn, R **16 A3**
Severn Beach *Avon* **16 A3**
Shaftesbury *Dorset* **9 F2**
Shalford *Surrey* **19 E6**
Shanklin *I of Wight* **10 C6**
Shap *Cumb* **53 E3**
Shapinsay, I *Orkney* **89 B6**
Sharnbrook *Beds* **29 E2**
Sharpness *Glos* **16 B2**
Shaw *Gtr Man* **43 E1**
Shawbury *Salop* **34 C2**
Sheerness *Kent* **21 E4**
Sheffield *S Yorks* **43 H3**
Shefford *Beds* **29 F4**
Shell Bay *Dorset* **9 G5**
Shelve *Salop* **34 A4**
Shenfield *Essex* **20 C2**
Shenley *Herts* **19 F2**
Shepperton *Surrey* **19 E5**
Sheppey, I *Kent* **21 E4**
Shepshed *Leics* **36 B3**
Shepton Mallet *Som* **16 B6**
Sherborne *Dorset* **8 D3**
Sherburn-in-Elmet *N Yorks* **49 G5**
Shere *Surrey* **19 E6**
Sheriff Hutton *N Yorks* **49 H2**
Sheriff Muir *Cent* **72 C4**
Sheringham *Norf* **39 F1**
Sherston *Wilts* **16 D3**
Sherwood Forest **44 B5**
Shetland Is, and reg **89**
Shiel, Loch *H'land* **68 F2**
Shiel Bridge *H'land* **68 E2**
Shiel Bridge *H'land* **80 A5**
Shieldaig *H'land* **78 F4**
Shifnal *Salop* **34 D3**
Shilbottle *N'land* **61 G1**
Shildon *Durham* **54 B2**
Shin, Loch *H'land* **85 E5**
Shipley *W Yorks* **48 D4**
Shipston-on-Stour *Warks* **27 G3**
Shipton-under-Wychwood *Oxon* **27 G5**
Shirehampton *Avon* **16 A4**
Shirenewton *Gwent* **16 A2**
Shirrell Heath *Hants* **10 C3**
Shoeburyness *Essex* **21 E3**
Shoreham-by-Sea *W Sussex* **11 H4**
Shorwell *I of Wight* **10 B6**
Shotley Bridge *Durham* **61 F6**
Shottermill *Surrey* **11 E2**
Shotts *S'clyde* **65 F3**
Shrewsbury *Salop* **34 C3**
Sidlaw Hills *Tay* **73 E2**
Sidmouth *Devon* **5 G2**
Siggleshorne *Humber* **51 F4**
Silchester *Hants* **18 B5**
Silloth *Cumb* **59 F6**
Silsden *W Yorks* **48 C4**
Silsoe *Beds* **29 E4**
Silverstone *Northants* **28 B3**
Singleton *W Sussex* **11 E4**
Sissinghurst *Kent* **12 D3**
Sittingbourne *Kent* **13 E1**
Sizewell *Suff* **31 H2**
Skateraw *Gramp* **77 H2**
Skegness *Lincs* **45 H5**
Skelmanthorpe *W Yorks* **43 G1**
Skelmersdale *Lancs* **42 A1**
Skelton *Cumb* **52 D2**
Skelton *Clev* **55 E3**
Skelwith Force, waterfall *Lancs* **52 D4**
Skewen *W Glam* **14 C2**
Skiddaw, mt *Cumb* **52 C2**
Skipton *N Yorks* **48 C3**
Skipwith *N Yorks* **49 H4**
Skirling *Borders* **65 G4**
Skye, I *H'land* **79 C5**
Slaidburn *Lancs* **47 G3**
Slaithwaite *W Yorks* **48 D6**
Slaley *N'land* **61 E5**
Slamannan *Cent* **65 E2**
Sleaford *Lincs* **37 F1**
Sleat, Sound of *H'land* **79 E7**
Sligachan Hotel *Skye* **79 C6**
Slimbridge *Glos* **26 C6**
Slingsby *N Yorks* **50 C1**
Slioch, mt *H'land* **80 A1**
Slough *Berks* **18 D3**
Sma' Glen *Tay* **72 C2**
Smailholm *Borders* **66 D5**
Smethwick *W Mid* **35 F5**
Smoo Cave *H'land* **84 D2**
Snaefell, mt *I of Man* **46 B4**
Snaith *Humber* **49 H5**
Snape *Suff* **31 G2**
Snetterton *Norf* **38 D5**
Snitterfield *Warks* **27 F2**
Snizort, Loch *Skye* **78 B3**
Snowdon, mt *Gwyn* **40 C6**
Soay, I *Skye* **79 C7**
Soham *Cambs* **30 B1**
Solent, The **10 C5**
Solihull *W Mid* **35 G6**
Solva *Dyfed* **22 A3**
Somercoates *Derby* **43 H5**
Somerset, co **8 A1**
Somersham *Cambs* **30 B1**
Somerton *Som* **8 C2**
Sonning *Berks* **18 C4**
Soutergate *Lancs* **46 D1**
South Bank *Clev* **54 D3**
South Brent *Devon* **4 D4**
South Cave *Humber* **50 D5**
South Cerney *Glos* **17 E2**
South Downs *E & W Sussex* **11 E3**
South Foreland *Kent* **13 H3**
South Glamorgan, co **15 F4**
South Kirkby *W Yorks* **49 F6**
South Molton *Devon* **7 E3**
South Ockendon *Essex* **20 C3**
South Petherton *Som* **8 C3**
South Ronaldsay, I *Orkney* **89 B7**
South Shields *Tyne/Wear* **61 H4**
South Uist, I *W Isles* **88 E3**
South Willingham *Lincs* **45 F3**
South Yorkshire, co **44**
Southam *Warks* **27 H2**
Southampton *Hants* **10 B3**
Southampton Water *Hants* **10 B4**
Southborough *Kent* **12 C3**
Southend *S'clyde* **62 D6**
Southend-on-Sea *Essex* **21 E3**
Southery *Norf* **38 B5**
Southminster *Essex* **21 E2**
Southport *Mersey* **46 D6**
Southrop *Glos* **27 G6**
Southsea *Hants* **10 D5**
Southwark *London* **19 G4**
Southwell *Notts* **44 B6**
Southwick *W Sussex* **11 H4**
Southwold *Suff* **31 H1**
Soutra Hill *Loth* **66 C3**
Sowerby Bridge *W Yorks* **48 C5**
Spalding *Lincs* **37 G2**
Sparkford *Som* **8 D2**
Spean Bridge *H'land* **74 D3**
Speeton *N Yorks* **51 F1**
Speke *Lancs* **42 A3**
Spenborough *W Yorks* **48 D5**
Spencers Wood *Berks* **18 C5**
Spennymoor *Durham* **54 B2**
Spey, R **81 H5**
Spey Bay *Gramp* **82 C1**
Spilsby *Lincs* **45 G4**
Spithead **10 C5**
Spittal of Glenshee *Tay* **76 B4**
Spofforth *N Yorks* **49 F3**
Springfield *Fife* **73 F3**
Sproatley *Humber* **51 F5**
Sprouston *Borders* **67 E5**
Squires Gate *Lancs* **46 D5**
Stadhampton *Oxon* **18 B2**
Staffa, I *S'clyde* **69 B5**
Staffin *Skye* **78 C3**
Stafford *Staffs* **35 F2**
Staffordshire, co **35 E2**
Stagshaw Bank *N'land* **61 E4**
Staindrop *Durham* **54 A3**
Staines *Surrey* **19 E4**
Stainforth *S Yorks* **49 H6**
Staithes *N Yorks* **55 F3**
Stalbridge *Dorset* **9 E3**
Stalham *Norf* **39 G2**
Stalybridge *Gtr Man* **43 F2**
Stamford *Lincs* **37 E4**
Stamfordham *N'land* **61 F4**
Standish *Lancs* **42 B1**
Standlake *Oxon* **17 G2**
Stanford-in-the-Vale *Oxon* **17 G2**
Stanford-le-Hope *Essex* **20 C3**
Stanhope *Durham* **53 H1**
Stanley *Durham* **61 G6**
Stanley *Tay* **73 E2**
Stanley *W Yorks* **49 E5**
Stanley Force, waterfall *Cumb* **52 B5**
Stannington *N'land* **61 G4**
Stansted *Essex* **29 H5**
Stanton *Suff* **30 D1**
Stanton Harcourt *Oxon* **17 H1**
Stanwix *Cumb* **60 A5**
Stapleford *Cambs* **29 H3**
Stapleford *Notts* **36 B1**
Stapleford *Wilts* **9 G1**
Stapleford Abbotts *Essex* **20 B2**
Starbeck *N Yorks* **49 E3**
Start Pt *Devon* **5 E6**
Staunton *Glos* **26 C4**
Staunton *Glos* **26 B6**
Staunton-on-Wye *Heref/Worcs* **25 H3**
Staveley *Cumb* **52 D6**
Staveley *Derby* **43 H4**
Staverton *Glos* **26 D5**
Steall Fall *H'land* **74 C4**
Steeple Aston *Oxon* **27 H5**
Stevenage *Herts* **29 F5**
Stevenston *S'clyde* **64 A4**
Stewarton *S'clyde* **64 B4**
Steyning *W Sussex* **11 G4**
Stibb Cross *Devon* **6 C4**
Stickford *Lincs* **45 G5**
Stickney *Lincs* **45 G5**
Stilton *Cambs* **37 F5**
Stirling *Cent* **72 B5**
Stithians *Corn* **2 C4**
Stock *Essex* **20 D2**
Stockbridge *Hants* **10 B2**
Stockport *Gtr Man* **42 D2**
Stocksbridge *S Yorks* **43 G2**
Stockton Heath *Ches* **42 B3**
Stockton-on-Tees *Clev* **54 D3**
Stockwith *Lincs* **44 C2**
Stoke Canon *Devon* **7 G5**
Stoke Ferry *Norf* **38 B4**
Stoke Fleming *Devon* **5 E5**
Stoke-on-Trent *Staffs* **42 D6**
Stoke Poges *Bucks* **18 D3**
Stokenchurch *Bucks* **18 C2**
Stokesley *N Yorks* **54 D4**
Stone *Staffs* **35 E1**
Stonefield *S'clyde* **64 D3**
Stonehaven *Gramp* **77 H3**
Stonehenge *Wilts* **9 H1**
Stonehouse *Glos* **16 C1**
Stonehouse *S'clyde* **65 E4**
Stoneykirk *Dumf/Gal* **57 B7**
Stony Stratford *Bucks* **28 C4**
Stornoway *Lewis* **88 C2**
Storrington *W Sussex* **11 G4**
Stourbridge *W Mid* **35 E5**
Stourport *Heref/Worcs* **26 C1**
Stow *Borders* **66 C4**
Stow-on-the-Wold *Glos* **27 F5**
Stowmarket *Suff* **31 E2**
Strachan *Gramp* **77 F2**
Strachur *S'clyde* **70 C4**
Stradbroke *Suff* **31 F1**
Stradishall *Suff* **30 C3**
Stradsett *Norf* **38 B4**
Straiton *S'clyde* **56 D3**
Stranraer *Dumf/Gal* **57 A6**
Stratford *London* **19 G3**
Stratford St Mary *Essex* **31 E4**
Stratford-upon-Avon *Warks* **27 F2**
Strath Glass *H'land* **80 D4**
Strath Halladale *H'land* **86 B3**
Strathaven *S'clyde* **64 D4**
Strathblane *S'clyde* **72 A6**
Strathclyde, reg **70 A5**
Strathdon *Gramp* **82 C5**
Strathkanaird *H'land* **85 B6**
Strathmiglo *Fife* **73 E3**
Strathmore *Tay* **72 D2**
Strathpeffer *H'land* **81 E2**
Strathy *H'land* **86 B2**
Strathyre *Cent* **72 A3**
Stratton *Corn* **6 B4**
Streatley *Berks* **18 B3**
Street *Som* **8 C1**
Strensall *N Yorks* **49 G2**
Strete *Devon* **5 E5**
Stretford *Gtr Man* **42 D2**
Stretham *Cambs* **30 A1**
Stretton *Ches* **42 C3**
Strichen *Gramp* **83 C2**
Strid, The, waterfall *N Yorks* **48 D3**
Striven, Loch *S'clyde* **63 G1**
Stroma, I *H'land* **86 F1**
Stromeferry *H'land* **80 A4**
Stromness *Orkney* **89 A6**
Stronachlachar *Tay* **71 E4**
Stronsay, I *Orkney* **89 C6**
Strontian *H'land* **74 A5**
Strood *Kent* **20 D4**
Stroud *Glos* **16 D1**
Struy *H'land* **80 D3**
Studland *Dorset* **9 G5**
Studley *Warks* **27 E2**
Sturminster Newton *Dorset* **9 E3**
Sudbury *Suff* **30 D4**
Suffolk, co **30 C2**
Suilven, mt *H'land* **85 B5**
Sunburgh & Hd *Shet* **89 E8**
Summercourt *Corn* **2 D3**
Sunbury *Surrey* **19 E4**
Sunderland *Tyne/Wear* **61 H5**
Sunningdale *Berks* **18 D4**
Surbiton *London* **19 F5**
Surrey, co **19 E6**
Sutterton *Lincs* **37 G1**
Sutton *Cambs* **37 H6**
Sutton *London* **19 F5**
Sutton Coldfield *W Mid* **35 G4**
Sutton-in-Ashfield *Notts* **44 A5**
Sutton-on-Sea *Lincs* **45 H3**
Sutton Scotney *Hants* **10 B1**
Sutton upon Trent *Notts* **44 C4**
Swadlincote *Derby* **35 H3**
Swaffham *Norf* **38 C4**
Swainswick *Som* **16 C4**
Swallow Falls *Gwyn* **40 D5**
Swanage *Dorset* **9 G6**
Swanscombe *Kent* **20 C4**
Swansea *W Glam* **14 C2**
Swanton Morley *Norf* **39 E3**
Sway *Hants* **10 A5**
Swinbrook *Oxon* **27 G6**
Swinderby *Lincs* **44 C5**
Swindon *Wilts* **17 F3**
Swineshead *Lincs* **37 G1**
Swinton *Borders* **67 E4**
Swinton *Gtr Man* **42 C1**
Swinton *S Yorks* **43 H2**
Syerston *Notts* **44 C6**
Symington *S'clyde* **64 B5**
Symington *S'clyde* **65 F5**
Sywell *Northants* **28 D1**
Tadcaster *N Yorks* **49 G4**
Tadley *Hants* **18 B5**
Tain *H'land* **87 B7**
Tal-sarnau *Gwyn* **32 D1**
Tal-y-cafn *Clwyd* **41 E4**
Talgarth *Powys* **25 F4**
Talybont *Dyfed* **32 D5**
Tamworth *Staffs* **35 G4**
Tangmere *W Sussex* **11 E4**
Tarbat Ness *H'land* **87 C7**
Tarbert *Harris* **88 B3**
Tarbert *S'clyde* **63 E1**
Tarbet *S'clyde* **71 E4**
Tarbolton *S'clyde* **64 B6**
Tarland *Gramp* **82 D6**
Tarporley *Ches* **42 B5**
Tattershall *Lincs* **45 F5**
Tatton Park *Ches* **42 C3**
Taunton *Som* **8 A2**
Taunton Deane, Vale of *Som* **8 A2**
Tavistock *Devon* **4 B3**
Tay, Loch *Tay* **72 A2**
Tay, R *Tay* **73 E3**
Taynuilt *S'clyde* **70 B2**
Tayport *Fife* **73 G2**
Tayside, reg **76 B5**
Tebay *Cumb* **53 F4**
Tedburn St Mary *Devon* **4 D2**
Teddington *London* **19 F4**
Teignmouth *Devon* **5 E3**
Telford *Salop* **34 D3**
Tenbury Wells *Heref/Worcs* **26 B1**
Tenby *Dyfed* **22 D5**
Tendring *Essex* **31 E5**
Tenterden *Kent* **13 E3**
Ternhill *Salop* **34 C2**
Tetbury *Glos* **16 D2**
Tetsworth *Oxon* **18 B2**
Tettenhall *W Mid* **35 E4**
Teversham *Cambs* **30 A2**
Tewkesbury *Glos* **26 D4**
Thame *Oxon* **18 C1**
Thames Ditton *Surrey* **19 F5**
Thamesmead *London* **20 B4**
Thanet, I of *Kent* **13 H1**
Thaxted *Essex* **30 B4**
Theale *Berks* **18 B4**
Thetford *Norf* **38 D6**
Theydon Bois *Essex* **20 B2**
Thirsk *N Yorks* **49 F1**
Thirston *N'land* **61 F2**
Thornaby-on-Tees *Clev* **54 D3**
Thornbury *Avon* **16 B3**
Thorne *S Yorks* **50 C6**
Thorney *Cambs* **37 G4**
Thorney I *W Sussex* **10 D4**
Thornhill *Cent* **71 G4**
Thornhill *Dumf/Gal* **58 D2**
Thornhill *W Yorks* **49 E6**
Thornton Cleveleys *Lancs* **46 D4**
Thornton Force, waterfall *N Yorks* **47 G1**
Thorpe-le-Soken *Essex* **31 F5**
Thorpe-on-the-Hill *Lincs* **44 D4**
Thorpeness *Suff* **31 H2**
Thrapston *Northants* **37 E6**
Three Cocks *Powys* **25 F4**
Threlkeld *Cumb* **52 C3**
Threshfield *N Yorks* **48 C2**
Thruxton *Hants* **10 A1**
Thurlow *Suff* **30 B3**
Thursby *Cumb* **59 H6**
Thurso *H'land* **86 D1**
Tibberton *Salop* **34 D3**
Ticehurst *E Sussex* **12 C4**
Tickhill *S Yorks* **44 B2**
Tideswell *Derby* **43 F4**
Tighnabruaich *S'clyde* **63 F1**
Tilbury *Essex* **20 C4**
Tillicoultry *Cent* **72 C5**
Tilshead *Wilts* **17 E6**
Tintagel *Corn* **6 A6**
Tintern Abbey *Gwent* **16 A2**

Tipton *W Mid* **35 F5**
Tiptree *Essex* **30 D6**
Tiree, I *S'clyde* **69 A7**
Tisbury *Wilts* **9 F2**
Titchfield *Hants* **10 C4**
Tiverton *Devon* **7 G4**
Tobermory *Mull* **68 C3**
Todmorden *W Yorks* **48 C5**
Tollerton *Notts* **36 C1**
Tollesbury *Essex* **21 E1**
Tolleshunt D'Arcy *Essex* **21 E1**
Tomatin *H'land* **81 G4**
Tomdoun *H'land* **74 C2**
Tomintoul *Gramp* **82 B5**
Tonbridge *Kent* **12 C2**
Tongue *H'land* **84 F2**
Topcliffe *N Yorks* **49 F1**
Topsham *Devon* **5 F2**
Torbay *Devon* **5 E4**
Torcross *Devon* **5 E6**
Torpoint *Corn* **3 H3**
Torquay *Devon* **5 E4**
Torrance *S'clyde* **64 D2**
Torridon *H'land* **80 A2**
Torver *Cumb* **52 C5**
Totland *I of Wight* **10 A5**
Totley *S Yorks* **43 G3**
Totnes *Devon* **5 E4**
Tottenham *London* **19 G3**
Tottington *Lancs* **42 D1**
Totton *Hants* **10 B3**
Tow Law *Durham* **54 A1**
Towcester *Northants* **28 C3**
Tower Hamlets *London* **19 G3**
Tranent *Loth* **66 B2**
Traquair *Borders* **66 B5**
Trawden *Lancs* **48 B4**
Tredegar *Mid Glam* **15 F1**
Treforest *Mid Glam* **15 F3**
Tregaron *Dyfed* **24 C2**
Tregony *Corn* **3 E4**
Treharris *Mid Glam* **15 F2**
Trelleck *Gwent* **16 A1**
Treorci *Mid Glam* **15 E2**
Tresco, I *Scilly Is.* **2 A1**
Tresparrett Posts *Corn* **6 A5**
Trimdon *Durham* **54 C2**
Trimley *Suff* **31 F4**
Tring *Herts* **18 D1**
Troon *S'clyde* **64 B5**
Trossachs, The *Cent* **71 F4**
Trowbridge *Wilts* **16 D4**
Trumpington *Cambs* **29 H2**
Truro *Corn* **2 D4**
Tugby *Leics* **36 D4**
Tulloch *H'land* **75 E3**
Tumby *Lincs* **45 F5**
Tummel, Loch *Tay* **75 H5**
Tummel Bridge *Tay* **75 G5**
Tunbridge Wells, Royal *Kent* **12 C3**
Tunstall *Staffs* **42 D5**
Turnberry *S'clyde* **56 C3**
Turnditch *Derby* **43 G6**
Turnershill *W Sussex* **11 H2**
Turnhouse *Loth* **65 G2**
Turriff *Gramp* **83 F2**
Turton *Lancs* **47 G6**
Tutbury *Staffs* **35 H2**
Tuxford *Notts* **44 C4**
Tweed, R **67 F3**
Tweedmouth *N'land* **67 F3**
Tweedsmuir *Borders* **65 G6**
Twickenham *London* **19 F4**
Two Bridges *Devon* **4 C3**
Twycross *Leics* **36 A4**
Twyford *Berks* **18 C4**
Twyford *Bucks* **28 B5**
Twyford *Hants* **10 B3**
Twynholm *Dumf/Gal* **58 C6**
Tyldesley *Gtr Man* **42 C1**
Tyn-y-Groes *Gwyn* **40 D4**
Tyndrum *Cent* **71 E2**
Tyne, R *N'land, etc* **61 G5**
Tyne and Wear, co **61 H4**
Tynemouth *Tyne/Wear* **61 H4**
Tywyn *Gwyn* **32 D4**
Tywyn *Gwyn* **41 E3**
Uckfield *E Sussex* **12 B4**
Uddingston *S'clyde* **64 D3**
Uffculme *Devon* **7 H4**
Uig *Lewis* **88 A2**
Uig *Sky* **78 B3**
Ulceby *Lincs* **51 E6**
Ulceby Cross *Lincs* **45 G4**
Uldale *Cumb* **52 C2**
Ullapool *H'land* **85 B7**
Ullswater *Cumb* **52 D3**
Ulva, I *Mull* **68 C4**
Ulverston *Cumb* **46 D1**
Unapool *H'land* **84 C4**
Unst, I *Shet* **89 F5**
Upavon *Wilts* **17 F5**
Uphall *Loth* **65 G2**
Upham *Hants* **10 C3**
Up Holland *Gtr Man* **42 B1**
Upper Tean *Staffs* **35 F1**
Uppingham *Leics* **36 D4**
Upton-upon-Severn *Heref/Worcs* **26 D4**
Urmston *Gtr Man* **42 D2**
Urquhart *Gramp* **82 C1**
Usk *Gwent* **15 H2**
Uttoxeter *Staffs* **35 G1**
Uxbridge *London* **19 E3**
Valley *Gwyn* **40 A3**
Vatersay, I *W Isles* **88 D4**
Venachar, Loch *Cent* **71 G4**
Ventnor *I of Wight* **10 C6**
Virginia Water *Surrey* **18 D4**
Voil, Loch *Tay* **71 F3**
Vyrnwy, L *Powys* **33 F2**
Waddesdon *Bucks* **28 C5**
Waddington *Lincs* **44 D4**
Wadebridge *Corn* **3 E1**
Wadhurst *E Sussex* **12 C4**
Wainfleet *Lincs* **45 H5**
Wakefield *W Yorks* **49 E6**
Wakes Colne *Essex* **30 D5**
Walford *Heref/Worcs* **25 H1**
Walkden *Lancs* **42 C1**
Walkerburn *Borders* **66 B5**
Wallasey *Mersey* **41 H2**
Wallingford *Oxon* **18 B3**
Walls *Shet* **89 D7**
Wallsend *Tyne/Wear* **61 G4**
Walmer *Kent* **13 H2**
Walney I *Cumb* **46 C2**
Walsall *W Mid* **35 F4**
Walsall Wood *W Mid* **35 F4**
Walsingham *Norf* **38 D1**
Waltham Abbey *Essex* **19 G2**
Waltham Cross *Herts* **19 G2**
Waltham Forest *London* **19 G3**
Waltham-on-the-Wolds *Leics* **36 D2**
Walthamstow *London* **19 G3**
Walton *Cumb* **60 B5**
Walton-le-dale *Lancs* **49 F5**
Walton-on-Thames *Surrey* **19 E5**
Walton-on-the-Hill *Surrey* **19 F5**
Walton-on-the-Naze *Essex* **13 F6**
Wandsworth *London* **19 F4**
Wangford *Suff* **31 H1**
Wanlockhead *Dumf/Gal* **58 D1**
Wanstead *London* **19 G3**
Wantage *Oxon* **17 G3**
Warboys *Cambs* **37 G6**
Wardington *Oxon* **27 H3**
Wardle *Gtr Man* **48 B6**
Ware *Herts* **19 G1**
Wareham *Dorset* **9 F5**
Wargrave *Berks* **18 C4**
Wark *N'land* **60 D4**
Warkworth *N'land* **61 G1**
Warley *W Mid* **35 F5**
Warlingham *Surrey* **12 A1**
Warminster *Wilts* **16 D6**
Warnham *W Sussex* **11 G2**
Warrington *Lancs* **42 B3**
Warsop *Notts* **44 B3**
Warton *Lancs* **47 E5**
Warwick *Cumb* **60 A5**
Warwick *Warks* **27 G2**
Warwickshire, co **27 F1**
Wash, The **38 A1**
Washington *Tyne/Wear* **61 G5**
Washington *W Sussex* **11 G4**
Wast Water *Cumb* **52 B4**
Watchet *Som* **7 H1**
Waterbeach *Cambs* **30 A2**
Waterloo *Hants* **10 D4**
Watford *Herts* **19 E2**
Wath upon Dearne *S Yorks* **43 H1**
Watling Street *Northants* **28 C3**
Watlington *Oxon* **18 B2**
Watten *H'land* **86 E2**
Watton *Norf* **38 D4**
Watton-at-Stone *Herts* **29 G5**
Wealdstone *London* **19 F3**
Wednesbury *W Mid* **35 F5**
Wednesfield *W Mid* **35 F4**
Weedon Bec *Northants* **28 B2**
Week St Mary *Corn* **6 B5**
Weeley *Essex* **31 E5**
Welbeck Abbey *Notts* **44 A4**
Welford *Northants* **36 C6**
Wellburnspout, waterfall *Dumf/Gal* **59 G2**
Wellingborough *Northants* **28 D1**
Wellington *Salop* **34 D3**
Wellington *Som* **8 A2**
Wells *Som* **16 B6**
Wells next the Sea *Norf* **38 D1**
Welshampton *Salop* **34 B1**
Welshpool *Powys* **33 H4**
Welwyn *Herts* **29 F6**
Welwyn Garden City *Herts* **19 F1**
Wem *Salop* **34 C2**
Wembley *London* **19 F3**
Wemyss Bay *S'clyde* **63 H1**
Wendover *Bucks* **18 D1**
Wendron *Corn* **2 C5**
Wenlock Edge *Salop* **34 B5**
Wensleydale *N Yorks* **54 A5**
Wenvoe *S Glam* **15 F4**
Weobley *Heref/Worcs* **25 H3**
West Auckland *Durham* **54 B2**
West Bridgford *Notts* **36 B1**
West Bromwich *W Mid* **35 F5**
West Calder *Loth* **65 G3**
West Glamorgan, co **14 C2**
West Gordon *Borders* **66 D4**
West Haddon *Northants* **28 B1**
West Ham *London* **20 A3**
West Kilbride *S'clyde* **64 A4**
West Kirby *Mersey* **41 G3**
West Linton *Borders* **65 G3**
West Meon *Hants* **10 D3**
West Mersea *Essex* **21 F1**
West Midlands, co **35 F5**
West Sussex, co **11 F3**
West Thurrock *Essex* **20 C4**
West Wycombe *Bucks* **18 C2**
West Yorkshire, co **48 C5**
Westbury *Wilts* **16 D6**
Westbury-upon-Severn *Glos* **26 C6**
Westerham *Kent* **12 B2**
Western Isles, reg **88**
Westgate-on-Sea *Kent* **13 H1**
Westhoughton *Lancs* **42 C1**
Westminster *London* **19 F3**
Weston-super-Mare *Avon* **15 G5**
Westonbirt *Glos* **16 D3**
Westray, I *Orkney* **89 B5**
Westruther *Borders* **66 D3**
Westward Ho! *Devon* **6 C2**
Wetherby *W Yorks* **49 F3**
Wetwang *Humber* **50 D3**
Weybridge *Surrey* **19 E5**
Weyhill *Hants* **10 A1**
Weymouth *Dorset* **9 E6**
Whaley Bridge *Derby* **43 E3**
Whalley *Lancs* **47 G4**
Whalsay, I *Shet* **89 F7**
Whalton *N'land* **61 F3**
Wharfedale *N Yorks* **48 D3**
Wheathampstead *Herts* **19 F1**
Wheatley *Oxon* **18 B1**
Whickham *Tyne/Wear* **61 G5**
Whiddon Down *Devon* **4 D2**
Whimple *Devon* **5 F1**
Whipsnade *Beds* **29 E6**
Whitburn *Tyne/Wear* **61 H5**
Whitburn *Loth* **65 F2**
Whitby *N Yorks* **55 G4**
Whitchurch *Bucks* **28 C5**
Whitchurch *S Glam* **15 F3**
Whitchurch *Hants* **10 B1**
Whitchurch *Heref/Worcs* **26 B5**
Whitchurch *Salop* **34 C1**
White Horse, Vale of *Berks* **17 G2**
White Waltham *Berks* **18 D4**
Whitefield *Gtr Man* **42 D1**
Whitehaven *Cumb* **52 A3**
Whitehills *Gramp* **83 E1**
Whitekirk *Loth* **66 D1**
Whiteparish *Wilts* **10 A3**
Whithorn *Dumf/Gal* **57 E8**
Whiting Bay *Arran* **63 G5**
Whitland *Dyfed* **22 D4**
Whitletts *S'clyde* **64 B6**
Whitley *W Yorks* **49 E6**
Whitley Bay *Tyne/Wear* **61 H4**
Whitstable *Kent* **13 F1**
Whittingham *N'land* **60 F1**
Whittington *Salop* **34 A2**
Whittlesey *Cambs* **37 G4**
Whitton *Powys* **25 G2**
Whitwell *I of Wight* **10 C6**
Whitworth *Lancs* **48 B6**
Wick *H'land* **86 F3**
Wickford *Essex* **20 D2**
Wickham *Hants* **10 C4**
Wickham Market *Suff* **31 G3**
Wickwar *Avon* **16 C3**
Widdington *Essex* **30 A4**
Widecombe-in-the-Moor *Devon* **4 D3**
Widmerpool *Notts* **36 C2**
Widnes *Ches* **42 B3**
Wigan *Gtr Man* **42 B1**
Wigginton *N Yorks* **49 G2**
Wight, Isle of *Hants* **10 B6**
Wigmore *Heref/Worcs* **25 H1**
Wigston Magna *Leics* **36 C4**
Wigton *Cumb* **52 C1**
Wigtown *Dumf/Gal* **57 E7**
Wilburton *Cambs* **29 H1**
Willenhall *W Mid* **35 F4**
Willersley *Heref/Worcs* **25 G3**
Willesden *London* **19 F3**
Willingham *Cambs* **29 H1**
Willington *Derby* **35 H2**
Willington *Durham* **54 B2**
Williton *Som* **7 H1**
Wilmington *Kent* **20 B4**
Wilmslow *Ches* **42 D3**
Wilton *Wilts* **9 G2**
Wiltshire, co **16 D5**
Wimbledon *London* **19 F4**
Wimborne Minster *Dorset* **9 G4**
Wincanton *Som* **9 E2**
Winchburgh *Loth* **65 G2**
Winchcombe *Glos* **27 E4**
Winchelsea *E Sussex* **13 E5**
Winchester *Hants* **10 C2**
Windermere *Cumb* **52 D5**
Windsor, New *Berks* **18 D4**
Windsor Great Park *Berks* **18 D4**
Windygates *Fife* **73 F4**
Winfrith Heath *Dorset* **9 E5**
Wingham *Kent* **13 G2**
Winnersh *Berks* **18 C4**
Winscales *Cumb* **52 A4**
Winsford *Ches* **42 C4**
Winslow *Bucks* **28 C5**
Winstanley *Lancs* **42 B2**
Winster *Derby* **43 G5**
Winterbourne Stoke *Wilts* **9 G1**
Winteringham *Humber* **50 D5**
Winterton *Humber* **50 D6**
Winterton *Norf* **39 H3**
Wirksworth *Derby* **43 G5**
Wirral Pen *Ches* **41 H3**
Wisbech *Cambs* **37 H3**
Wisborough Green *W Sussex* **11 F3**
Wishaw *S'clyde* **65 E3**
Witchampton *Dorset* **9 G4**
Witham *Essex* **21 E1**
Witheridge *Devon* **7 F4**
Withern *Lincs* **45 H3**
Withernsea *Humber* **51 G5**
Withington *Glos* **27 E6**
Withington *Gtr Man* **42 D2**
Withington *Heref/Worcs* **26 B3**
Withnell *Lancs* **47 G5**
Witley *Surrey* **11 F1**
Witney *Oxon* **17 G1**
Wittering *Cambs* **37 F4**
Wittering, E and W *W Sussex* **11 E5**
Witton-le-Wear *Durham* **54 B2**
Wiveliscombe *Som* **7 H2**
Wivenhoe *Essex* **31 E5**
Woburn Park *Beds* **28 D4**
Woburn Sands *Beds/Bucks* **28 D4**
Woking *Surrey* **19 E5**
Wokingham *Berks* **18 C4**
Wolsingham *Durham* **54 A2**
Wolston *Warks* **27 H1**
Wolverhampton *W Mid* **35 E4**
Wolverton *Bucks* **28 C4**
Wolvey *Warks* **36 A5**
Wolviston *Clev* **54 D3**
Wombwell *S Yorks* **43 H1**
Womersley *N Yorks* **49 G6**
Wonersh *Surrey* **19 E6**
Wood End *Warks* **27 F1**
Woodbridge *Suff* **31 G3**
Woodchester *Glos* **16 D2**
Woodchurch *Kent* **13 E3**
Woodford *London* **20 B3**
Woodford Halse *Northants* **28 B3**
Woodhall Spa *Lincs* **45 F5**
Woodhead *Ches* **43 F2**
Woodstock *Oxon* **27 H5**
Woofferton *Salop* **26 A1**
Wookey Hole *Som* **16 A6**
Woolacombe *Devon* **6 C1**
Wooler *N'land* **67 F5**
Woolsington *N'land* **61 G4**
Woolston *Hants* **10 B4**
Woolton *Lancs* **42 A3**
Woolwich *London* **19 H4**
Woore *Salop* **42 C6**
Wootton Bassett *Wilts* **17 E3**
Wootton Glanville *Dorset* **9 E3**
Worcester *Heref/Worcs* **26 D2**
Workington *Cumb* **52 A2**
Worksop *Notts* **44 B3**
Worle *Avon* **15 H5**
Worlingham *Suff* **39 H5**
Wormit *Fife* **73 G2**
Worsbrough *S Yorks* **43 H1**
Worsley *Lancs* **42 C2**
Worthing *W Sussex* **11 G4**
Wotton-under-Edge *Glos* **16 C2**
Wragby *Lincs* **45 E3**
Wragby *W Yorks* **49 F6**
Wrath, C *H'land* **84 C1**
Wrekin, The, mt *Salop* **34 C3**
Wrentham *Suff* **31 H1**
Wrexham *Clwyd* **42 A6**
Wrightington *Lancs* **47 F6**
Writtle *Essex* **20 C1**
Wrotham *Kent* **12 C1**
Wroughton *Wilts* **17 F3**
Wroxham *Norf* **39 G3**
Wye *Kent* **13 F2**
Wyke Regis *Dorset* **8 D6**
Wylye *Wilts* **9 G1**
Wymeswold *Leics* **36 B2**
Wymondham *Norf* **39 E4**
Yapton *Sussex* **11 F4**
Yardley *W Mid* **35 G5**
Yardley Chase *Northants* **28 D2**
Yarm *Clev* **54 C3**
Yarmouth *of Wight* **10 B5**
Yarrow Church *Borders* **66 B5**
Yatton *Avon* **16 A5**
Yeadon *W Yorks* **49 E4**
Yealmpton *Devon* **4 C5**
Yell, I *Shet* **89 E6**
Yelverton *Devon* **4 B4**
Yeovil *Som* **8 D3**
Yiewsley *London* **19 E3**
Yoker *S'clyde* **64 C2**
York *N Yorks* **49 G3**
Youlgreave *Derby* **43 G4**
Yoxall *Staffs* **35 G3**
Yoxford *Suff* **31 G2**
Ystalyfera *W Glam* **14 D1**
Ystrad Aeron *Dyfed* **24 B3**
Ystrad Mynach *Mid Glam* **15 F2**
Ystrad Rhondda *Mid Glam* **15 E2**
Ystradgynlais *Powys* **24 D6**
Zennor *Corn* **2 A4**

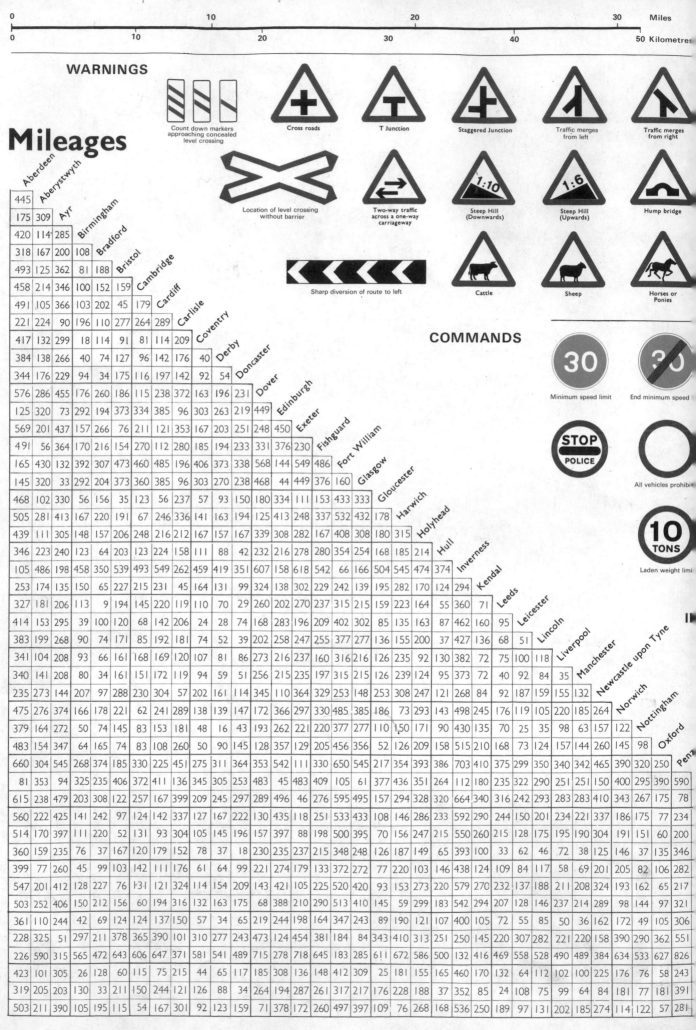

Scale: Miles 0 — 10 — 20 — 30   Kilometres 0 — 10 — 20 — 30 — 40 — 50

WARNINGS

- Count down markers approaching concealed level crossing
- Cross roads
- T Junction
- Staggered Junction
- Traffic merges from left
- Traffic merges from right
- Location of level crossing without barrier
- Two-way traffic across a one-way carriageway
- Steep Hill (Downwards) 1:10
- Steep Hill (Upwards) 1:6
- Hump bridge
- Sharp diversion of route to left
- Cattle
- Sheep
- Horses or Ponies

COMMANDS

- **30** Minimum speed limit
- **30** End minimum speed
- **STOP POLICE**
- All vehicles prohibited
- **10 TONS** Laden weight limit

Mileages

City order along the diagonal: Aberdeen, Aberystwyth, Ayr, Birmingham, Bradford, Bristol, Cambridge, Cardiff, Carlisle, Coventry, Derby, Doncaster, Dover, Edinburgh, Exeter, Fishguard, Fort William, Glasgow, Gloucester, Harwich, Holyhead, Hull, Inverness, Kendal, Leeds, Leicester, Lincoln, Liverpool, Manchester, Newcastle upon Tyne, Norwich, Nottingham, Oxford, Penzance

```
445
175 309
420 114 285
318 167 200 108
493 125 362  81 188
458 214 346 100 152 159
491 105 366 103 202  45 179
221 224  90 196 110 277 264 289
417 132 299  18 114  91  81 114 209
384 138 266  40  74 127  96 142 176  40
344 176 229  94  34 175 116 197 142  92  54
576 286 455 176 260 186 115 238 372 163 196 231
125 320  73 292 194 373 334 385  96 303 263 219 449
569 201 437 157 266  76 211 121 353 167 203 251 248 450
491  56 364 170 216 154 270 112 280 185 194 233 331 376 230
165 430 132 392 307 473 460 485 196 406 373 338 568 144 549 486
145 320  33 292 204 373 360 385  96 303 270 238 468  44 449 376 160
468 102 330  56 156  35 123  56 237  57  93 150 180 334 111 153 433 333
505 281 413 167 220 191  67 246 336 141 163 194 125 413 248 337 532 432 178
439 111 305 148 157 206 248 216 212 167 157 167 339 308 282 167 408 308 180 315
346 223 240 123  64 203 123 224 158 111  88  42 232 216 278 280 354 254 168 185 214
105 486 198 458 350 539 493 549 262 459 419 351 607 158 618 542  66 166 504 545 474 374
253 174 135 150  65 227 215 231  45 164 131  99 324 138 302 229 242 139 195 282 170 124 294
327 181 206 113   9 194 145 220 119 110  70  29 260 202 270 237 315 215 159 223 164  55 360  71
414 153 295  39 100 120  68 142 206  24  28  74 168 283 196 209 402 302  85 135 163  87 462 160  95
383 199 268  90  74 171  85 192 181  74  52  39 202 258 247 255 377 277 136 155 200  37 427 136  68  51
341 104 208  93  66 161 168 169 120 107  81  86 273 216 237 160 316 216 126 235  92 130 382  72  75 100 118
340 141 208  80  34 161 151 172 119  94  59  51 256 215 235 197 315 216 126 239 124  95 373  72  40  92  84  35
235 273 144 207  97 288 230 304  57 202 161 114 345 110 364 329 253 148 253 308 247 121 268  84  92 187 159 155 132
475 276 374 166 178 221  62 241 289 138 139 147 172 366 297 330 485 385 186  73 293 143 498 245 176 119 105 220 185 264
379 164 272  50  74 145  83 153 181  48  16  43 193 262 221 220 377 277 110 150 171  90 430 135  70  25  35  98  63 157 122
483 154 347  64 165  74  83 108 260  50  90 145 128 357 129 205 456 356  52 126 209 158 515 210 168  73 124 157 144 260 145  98
660 304 545 268 374 185 330 225 451 275 311 364 353 542 111 330 650 545 217 354 393 386 703 410 375 299 350 340 342 465 390 320 250
 81 353  94 325 235 406 372 411 136 345 305 253 483  45 483 409 105  61 377 436 351 264 112 180 235 322 290 251 251 150 400 295 390 590
615 238 479 203 308 122 257 167 399 209 245 297 289 496  46 276 595 495 157 294 328 320 664 340 316 242 293 283 283 410 343 267 175  78
560 222 425 141 242  97 124 142 337 127 167 222 130 435 118 251 533 433 108 146 286 233 592 290 244 150 201 234 221 337 186 175  77 234
514 170 397 111 220  52 131  93 304 105 145 196 157 397  88 198 500 395  70 156 247 215 550 260 215 128 175 195 190 304 191 151  60 200
360 159 235  76  37 167 120 179 152  78  37  18 230 235 237 215 348 248 126 187 149  65 393 100  33  62  46  72  38 125 146  37 135 346
399  77 260  45  99 103 142 111 176  61  64  99 221 274 179 133 372 272  77 220 103 146 438 124 109  84 117  58  69 201 205  82 106 282
547 201 412 128 227  76 131 121 324 114 154 209 143 421 105 225 520 420  93 153 273 220 579 270 232 137 188 211 208 324 193 162  65 217
503 252 406 150 212 156  60 194 316 132 163 175  68 388 210 290 513 410 145  59 299 183 542 294 207 128 146 237 214 289  98 144  97 321
361 110 244  42  69 124 124 137 150  57  34  65 219 244 198 164 347 243  89 190 121 107 400 105  72  55  85  50  36 162 172  49 105 306
228 325  51 297 211 378 365 390 101 310 277 243 473 124 454 381 184  84 343 410 313 251 250 145 220 307 282 221 220 158 390 290 362 551
226 590 315 565 472 643 606 647 371 581 541 489 715 278 718 645 183 285 611 672 586 500 132 416 469 558 528 490 489 384 634 533 627 826
423 101 305  26 128  60 115  75 215  44  65 117 185 308 136 148 412 309  25 181 155 165 460 170 132  64 112 102 100 225 176  76  58 243
319 205 203 130  33 211 150 244 121 126  88  34 264 194 287 261 317 217 176 228 188  37 352  85  24 108  75  99  64  84 181  77 181 391
503 211 390 105 195 115  54 167 301  92 123 159  71 378 172 260 497 397 109  76 268 168 536 250 189  97 131 202 185 274 114 122  57 281
```

Distances assume the use of ferries where appropriate